Ten Problems of Consciousness

Representation and Mind
Hilary Putnam and Ned Block, editors

Ten Problems of Consciousness
A Representational Theory of the Phenomenal Mind

Michael Tye

A Bradford Book
The MIT Press
Cambridge, Massachusetts
London, England

This book was set in Sabon by Compset, Inc. and was printed and bound in the United States of America.

Library of Congress Cataloging-in-Publication Data

Tye, Michael.
    Ten problems of consciousness : a representational theory of the phenomenal mind / Michael Tye.
        p.   cm. — (Representation and mind)
    "A Bradford book."
    Includes bibliographical references and index.
    ISBN 0-262-20103-8
    1. Consciousness. 2. Philosophy of mind. 3. Mental representation. I. Title. II. Series.
    B105.C477T84 1995
    128'.2—dc20   95-19301
                                                                                   CIP

For John, Neil, and Paul

Contents

Acknowledgments

I have been thinking about consciousness on and off since 1984, the spring of which I spent in Oxford. While there I wrote a paper, subsequently published in *Mind* (1986), in which I tried to defend a materialist view of experience and feeling against some familiar philosophical objections. At the time, I uncritically accepted the view that the troublesome phenomenal, or "what it is like," aspect of experiences had nothing to do with their representational contents, and I supposed that neurophysiology would ultimately tell the full story. In the course of reflecting on this pair of assumptions in later years, I came to think that I had made a serious mistake. Not only are the phenomenal or felt aspects of our mental lives representational but also (relatedly) they are not even in the head at all. So, neurophysiology certainly will not reveal to us what it is like to smell a skunk or to taste a fig. Look at the neurons for as long as you like, and you still will not find phenomenal consciousness.

The present book is an attempt to explain why my earlier assumptions should be rejected and to propose an alternative positive theory. The traditional view that what it is like is a matter of intrinsic, head-bound (or soul-bound) qualities has been in peaceful slumber for too long. What follows is an attempt to rouse it and shake it apart. Sleeping dogmas should not be left to lie undisturbed. The thesis that phenomenal character is representational is an idea whose time has come.

Many people have influenced the writing of this work. I gave a series of eight seminars on consciousness at King's College, London, in spring 1993, attended by many of the King's philosophy faculty, and their vigorous criticisms were useful to me in many ways. I also gave four lectures at the University of Mexico in the late summer of 1993, which helped me to sharpen my position further. And bits and pieces of the book have been read at philosophy colloquia at universities in the United States and Europe.

Of the numerous people with whom I have had helpful discussions, I would like to thank Maite Escurdia Olavarriet, Terry Horgan, Keith Hossack, Brian McLaughlin, David Papineau, Lauretta Reeves, Mark Sainsbury, Gabriel Segal, Sydney Shoemaker, Barry Smith, Richard Sorabji, Rob Stainton, and Gerry Vision in particular. I am also indebted to several past or present students, especially Dan Krasner, Robert Lurz, Mike Thau, and Abraham Witonsky. I am especially grateful to Ned Block, Fred Dretske, and Stephen White, all of whom were kind enough to read an earlier draft of this book and to make many useful comments. The present book is very different from what it would have been without their criticisms. Last but not least, I would like to thank Jim Gibbs for drawing the cartoons.

The material in the book is very largely new. Some sections in chapter 4 appear in slightly different form in "A Representational Theory of Pains and their Phenomenal Character," *Philosophical Perspectives* 9 (1995) (to be reprinted in *The Nature of Consciousness: Philosophical and Scientific Debates*, ed. Block, Flanagan, and Güzeldere [Cambridge, Mass.: MIT Press, Bradford Books, 1996]. The first two pages of chapter 5 also comprise "What What It's Like Is Really Like," *Analysis,* 55 (1995), 125–126. The appendix is taken from material in my "Blindsight, the Absent Qualia Hypothesis, and the Mystery of Consciousness," in *Philosophy and Cognitive Science,* suppl. 34 to *Philosophy,* ed. by C. Hookway and D. Peterson (1993), 19–40.

Introduction

Bertrand Russell once remarked, "Philosophy is a reluctant mistress—one can only reach her heart with the cold steel in the hand of passion." Anyone who has grappled with the philosophical puzzles of consciousness will appreciate the truth in this remark. Consciousness is mystifying, and the more one reflects on it, the more mystifying it is apt to seem. Nonetheless, I think that a philosophical theory of consciousness is possible, and I propose to elaborate a global view that seems to me to provide an illuminating framework within which to understand the kind of consciousness that has generated most perplexity: so-called phenomenal consciousness.

One difficulty in assessing philosophical theories of consciousness is that it is not always clear what they are theories *of*; nor is it always clear just what are the puzzles or problems that the theories are intended to solve. For example, it is sometimes said that the subjectivity of experience presents an insurmountable obstacle to materialist or physicalist theories of consciousness. But there is no one sort of subjectivity associated with experience, and neither is there any single problem. Unfortunately, the different kinds of subjectivity are frequently conflated, even by prominent philosophers. The result is that many people are perplexed, but not all of them are perplexed for the right reasons.

I have tried very hard in the present work to specify clearly the target domain and the target problems. The target domain, as I indicated in the opening paragraph, is *phenomenal* consciousness. For the purposes of this introduction, it suffices to say that phenomenal consciousness is the sort of consciousness that is integral to experiences and sensations—for example, the experience of red, the sensation of pain, the feeling of elation.

The target problems, of which there are ten, are each concerned with an important aspect of phenomenal consciousness. The goal is to articulate a theory that solves *all* the problems. I emphasize the term 'all' here, since theories abound that address some of the problems I elucidate. And some of these theories seem to me plausible, as far as they go. But articulating a theory that comes to grips with all of the problems is extraordinarily difficult.

Why the focus on phenomenal consciousness? After all, the feeling of pain, to take just one example, seems a rather primitive, straightforward state that is very widespread in nature. What can be so mystifying about that? The answer, I suggest, is that at the heart of philosophical reflection on phenomenal consciousness lies a special paradox. This paradox must be solved if the phenomenal mind is to be properly understood. The way to approach the paradox, I maintain, is through a consideration of those of the ten problems that are not directly implicated in the reasoning that leads to its formulation. Solving these less-central problems provides us with the beginnings of a path through some of the denser philosophical thickets.

The book is organized into two parts. The first part lays out the domain, the problems, and the paradox; it also summarizes all the options currently available in the literature on phenomenal consciousness, together with the difficulties they face. The second part articulates the proposed theory. Part I is written in a way that should be accessible to anyone at all who has any interest in consciousness. To assist the reader, I have added summaries of the more important points in special gray boxes in the text, and I have used white boxes to mark off more-sophisticated points that are not crucial to understanding the overall view. I have even included some cartoons in the text to accompany the puzzles. Consciousness is so perplexing that one might as well smile at the problems it creates.

Part II is divided into five chapters. This part of the book is, of necessity, more complex than the first two chapters. But again, I have used boxes as in part I, and I have striven to make my approach broadly accessible. The overall strategy is to develop a theory piece by piece and to explain, as I go along, how it handles the various puzzles.

The first chapter of part II (chapter 4) examines the question of what it is about our pains, afterimages, itches, and other mental objects of experience and feeling that is responsible for their necessary privacy and necessary ownership. Why can't you feel my pains? Why can't there be pains that are felt by nobody at all? A number of different proposals are considered, including one that denies (on the basis of thought experiments about split brains) that pains and other such mental objects cannot be shared, and a new theory is suggested.

Chapter 4 argues for a position that runs strongly counter to philosophical orthodoxy. It is customary to divide experiences and feelings into two subclasses: those that represent things and those that do not. Consider, for example, my seeming to see a bright, gold coin on the ground before me. The visual experience I undergo has a certain raw feel or phenomenal character to it. There is something it is like for me to undergo the experience, just as there is something it is like for me to hear the squeal of chalk against a blackboard or to smell a skunk. Seeming to see a bright, gold coin on the ground is a state with "technicolor phenomenology" (McGinn 1990). It is also a state with representational content: it represents the world as being a certain way.

Consider now my feeling an itch or my feeling depressed (without there being anything in particular about which I am depressed). These states, again, have a phenomenal character. There is something it is like to undergo them. But on the face of it, they lack any representational content. In chapter 4, I argue against this view. In my view, *all* experiences and feelings have representational content, not just perceptual experiences.

Chapter 5 addresses the question of the relationship of phenomenal character to representational content. Here, again, I go against philosophical orthodoxy. The received view is that the way things phenomenally look or taste or smell is distinct from the representational contents of the experiences they produce. I argue that this is not so, that phenomenal character can be identified with representational content of a certain sort, and I explain just what this sort of content is.

In chapter 6, I show that the view elaborated in the preceding chapter allows us to understand what sort of mechanism is responsible for generating phenomenal consciousness in the brain, and I provide an account of how it is that feelings and experiences have the feature, made famous by Thomas Nagel, of perspectival subjectivity. I also discuss the explanatory gap that seems to exist between feelings and experiences, on the one hand, and objective, physical states of the brain, on the other.

In the final chapter, I turn my attention to a number of imaginary cases, some of which involve creatures whose experiences are systematically inverted relative to those of others and some of which focus on creatures without any experiences at all (in particular, on "zombies," as they are often called in the philosophical literature). I examine these and other cases from the perspective of the theory that I develop, and I discuss the use of imaginability as a tool in deciding between different philosophical theories of consciousness.

I have been unable to resist the temptation to include a nonphilosophical appendix, in which I discuss some empirical work on a psychological impairment in consciousness known as blindsight (as well as relatedly certain other visual impairments). I do so in part because blindsight figures in some of the earlier philosophical chapters, and it may be helpful to some readers to have the background psychological context elucidated further, and in part because the impairment itself is so fascinating. Boldly (and perhaps rashly) going where philosophers usually fear to tread, I also make a very tentative empirical proposal, much influenced by recent work in cognitive science on visual agnosia, for understanding blindsight.

I recently heard one well-known philosopher ask another, who had been propounding his theory of consciousness, whether he had heard the story of the man who claimed to have built a perpetual-motion machine. This man had housed his construction in a huge laboratory, which was packed full of the various component parts. There were enormous wheels, pistons the size of trees, cogs, gears, tubing all over the place, endless levers. In fact, the man proudly announced to visitors, there was *everything* he required for his perpetual motion machine except for one insignificant thing, which he had not managed to lay his hands on yet. All he still needed, he said, as he wagged a forefinger up and down repeatedly, was a little device that would do that forever!

I hope that I have succeeded in constructing a theory that is in no need of such a device. Still, were some philosophers to respond to my view by asking rhetorically, "Is that all there is?" (in the style of Peggy Lee's hit song from the sixties)—and there are always philosophers happy to play this role—I would not be unduly perturbed. There is, to be sure, much more to be said on the topic of phenomenal consciousness, even within my general approach. But there is, I believe, no special ingredient, undreamt of in my philosophy, that must be called on to finish the picture.

I

1

The Ten Problems

I taste a lemon, smell rotten eggs, feel a sharp pain in my elbow, see the color red. In each of these cases, I am the subject of a very different feeling or experience. For feelings and perceptual experiences, there is always something it is *like* to undergo them, some phenomenology that they have. As the phenomenal or felt qualities of experiences change, the experiences themselves change, but if the phenomenal or "what it is like" aspects disappear altogether, then there is no experience left at all. I shall say that phenomenal consciousness is present just in case there is a mental state present that is phenomenally conscious, and I shall say that a mental state is phenomenally conscious just in case there is some immediate subjective "feel" to the state, some distinctive experiential quality.

Philosophers sometimes maintain that there could be creatures (androids, say) capable of abstract thought and speech, but whose inner states have no phenomenal or sensational character to them. Lacking any phenomenal consciousness, it seems plausible to suppose that such creatures could have no clear concept of what anything is like in the phenomenal sense, no real idea of how things subjectively seem and feel (see section 1.3). But for the rest of us, anchored in the real world, the simple examples I have given should suffice as a pretheoretical starting point. The problems we are concerned with in this book all pertain to one or another aspect of phenomenal consciousness.

1.1 Phenomenal Consciousness Introduced

Which states are phenomenally conscious? Philosophers do not always agree, but the following would certainly be included on my own list. (1)

Perceptual experiences, for example, experiences of the sort involved in seeing green, hearing loud trumpets, tasting licorice, smelling the sea air, running one's fingers over sandpaper. (2) Bodily sensations, for example, feeling a twinge of pain, feeling an itch, feeling hungry, having a stomachache, feeling hot, feeling dizzy. Think here also of experiences like those present during orgasm or while running flat-out. (3) Felt reactions or passions or emotions, for example, feeling delight, lust, fear, love, grief, jealousy, regret. (4) Felt moods, for example, feeling happy, depressed, calm, bored, tense, miserable.[1]

Should we include any mental states that are not feelings and experiences? Consider my desire to eat ice cream. Is there not something it is like for me to have this desire? If so, is not this state phenomenally conscious? And what about the belief that I am a very fine fellow? Or the memory that September 2 is the date on which I first fell in love? Is there not some phenomenal flavor to both of these states? In the former case, some phenomenal sense of pride and ego, and in the latter some feeling of nostalgia?

It seems to me not implausible to deal with these cases by arguing that insofar as there is any phenomenal or immediately experienced felt quality to the above states, this is due to their being accompanied by sensations or images or feelings that are the real bearers of the phenomenal character. Take away the feelings and experiences that happen to be associated with the above states in particular cases, and there is no phenomenal consciousness left.

On this view, in and of itself there is nothing it is like to remember that September 2 is the date on which I first fell in love. I might remember this fact (perhaps I read it in an old diary) but feel nothing at all. It is all ancient history to me now. No spark of feeling is produced. Likewise, desires are not inherently phenomenally conscious. I need not *feel* a desire for the desire to exist. Still we do often experience a feeling of being "pulled" or "tugged" when we strongly desire something. There may also be accompanying images in various modalities.

What should we say about strong emotional reactions that are directed at specific things, for example, being violently angry that the car was wrecked, being terrified that there are sharks nearby, being disgusted that the house is so filthy? Do these states have an immediate felt aspect, an internal phenomenal character? The natural reply here is to say that the states involved are really hybrid, having both a feeling and a thought or belief as components. So being violently angry that the car was wrecked is a matter of believing that the car was wrecked and thereby being caused to feel anger. Likewise, being terrified that there are sharks nearby is a matter of thinking that there are sharks nearby and thereby being caused to feel great fear. A parallel account may be given for the example of disgust. The obvious suggestion, then, is that in each case there is something it is like to undergo the component feeling, but the belief or thought in itself has no intrinsic phenomenal aspect.

Some philosophers do not like to use the term 'consciousness' in the way I have in these early pages. They insist that consciousness is a matter of turning one's attention inward and thinking about what is going on in one's own mind.[2] In this connection, it is interesting to note that no less a philosopher than John Locke seems to have held such a view. In his *Essay Concerning Human Understanding* (bk. II, chap. 1, sec. 19), Locke remarks, "Consciousness is the perception of what passes in a Man's own mind." Locke, however, certainly does not deny the reality of experiences and feelings. And with good reason. Consider, for example, the bodily sensation of pain or the visual sensation of bright purple. There is something it is like to undergo these states. So of course phenomenal consciousness, as I have characterized it, is real.

Do animals other than humans undergo phenomenally conscious states? It certainly seems that way. Dogs often growl or whimper during REM (rapid eye movement) sleep. Surely, they are undergoing experiences when they do so, just as we are during our dreams. What seems much less plausible is the idea that in every such case, there is consciousness of above higher-order type, and hence thought directed on other mental states. After all, one important difference between humans and other animals is that the former are much more reflective than the latter. So with nonhuman animals there is generally much less higher-order consciousness. It is very hard to deny that there is phenomenal consciousness, however. It would be absurd to suppose that there is nothing it is like for a dog that chews a favorite bone or a cat that prefers chopped liver for its dinner over anything else it is offered.

Here is another example that suggests that phenomenal consciousness can be present without higher-order consciousness. People who entirely lose their sense of smell, through damage to their olfactory tracts, are typically shocked and troubled by what has happened to them. Consider the following description of the effects by one such person:

Sense of smell? I never gave it a thought. You don't normally give it a thought. But when I lost it—it was like being struck blind. Life lost a good deal of its savour—one doesn't realise how much 'savour' *is* smell. You *smell* people, you *smell* books, you *smell* the city, you *smell* the spring—maybe not consciously but as a rich unconscious background to anything else. My whole world was suddenly radically poorer. (Sacks 1987, p. 159).

This particular subject is reported, after the injury, to have had an acute desire to "remember the smell-world to which he had paid no conscious attention . . . but which had formed the very ground base of life" (Sacks 1987, p. 159).

These descriptions support the view that phenomenally conscious states need not be conscious in a higher-order way. We are assailed constantly with smells of one sort or another. Typically, we do not notice them. We pay no attention to how things smell unless they are out of the ordinary. Our minds are normally focused on other matters. But the olfactory experiences are there, whether or not we reflect on them or attend to the things producing them. There is something it is like for us to smell people, books, the city, the spring—something the absence of which would certainly capture our attention were we unfortunate enough to lose our sense of smell altogether.

What is true here for smell, I might add, is intuitively true for touch and sound and general bodily feeling. As I type these words, I have auditory sensations of my computer humming quietly, a heating fan purring, distant traffic. I feel my legs crossed, as I sit on my chair. There is a slight sensation of pressure around my neck from my shirt collar. I feel my feet touching the floor, my wrists resting against the edge of my desk as my fingers make contact with the keyboard. These sensations do not themselves come into existence as I focus on them. They are there even if, as is usually the case, my attention is directed elsewhere. Or so, at least, it is normally supposed.

The thesis that phenomenal consciousness is real and distinct from higher-order consciousness is sometimes resisted on the grounds that accepting phenomenal consciousness automatically necessitates accepting that the ways things phenomenally look and feel are fixed from birth or shortly thereafter, once the receptor cells are matured. But this is just not so. As long as you agree that there is something it is like for you to undergo some mental states, that some mental states have a subjective or phenomenal character to them, you have granted phenomenal consciousness, whatever your views on its variability. So, for example, you do not need to hold that the subjective character of the taste of beer remains fixed and unchanging from the first sip, as Winston Churchill implicitly seems to do in the following exchange (in Muir 1976, p. 294):

Lady Spencer Churchill: I hate the taste of beer.
Winston Churchill: So do many people—to begin with. It is, however, a prejudice that many have been able to overcome.

There is, then, no inconsistency in claiming both that there is phenomenal consciousness and that phenomenal character is sometimes causally influenced by higher-level cognitive processing, for example, relevant beliefs.

Another objection to phenomenal consciousness, which also misses the point, is based on the claim that it goes hand in hand with the implausible view that there is a single place in the brain where phenomenal experiences are located (Dennett's Cartesian Theater[3]). The premise here is straightforwardly false. Advocates of the reality of phenomenal consciousness are not committed to holding that experiences and feelings are all localized in just one neural region.[4] They could be found in a variety of different places in the brain (assuming it makes sense to suppose that they are spatially located at all).

Box 1.1

Here is a fascinating scientific case, in which it may initially seem that there is no change in phenomenal consciousness, but which, on reflection, may be viewed in a different way. Unilateral visual neglect is a striking impairment, which is typically brought about by brain damage in the parietal lobe. Patients with this deficit typically have great difficulty in noticing, or attending to, stimuli in one half of the visual field. The deficit often persists, moreover, despite free movement of the head and eyes. So it is not usually taken to indicate basic "sensory loss" in the relevant field. More on this below.

Box 1.1 *continued*

One patient, P. S., a forty-nine-year-old woman, with unilateral neglect was presented simultaneously with two vertically aligned dark green line drawings of a house.[5] In one of these drawings, the house had bright red flames emerging from the left side. In other respects, the drawings were matched. P. S. was asked what she saw. She identified each drawing as being of a house. P. S. was then asked whether the two drawings were the same or different. She judged them to be the same. On a number of different trials she never noticed the flames on the left. However, when she was asked which house she would prefer to live in, eighty percent of the time she chose the house without flames. This choice she made only when she was compelled to pick one or the other, since she believed the two houses to be alike and the question "silly."

In some subsequent trials, P. S. was shown simultaneously a new pair of vertically aligned drawings, one of a house with flames on the *right* side and the other normal. She immediately noticed the flames and preferred the other house. Then, in five final trials, she was presented with the original pair of drawings again. In the first four cases, she noticed no difference but chose the nonburning house. In the fifth, she finally noticed the flames on the left (remarking "Oh my God, this is on fire!")

The conclusion drawn by Marshall and Halligan (the authors of the article from which this case study is taken) is that "the 'neglected' stimulus can exert an influence upon cognitive functioning, albeit at some pre-attentional, pre-conscious level" (1988, p. 767). Now, we can all agree that what the above case clearly illustrates is the absence of any thoughts or beliefs with respect to the flames or any of their features (e.g., their color) *prior* to the final trial. P. S. simply does not *notice* the flames. In the last trial, however, given the earlier cue of the house with the flames on the right, she does notice them. So the "neglected" stimulus is clearly preconscious in the sense that she does not register it cognitively prior to the final trial.

What is not so clear is whether there is any difference in the phenomenal consciousness of P. S. as she views each member of the pair of drawings in the first set of trials. Does the house with the flames on the left *look* any different to her than the normal house? Is there any difference in what it is like for her as she views the two houses? Clearly, she is not conscious that they look any different. She has no higher-order consciousness of any difference in her phenomenal state. But not noticing that there is any difference in how things look (in what it is like) does not directly entail that there is no difference. And if there is *never* any difference in how the two houses look, how is it that insight is achieved, on the basis of viewing, in the final trial? If, immediately prior to her saying "Oh my God, this is on fire!" the two houses had looked to her to be exactly alike, if her

Box 1.1 *continued*

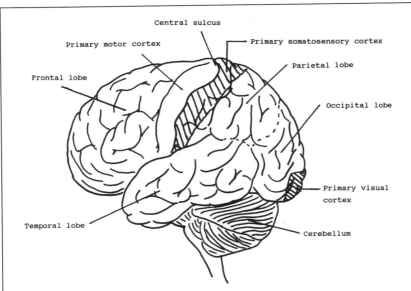

Figure 1.1
Side view of the cerebral cortex

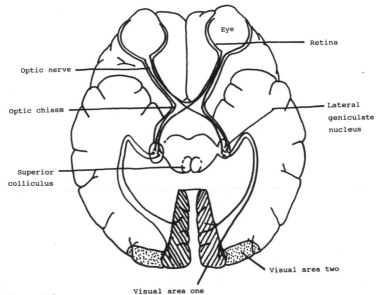

Figure 1.2
A cross section of the cerebral cortex, seen from above

Box 1.1 *continued*

experiences had themselves been phenomenally identical, then what was it that triggered the correct identification?

I do not wish to claim here that this question has *no* answer if the two houses looked exactly alike to P. S. But the hypothesis of a phenomenal difference does provide *one* plausible explanation. Moreover, as the authors of the study acknowledge, there was no "sensory loss" for P. S. So her early visual processing in the post-geniculate region of the brain and the visual areas one and two in the occipital lobe (see figures 1.1 and 1.2 above) was like that of normally sighted subjects (unlike the case of blindsight, as we shall see later). The brain damage occurred in the higher-level attentional system located in the parietal lobe.

On this proposal, then, what P. S. failed to do, prior to being presented with the cue of the house with the flames on the right, was to respond consciously, at a conceptual level, to a phenomenal difference in her experiences. But the difference was there, in position to trigger such a response, before she actually responded. The two houses did *look* different to her.

We are now ready to turn our attention to the ten problems of consciousness. These problems are so perplexing that some philosophers have despaired of ever solving them. I think that this reaction is mistaken. But it cannot be denied that the problems are very challenging indeed.

1.2   The Problem of Ownership

Just what kind of thing is phenomenal consciousness? In particular, is it an ordinary physical phenomenon, as much a part of the objective, natural world as, say, electromagnetism or lightning or the firing of neurons or the process of digestion? Many philosophers have thought not. The first problem I want to raise is one that must be faced by any philosopher who wants to hold that phenomenally conscious states are physical. The problem is that of explaining how the mental objects of experience and feeling—particular pains, afterimages, appearance, tickles, itches, for example—*could* be physical, given that they are necessarily owned and necessarily private to their owners. Unless these objects are themselves physical, the phenomenal states involving them, states like having a yellow afterimage or feeling a tickle, cannot themselves be physical either.

Let us take a concrete example to illustrate the problem. Suppose that you are lying in the sun with your eyes closed. You have not a care in the world. Life is good. Suddenly you feel intense, burning pain in your left leg—a stray American pit bull has chosen you for lunch. There is something it is like for you at this decidedly unlucky moment.

This is an objective fact about you, not dependent for its existence on anyone else's seeing or thinking about your situation. But the pain you are feeling—that particular pain—is private to you. It is yours alone, and necessarily so. No one else could have that particular pain. Of course, conceivably somebody else could have a pain that felt just like your pain, but only you could have that very pain. What is true for this one pain is true for pains generally. Indeed, it is true for all mental objects of experience. None of these items of experience can be shared. I can't have your visual images or feel your tickles, for example. Your images and tickles necessarily belong to you.

The problem, in part, is that ordinary physical things do not seem to be owned in this way. For example, my pit bull is something you could own, in the unlikely event that you wanted to do so. Likewise, my tie or my car. But the problem runs deeper, because any pain or itch or image is always *some creature's* pain or itch or image. Likewise, any appearance is always an appearance *to* some creature or other. Each mental object of experience necessarily has *an* owner. So pains, for example, in this respect are not like dogs or tables or even legs. Legs can exist amputated, and dogs and tables can belong to no one at all. Pains, however, *must* have owners.

The challenge for the philosopher who wants to hold that experiences and feelings are wholly physical is to explain how it is that pains and other mental objects of experience can have the above features if they really are just ordinary physical things.

Box 1.2

The Problem of Ownership

If pains, itches, and afterimages are physical, then why can't you feel my pains or itches, or have my afterimages? Why can't there be a pain or an itch or an afterimage that belongs to no sentient creature at all?

1.3   The Problem of Perspectival Subjectivity

This problem is again, in the first instance, a problem for the physicalist about phenomenal experience. It can be illustrated in a number of different ways. Let us begin by returning to the example of the pit bull. Consider again the experience you underwent as the pit bull sank its teeth into your leg. It seems highly plausible to suppose that *fully* comprehending the specific type of experience or feeling to which you were subject requires knowing what it is like to undergo that type of experience or feeling. And knowing what it is like to undergo an experience requires one to have a certain experiential point of view or perspective. In the case of the pit bull, knowing what it is like requires either that one has oneself been unfortunate enough to have had phenomenologically similar experiences during a dog attack or that one can imagine such experiences on the basis of other pain experiences one has undergone.

This is why a child born without the capacity to feel pain and kept alive in a very carefully controlled environment could never come to know what it was like for you to experience what you did. Such a

"I THOUGHT THE MOVIE WOULD STINK. NOW, EXPERIENTIALLY SPEAKING, THIS PROPOSITION HAS BEEN VERIFIED. IT STUNK."

child could never herself adopt the relevant perspective. Lacking that perspective, she could never comprehend fully what that type of feeling was, no matter how much information was supplied about the firing patterns in your brain, the biochemical processes, the chemical changes.

Phenomenally conscious states, then, are subjective in that fully comprehending *them* requires adopting a certain experiential point of view. In this way, they are perspectival. But physical states are not perspectival. Understanding fully what lightning or gold is does not require any particular experiential point of view. For example, one need not undergo the experiences normal human beings undergo as they watch the sky in a storm or examine a gold ring. A man who is blind and deaf cannot experience lightning by sight or hearing at all, but he can understand fully just what it is, namely, a certain sort of electrical discharge between clouds. Similarly, if gold presents a very different appearance to Martians, say, this does not automatically preclude them from fully grasping what gold is, namely, the element with atomic number 79. Physical items, then, are not perspectivally subjective. They are, in the relevant way, objective.[6]

We can now appreciate why an android who is incapable of any feeling or experience at all would seem to lack the resources to grasp the concept of phenomenal consciousness. Lacking any phenomenal consciousness herself, she would not know what it is like to be phenomenally conscious. And not knowing that, she could not occupy *any* experiential perspective. So she could not fully understand the nature of phenomenal consciousness; nor could she properly grasp the meaning of the term 'phenomenal consciousness'.

The problem of perspectival subjectivity can be illustrated in other ways. Consider a brilliant scientist of the future, Mary, who has lived in a black-and-white room since birth and who acquires information about the world via banks of computers and black-and-white television screens depicting the outside world.[7] Suppose that Mary has at her disposal in the room all the objective, physical information there is about what goes on when humans see roses, trees, sunsets, rainbows, and other phenomena. She knows everything there is to know about the surfaces of the objects, the ways in which they reflect light, the changes on the retina and in the optic nerve, the firing patterns in the visual cortex, and so on. Still there is something she does not know. She does not know what it is like to see red or green or the other colors. This is shown by the fact that when she finally steps outside her room and looks at a rose, say, she will certainly learn something. Only then will she appreciate what it is like to see red. So, physicalism is incomplete.

Alternatively, suppose we make contact with some extraterrestrials and scientists from earth eventually come to have exhaustive knowledge of their physical states. It turns out that their physiology is very different from that of any earth creatures. Surely our scientists can wonder what it feels like to be an extraterrestrial, whether their feelings and experiences are the same as ours. But if they can wonder this, then they are not yet in a position to know everything by means of their objective, scientific investigations. There is something they do not yet know, namely, what it is like for the extraterrestrials. This is something subjective, something not contained in the information about the objective facts already available to them.

Box 1.3

The Problem of Perspectival Subjectivity

What accounts for the fact that fully comprehending the nature of pain
or the feeling of depression or the visual experience of red requires having
the appropriate experiential perspective (that conferred by being oneself
the subject of these or closely related experiences)?

1.4   The Problem of Mechanism

Neural states are not themselves perspectivally subjective. But phenomenally conscious states are. Somehow, physical changes in the soggy gray-
and-white matter composing our brains produce feeling, experience,
"technicolor phenomenology" (McGinn 1991). How is it that items that
are generated by nonperspectival items can be perspectival? What is it
about the brain that is responsible for the production of states with a
perspectivally subjective character? These questions ask for a specification
of the *mechanism* that underlies the generation of perspectivally subjective
entities by nonperspectival ones, and that closes the explanatory gap we
intuitively feel between the two. This explanatory gap is the one puzzling
T. H. Huxley when he commented in 1866, "How it is that anything so
remarkable as a state of consciousness comes about as a result of irritating
nervous tissue, is just as unaccountable as the appearance of Djin when
Aladdin rubbed his lamp."

Here is a thought experiment that brings out the explanatory gap very
clearly. Suppose that scientists develop a device that can be attached to
the head and that permits the recipient to view physical changes in his
own brain. This device, which is sometimes called "an autocerebroscope,"
can be thought of as being something like the virtual-reality headgear
that is beginning to be marketed today except that what the recipient
sees in this case, via probes that pass painlessly through the skull, is the
inside of his own brain. Suppose you put the device on your head, and
lo and behold, firing patterns appear projected on a screen before your
eyes! As you move a hand control, further firing patterns from other

regions of the cortex appear before you. Imagine now that whenever you are tickled with a feather, you see that a certain fixed set of neurons in the somatosensory cortex is firing. At other times, when you are not being tickled, these neurons are dormant. Is it not going to seem amazing to you that *that* electrical activity generates the subjective tickle feeling? How on earth does that particular neural activity produce a *feeling* at all? And why does it feel like *that* rather than some other way?[8]

The need for a mechanism can also be appreciated when we reflect on some real-life examples from science. Consider the production of brittleness in a thin glass sheet or liquidity in water or digestion in a human being. In each case, there is a mechanism that explains how the higher-level property or process is generated from the lower-level one.

In the case of liquidity, for example, once we appreciate that liquidity is a disposition, namely, the disposition to pour easily, and we are told that in liquid water the H_2O molecules are free to slide past one another instead of being trapped in fixed locations (as they are in ice), we have no difficulty in seeing how liquidity is generated from the underlying molecular properties. There is no explanatory gap.

A similar account is available in the case of brittleness. Like liquidity, brittleness is a disposition. Brittle objects are disposed to shatter easily.

This disposition is produced in a thin glass sheet via the irregular alignment of crystals. Such an alignment results in there being weak forces holding the crystals together. So when a force is applied, the glass shatters. The generation of brittleness is now explained.

Digestion is a matter of undergoing a process whose function is to change food into energy. So digestion is a functionally characterized process. It follows that digestion takes place in a given organism via any set of internal changes that performs the relevant function for that organism. In this way, digestion is realized in the organism. In human beings, for example, digestion is realized chiefly by the action of certain enzymes secreted into the alimentary canal. These enzymes cause the food to become absorbable and hence available as energy by dissolving it and breaking it down into simpler chemical compounds. Once one grasps these facts, there is no deep mystery about how digestion is generated.

What the above examples strongly suggest is that, in the natural world, the generation of higher-level states or processes or properties by what is going on at lower neurophysiological or chemical or microphysical levels is grounded in mechanisms that *explain* the generation of the higher-level items. So if phenomenal consciousness is a natural phenomenon, a part of the physical world, there should be a mechanism that provides an explanatory link between the subjective and the objective. Given that there is such a mechanism, the place of phenomenally conscious states in the natural, physical domain is not threatened. But what could this mechanism be? We currently have no idea. Nor is it easy to see what scientific discoveries in biology, neurophysiology, chemistry, or physics could help us. For these sciences are sciences of the objective. And no fully objective mechanism could close the explanatory gap between the objective and the subjective. No matter how deeply we probe into the physical structure of neurons and the chemical transactions that occur when they fire, no matter how much objective information we acquire, we still seem to be left with something that cries out for a further explanation, namely, why and how *this* collection of neural and/or chemical changes produces *that* subjective feeling, or any subjective feeling at all.

Box 1.4

The Problem of Mechanism

How do objective, physical changes in the brain generate subjective feelings and experiences? What is the mechanism responsible for the production of the "what it is like" aspects of our mental lives?

1.5   The Problem of Phenomenal Causation

Phenomenal consciousness has effects on our behavior. The torture victim who screams is caused to do so by the awful felt quality of the pain he feels. The child who giggles uncontrollably as her father tickles her toes is caused to react in this way by the special phenomenal character of her experience. The woman who mistakenly turns on the wrong tap for a shower and is caused to gasp as the cold water runs down her back does so in response to the way the water feels to her. The wine connoisseur

"WELL..., I'D STOP MY SCREAMING IF YOU'D STOP EGGING HIM ON NOW, WOULDN'T I?"

who sips a glass of 1976 Chateau Latour and sighs contentedly is caused to react in this manner by the way the wine tastes to him. How the movie star with sex appeal looks in the previews to his latest film, *Too Hot to Touch,* causes many women to buy tickets. If anything in the world seems undeniable, it is that the subjective, phenomenal qualities of our experiences have behavioral effects.

But it also seems very difficult to deny that in each of the above cases, there is a complete physical explanation for the overt, public behavior, even though we do not as yet know all the details. Consider the specific bodily movements and noises that are produced by the torture victim. Their proximal causes are electrical impulses in the nerves. These impulses, in turn, are produced by firing patterns on the motor neurons, which themselves are caused by other firing patterns leading back to firing patterns on the sensory neurons. The details of this story are to be found in further scientific investigation, and the tale in its final form, as told by the neurophysiologist, chemist, and physicist will not mention any felt qualities as such. How, then, can the phenomenal character of the pain experiences make any difference to what we say or do?[9]

Box 1.5

The Problem of Phenomenal Causation

If there is a complete, objective, physical explanation for why our bodies move as they do, then how can the ways things seem to us, the ways they subjectively feel, make any difference to the behavior we produce?

1.6   The Problem of Super Blindsight

There is a condition known as blindsight that has been extensively studied in the last decade in psychology. People with blindsight have large blind areas or scotoma in their visual fields, due to brain damage in the post-geniculate region (typically the occipital cortex), and yet, under certain circumstances, they can issue accurate statements with respect to the contents of those areas (see Weiskrantz 1986). For example, blindsight subjects can make accurate guesses with respect to such things as presence, position, orientation, and movement of visual stimuli. They can also guess correctly as to whether an *X* is present or an *O*. Some blindsight patients can even make accurate color judgments about the blind field. Additionally, when a pattern is flashed into the blind region, it typically attracts the eye toward it just as with normally sighted subjects.

It appears, then, that, given appropriate instructions, blindsight subjects can function in a way that is significantly like normally sighted subjects with regard to the blind areas in their visual fields, without there being anything experiential or phenomenally conscious going on. There is, however, one immediate, obvious observable difference between blindsight subjects and the rest of us: they do not spontaneously issue any public reports about the contents of their blind fields. In each case, they

TED NEVER CEASED TO MARVEL AT HIS WIFE'S BLINDSIGHT.

respond only when they are forced to choose between certain alternative possibilities.[10] Moreover, they do not believe what they say.

Imagine now a person with blindsight who has been trained to will herself to respond, to guess what is in her blind field without being directed to guess, and who, through time, comes to believe the reports she issues with respect to a range of stimuli in her blind field. Imagine too that these reports are the same as those you and I would produce when confronted with the same stimuli. Call this "super blindsight." For a more familiar species of "blindsight" (one not needing any brain damage), see the cartoon above.

As far as I know, there are no actual super-blindsight subjects. But there could be. Their possibility raises some interesting and puzzling questions. What exactly is the difference between a super-blindsight subject's believing that there are such and such stimuli present and a normally sighted subject's experiencing that they are present? Is it just that the latter undergoes a state with a much richer *content* than the former, so that the difference resides in the fact that what is experienced has a wealth of detail to it that is missing in what is believed? More generally, how is the case of super blindsight to be treated by philosophical theories of phenomenal consciousness?

Box 1.6

The Problem of Super Blindsight

In what precisely does the difference between a super-blindsight subject's believing that certain stimuli are present (in the blind field) and a normally sighted subject's experiencing that those stimuli are present consist? More generally, how is the case of super blindsight to be handled by philosophical theories of phenomenal consciousness?

1.7   The Problem of Duplicates

Hollywood zombies are not difficult to spot. They inhabit the world of films, wandering around in a trancelike state, typically unable to control their behavior in a voluntary manner. They are usually very pale, prefer-

ring the night to the day for their carnivorous activities, and their clothes
are normally disheveled and old. Hollywood zombies, then, are significantly different from the rest of us at a functional level. Moreover, they
need not be wholly without phenomenal consciousness.[11] Philosophical
zombies, as I shall describe them, are a very different kettle of fish.

A philosophical zombie is a molecule-by-molecule duplicate of a sentient creature, a normal human being, for example, but who differs from
that creature in lacking *any* phenomenal consciousness. For me, as I lie
on the beach, happily drinking some wine and watching the waves, I
undergo a variety of visual, olfactory, and gustatory experiences. But my
zombie twin experiences nothing at all. He has no phenomenal consciousness. His sense organs convey information to him just as mine do, but
there is no internal phenomenology. Since my twin is an exact physical
duplicate of me, his inner psychological states will be *functionally* isomorphic with my own (assuming he is located in an identical environment[12]).
Whatever physical stimulus is applied, he will process the stimulus in the
same way as I do, and produce exactly the same behavioral responses.
So my zombie twin and I are not quite like the twins depicted below;
our reactions are absolutely identical.

Indeed, on the assumption that nonphenomenal psychological states
are functional states (that is, states definable in terms of their role or

function in mediating between stimuli and behavior), my zombie twin has just the same beliefs, thoughts, and desires as I do. For example, he too believes that the waves are large and that the wine is red. He differs from me only with respect to experience. For him, there is nothing it is like to stare at the waves or to sip wine.

The hypothesis that there can be philosophical zombies is not normally the hypothesis that such zombies are *nomically* possible, that their existence is consistent with the actual laws of nature. Rather the suggestion is that the hypothesis is coherent, that zombie replicas of this sort are at least *imaginable* and hence logically or metaphysically possible.

Philosophical zombies pose a serious threat to any sort of physicalist view of phenomenal consciousness. To begin with, if zombie replicas are possible, then phenomenal states are not identical with internal, objective, physical states, as the following simple argument shows. Suppose objective, physical state P can occur without phenomenal state S in some appropriate zombie replica (in the logical sense of 'can' noted above). But intuitively S cannot occur without S. Pain, for example, cannot be felt without pain. So P has a modal property S lacks, namely, the property of *possibly* occurring without S. By Leibniz's Law (the law that for anything x and for anything y, if x is identical with y, then x and y share *all* the same properties), S is not identical with P.

Second, if a person who is microphysically identical with me, located in an identical environment, can lack *any* phenomenal experiences, then facts pertaining to experience and feeling, facts about what it is like, are not necessarily fixed or determined by the objective microphysical facts. This the physicalist cannot allow, even if she concedes that phenomenally conscious states are not strictly identical with internal, objective, physical states. The physicalist, whatever her stripe, must believe at least that the microphysical facts determine all the facts, that any world that was exactly like ours in *all* microphysical respects (down to the smallest detail, to the position of every single boson, for example) would have to be like our world in all respects (having identical mountains, lakes, glaciers, trees, rocks, sentient creatures, cities, and so on).[13]

So the physicalist again has a serious problem. Phenomenal states, it seems, are not identical with internal, objective physical states; nor are they determined by physical states. This is the problem of microphysical duplicates.

Philosophical zombies are microphysical duplicates that lack phenomenal consciousness. Other duplicates lacking consciousness have also occupied philosophers. In particular, there has been considerable debate about possible functional duplicates that are not philosophical zombies. So, for example, one writer asks us to suppose that a billion Chinese people are each given a two-way radio with which to communicate with one another and with an artificial (brainless) body.[14] The movements of the body are controlled by the radio signals, and the signals themselves are made in accordance with instructions the Chinese people receive from a vast display in the sky, which is visible to all of them. The instructions are such that the participating Chinese people function like individual neurons and the radio links like synapses, so that together the Chinese people duplicate the causal organization of a human brain. Whether or not this system, if it were ever actualized, would *actually* undergo any feelings and experiences, it seems coherent to suppose that it might not. But if this is possible, then phenomenal experience is not functionally analyzable or determined. Functional organization is not what necessarily *fixes* phenomenal consciousness. What, then, does?

It is important to understand what is being claimed about the China-body system to appreciate the full force of the example. Again the crucial question is not whether it *would* in fact undergo experiences but whether it *might* not. Suppose a certain rock R were to be dropped. Would it fall to earth? Of course it would. The prevailing laws of nature are such that if R were dropped, it would fall. Consistent with those laws, assuming that nothing interferes, it is not coherent to suppose that R does anything else. But there is no logical inconsistency in supposing that the laws themselves are false, that other laws are operative. So even though it is true that if R were dropped it would fall, still it *might* not do so, where the force of 'might' here is metaphysical or logical and not just nomic.

This point can be made in terms of possible worlds. Think of the set of worlds in which our laws of nature obtain. These worlds are not the only possible ones. There are worlds in which our laws are replaced by others. The former worlds are the nomically possible ones. If R is dropped in any of these worlds, it falls (again assuming no outside interference). But in some of the other worlds, worlds that are metaphysically possible but nomically impossible, R does not fall.

These points are frequently obscured in discussions of the China-body system. Paul Churchland, in presenting what he takes to be the problem here for functionalism, writes,

[The] system . . . could presumably instantiate the relevant functional organization . . . and would therefore be the subject of mental states, according to functionalism. But surely, it is urged, the complex states that there play the functional roles of pain, pleasure, and sensations-of-color *would* not have intrinsic qualia as ours do, and *would* therefore fail to be genuine mental states. (Churchland 1990, p. 39; my italics)

The real issue, however, is not (or at least should not be) whether the China-body system *would* fail to have feelings and experiences but rather, as I note above, whether it is metaphysically impossible for the system to lack these states.[15] To decide that it is nomically impossible for the system to lack experiences is not to decide that it is metaphysically impossible. After all, it certainly seems that we can imagine the system itself being without any feelings and experiences, just as we can imagine the rock, R, floating in the air or moving away from the earth. But if we really can imagine these things, then they are metaphysically possible. And that entails that phenomenal consciousness is neither identical with, nor metaphysically determined by, functional organization. This is the problem of functional duplicates.

Box 1.7

The Problem of Duplicates

Are zombie replicas possible? Are total functional duplicates without any phenomenal consciousness possible? If so, what does this tell us about phenomenal consciousness?

1.8   The Problem of the Inverted Spectrum

The classic inverted spectrum argument goes as follows. Suppose that Tom has a very peculiar visual system. His visual experiences are systematically inverted with respect to those of his fellows. When Tom looks at red objects, for example, what it is like for him is the same as what it is like for other people when they look at green objects and vice versa. This peculiarity is one of which neither he nor others are aware. Tom has learned the meanings of color words in the usual way, and he applies these words correctly. Moreover, his nonlinguistic behavior is standard in every way.

Now, when Tom views a ripe tomato in good light, his experience is phenomenally, subjectively different from the experiences you and I undergo. But his experience is *functionally* just like ours. His experience is of the sort that is usually produced in him by viewing red objects (in

the same sort of way that our experiences of red are produced) and that usually leads him (again in parallel fashion) to believe that a red object is present. In short, his experience functions in just the same way as ours do. So the phenomenal quality of Tom's experience is not a matter of its functional role. This conclusion cannot be accepted by any philosopher who wants to analyze, or understand, phenomenal consciousness functionally. But what, if anything, is wrong with the above reasoning? This is the problem of the inverted spectrum.[16]

One way to fix the puzzle clearly in your mind is to imagine that you are operated on by surgeons who alter some of the connections between neurons in your visual system. These alterations have the effect of making neurons that used to fire as a result of retinal-cell activity produced by viewing red objects now fire in response to such cell activity produced by seeing green objects and vice versa. On awakening from the operation, you find the world very weird indeed. Your lawn now looks red to you, the trees are varying shades of red and purple, the flamingo statues that decorate your garden look light green instead of pink. These changes in your experiences will be reflected in your behavior, for example, in your verbal reports. So there will be straightforward evidence that an inversion has occurred.

Now suppose that the surgeons operated on you at birth, so that you learned to apply color vocabulary to things with anomalous looks. For you, these looks are not anomalous, of course. So you use color terms in precisely the same circumstances as everyone else. Is this not imaginable? If we agree it is, however difficult it might be in practice to produce such an inversion, then functionally identical inverted experiences are metaphysically possible. So functionalism cannot be the truth about phenomenal consciousness.

The problem of the inverted spectrum is sometimes presented with respect to a single individual who, after the operation described two paragraphs ago, adapts to it through time and eventually forgets that things ever looked any different to him. In this case, it is suggested, the later person is subject to visual experiences that are functionally isomorphic to the earlier ones but that are subjectively different.[17]

In a variant scenario, we are asked to consider another planet, Inverted Earth.[18] On Inverted Earth, things have complementary colors to those of their counterparts on earth. The sky is yellow, grass is red, ripe tomatoes

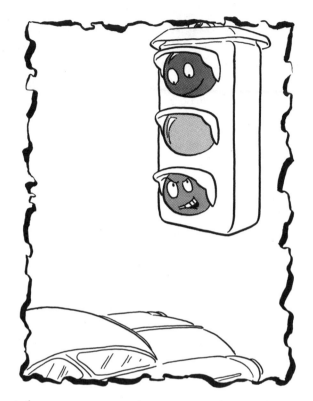

"I'M BORED—LET'S SWITCH PLACES."

are green, and so on. The inhabitants of Inverted Earth undergo psycho-logical attitudes and experiences with inverted functional roles, and hence, on a functional view of content, inverted intentional contents. They think that the sky is yellow, see that grass is red, and so on. However, they call the sky blue, the grass green, ripe tomatoes red, and so on, just as we do. Indeed, in all respects consistent with the alterations just described, Inverted Earth is as much like Earth as possible.

One night while you are asleep, a team of mad scientists insert color-inverting lenses in your eyes and take you to Inverted Earth, where you are substituted for your Inverted Earth twin, or doppelgänger. On awakening, you are aware of no difference, since the inverting lenses neutralize the inverted colors. You think that you are still where you were before. What it is like for you when you see the sky or anything else is just what it was like on earth. But after enough time has passed, after you have become sufficiently embedded in the language and physical environment of Inverted Earth, your intentional contents will come to match those of the other inhabitants. You will come to think that the sky is yellow, for example, just as they do, because the state that was earlier on earth normally caused by blue things is now normally caused by yellow things. So the later you will come to be subject to inner states that are functionally, and hence intentionally, inverted relative to the inner states of the earlier you, whereas the phenomenal aspects of your experiences will remain unchanged. It follows, as before, that what it is like for you cannot be grounded in the functional features of your mental states.[19]

What we have here, of course, is the converse of the traditional inverted-spectrum hypothesis. Although this version of the problem and the earlier ones are typically presented as challenges to those philosophers who want to think of pheneomenal consciousness functionally, it should be noted that they could be developed in ways that threaten a nonfunctional, physicalist approach to phenomenal states, too. For, if we can imagine microphysical zombies, as was supposed in the last problem, we can surely also imagine microphysical duplicates whose experiences are phenomenally inverted. Again, the claim here is not that such duplicates are nomically possible, merely that they are metaphysically possible. If this is so, if, for example, I could have a microphysical twin with experiences that were inverted relative to my own—and this does not seem difficult to imagine—then the problem of the inverted spectrum also becomes a challenge to the physicalist who rejects functionalism.

Box 1.8

The Problem of the Inverted Spectrum

Can two people who are functionally identical undergo experiences that are phenomenally inverted? Can one person, at different times, undergo experiences that are phenomenally inverted but functionally identical? Can there be phenomenal inversion in the case that there is microphysical duplication? What should we conclude about phenomenal consciousness from reflection on inverted experiences?

1.9   The Problem of Transparency

Focus your attention on a square that has been painted blue. Intuitively, you are directly aware of blueness and squareness as out there in the world away from you, as features of an external surface. Now shift your gaze inward and try to become aware of your experience itself, inside you, apart from its objects. Try to focus your attention on some intrinsic feature of the experience that distinguishes it from other experiences, something other than what it is an experience *of*. The task seems impossible: one's awareness seems always to slip through the experience to blueness and squareness, as instantiated together in an external object. In turning one's mind inward to attend to the experience, one seems to end up concentrating on what is outside again, on external features or properties. And this remains so, even if there really is no blue square in front of one—if, for example, one is subject to an illusion. Again, one experiences blue and square *as* features of an external surface, but introspection does not seem to reveal any further distinctive features of the experience over and above *what* one experiences in undergoing the illusion.

Visual experience, then, is transparent or diaphanous, as is phenomenal consciousness generally.[20] Take, for example, the case of pain. Focus your attention on some particular pain you are feeling, a pain in a leg, say. What do you end up focusing on? In my own case, I find myself attending to what I am experiencing in having the pain, namely, a painful disturbance in the leg. I experience the disturbance *as* located in the relevant part of my leg. But I cannot make myself aware of any features of my experience over and above, or apart from, what I am experiencing. My experience, after all, is not itself in my leg. This is shown by the fact that I could have an experience exactly like my actual one even if I had no legs, as long as my brain were stimulated electrically in the right way. But if I have a pain in my leg, *all* I end up focusing on, when I introspect my experience, is how things seem to be *in my leg*. How is this to be accounted for?

Box 1.9

The Problem of Transparency

How can experience be transparent in the above way? What is it about phenomenal consciousness that is responsible for its diaphanous character?

1.10 The Problem of Felt Location and Phenomenal Vocabulary

Suppose you feel a pain in a hand. You have an experience of something painful there. But there really is no pain inside your hand. Pains are mental objects, which depend for their existence on the appropriate neural activity, even though they are certainly sometimes caused by disturbances in limbs. Your experience, then, is mistaken or inaccurate: it tells you that there is a pain in your hand and really there is not. So your experience is *mis*representing how things are. But this seems highly counterintuitive: surely people who feel pains in hands are not normally subject to *illusions*.

One response to this problem is to say that when people feel pains in hands, there typically are pains in hands even though there are no pains

spatially inside hands. The term 'in', as it is used in pain discourse, has a special meaning quite different from its meaning in other contexts. This is supposedly why it is a fallacy to argue in the following way:

I have a pain in my thumb.
My thumb is in my mouth.
Therefore, I have a pain in my mouth.

If 'in' meant spatially inside, then the above argument would be valid, since the relation of being spatially inside is transitive (if x is inside y and y is inside z, then x is inside z). But the argument is not valid. So 'in' in the first premise and the conclusion must have a special meaning different from its meaning in the second premise.[21]

This view is often generalized to all terms used in connection with sensations that are also applied to external physical objects. Thus, green afterimages are not literally green; square afterimages are not literally square; stinging pains do not literally sting; burning smells do not literally burn; and so on. The problem now is to say what these terms *do* mean as applied to experiences, and how their meanings are connected to the meanings of the same terms, as applied to external things.

Box 1.10

The Problem of Felt Location and Phenomenal Vocabulary

If pains, itches, and tickles are not really where they feel to be, then are we all the subjects of illusions in having bodily sensations? What can it mean to say that a pain is in a leg or that it stings, if pains in legs are not really inside legs and do not really sting? What account can be given of the meaning of phenomenal vocabulary generally?

1.11   The Problem of the Alien Limb

This problem arises out of reflection on a psychological disorder. Subjects who have paralyzed legs or arms sometimes report that the limbs are alien or counterfeit. The well-known physician Oliver Sacks describes one such case in his book *The Man Who Mistook His Wife for a Hat*. A man who had just been admitted to the hospital for some tests, and who was left by the nurse in bed, managed to fall out of it onto the floor. He told Sacks that he had fallen asleep and that when he woke up, he found someone else's leg in bed with him—a severed leg, no less! He felt the leg gingerly with his hands, and it seemed well formed. But it was "peculiar" and cold. So he threw it out of bed. The trouble was that when he threw it, he somehow came along, too. And now, although he found it difficult to believe, the leg was attached to him.

Sacks tells us that the man then tried to tear the leg off his body. On being informed that it was *his own* leg that he was treating so roughly, he appeared absolutely dumbfounded and said, "this leg, this *thing* doesn't feel right, doesn't feel real—and it doesn't *look* part of me" (p. 57).

Remarkably, Sacks himself at one point had such a disorder (perhaps it is contagious!). In another of his writings, he describes his own experience. One of his legs, Sacks reports, "looked and felt uncannily alien—a lifeless replica attached to my body" (1984, p. 91). Later, after Sacks had regained feeling in his leg, he describes the transformation as follows:

Back in my room, on my bed, I hugged the redeemed leg, or rather cast, though even this seemed living now, transfused with the life of the leg. "You dear old

thing, you sweet thing," I found myself saying. "You've come back, you're real, you're part of me now." Its reality, its presence, its dearness were all one. (1984, p. 117)

Sacks, while he had the above disorder, was conscious of the alien leg when he looked at it. He had no difficulty in identifying it as a leg. But it did not *feel* to him like *his* leg. And the same is true for the man who fell out of bed. Presumably, this is at least in part why they both saw one leg as alien: given the lack of any bodily feeling of the above sort, neither believed the limb to be his own.

It appears, then, that there is an aspect to feeling, of the sort involved in bodily sensation, that somehow involves reference to the subject of the feeling. The claim here is not that this is necessarily always the case, but that it typically is. To take a more mundane case, consider a pain in a leg. There seems to be a sense in which what you experience, is not just that there is pain but that there is pain in *your* leg. Neither Sacks nor the man who fell out of bed had any such bodily experience with respect to the alien leg.

The philosophical questions that arise here are these: How can the subject of a feeling himself be involved in the feeling? Just what *is* the relationship of the self to the phenomenology of feeling?

Box 1.11

The Problem of the Alien Leg

How can I feel a pain in *my* leg? How do I get to be involved in my own feelings?

These are the ten problems of consciousness that will occupy us in one way or another for the rest of the book. Together they form perhaps the hardest nut to crack in all of philosophy. Now that they have been presented, it perhaps will seem less surprising to you that some philosophers of mind, not generally opposed to substantive philosophical theorizing, see little or no hope of coming to a satisfactory understanding of phenomenal consciousness.[22] But just how and why the problems are *so* deeply perplexing deserves further examination. It is the main topic of the next chapter.

2

Why the Problems Run So Deep

Now that we have an appreciation of just what the philosophical problems of consciousness are (at least insofar as phenomenal consciousness is concerned), it is worthwhile exploring the question of why they are so mystifying and how it is that phenomenal consciousness raises very special difficulties. What I am going to suggest is that a kind of paradox arises in our reflections on the puzzles. I call this the *paradox of phenomenal consciousness*.

This paradox is not a *formal* one like the the paradox of the liar. It does not issue in a formal contradiction via the rules of formal logic. Rather it is more like the paradox of the bald man. The latter paradox, which we owe to Eubulides in the fourth century B.C., goes as follows:

A man with no hairs is bald.
A single hair never makes the difference between being bald and not being bald (in other words, for any number N, if a man with N hairs is bald, then a man with $N + 1$ hairs is bald).
Therefore, a man with a million hairs is bald.

The conclusion follows from the premises by standard logical rules, and the premises certainly seem true. So apparently the conclusion must be true. Now there is here no formal contradiction of the sort found in the liar paradox. Instead, we have arrived at a true conclusion by apparently impeccable reasoning. And yet we know that our conclusion is false. Something of this sort obtains in the case of phenomenal consciousness, as we shall shortly see.

2.1   Must the Physical Be Objective?

Let us begin by returning to the problem of perspectival subjectivity. This problem is presented as a difficulty for the physicalist about phenomenally conscious states.

Phenomenally conscious states, it was urged, are subjective in that fully comprehending *them* requires adopting a certain experiential point of view. In this way, as I noted earlier, they are perspectival.[1] But physical items are not perspectival. Understanding fully what salt is, for example, does not require that one undergo the experiences normal human beings undergo as they view and taste salt. An alien who undergoes very different experiences on perceiving salt is not thereby precluded from understanding fully the nature of salt, namely, sodium chloride.

What can the physicalist, viewed here as the philosopher who believes that, in some sense yet to be explained, everything is physical, say in response to this pressing challenge? Phenomenally conscious states, for example, feeling pain, are alleged to have a property, perspectival subjectivity, that is, the property of being an x such that fully comprehending x requires adopting a certain experiential point of view, which no physical thing has. If this is so, then, by Leibniz's Law (which asserts that, for any x and y, if x and y are identical, then they share all the same properties), it follows that phenomenally conscious states (hereafter just phenomenal states) are *not* physical.

It appears that the physicalist must respond either by denying that phenomenal states are perspectivally subjective or by denying that being objective is a necessary condition for being physical.

Let us suppose for the moment that the physicalist about phenomenal consciousness opts for the latter reply. How can this strategy be defended? It will not do, I suggest, simply to assert that being objective is not a necessary condition for being physical without further defense, as, for example, John Searle does (1992). After all, there is a long-established tradition, according to which nothing that is not objective can be physical. Let us, then, examine some of the different meanings of 'physical'.

It is sometimes supposed that a general term is physical (that is, that it picks out a physical state or property or kind) just in case it occurs in some true theory of physics. This is evidently too narrow a definition, however; terms like 'acid', 'alkali', and 'DNA' lie outside the domain of physics, and yet they would normally be classified as physical. Perhaps we should say that a general term is physical just in case it occurs in some true theory of physics, chemistry, molecular biology, or neurophysiology. But it is far from clear that this is a satisfactory way to characterize the physical. If 'gene' and 'neuron' are now classified as physical terms, then why not go further and classify 'tsetse fly', 'crocodile', 'continent', and 'planet' (terms found in entomology, zoology, geology, and astronomy, respectively) as physical, too? The general problem here, of course, is that we have not been provided with any account of what physics, chemistry, molecular biology, and neurophysiology share in virtue of which they count as physical and the other sciences mentioned above do not.[2]

One way of avoiding this problem is to say that a general term is physical just in case it occurs in some true theory adequate for the explanation of the phenomena of nonliving matter. But there remain serious difficulties even here. Suppose that there are properties that are tokened or instantiated *only* in the brains of certain living creatures, and that these properties figure in neurophysiological laws. It seems to me ad hoc to deny that such properties are physical.[3] Yet this is what we must do according to the final definition.

How, then, is the term 'physical' to be understood? Even leaving to one side the problems that face the definitions mentioned above, none of these definitions is broad enough to allow us to count perspectivally subjective states as physical. Is there any other definition to which the physicalist about phenomenal states might appeal? It appears that the only sort of definition that could fit the bill is a very broad one indeed, according to which there is nothing in the natural world that is not physical, at least as the natural world in which we live is normally conceived. But what is it for something to be a part of the natural world?

There have been any number of different ways of understanding the term 'natural'. So different philosophers have had very different conceptions of what it is to be a naturalist about a given domain, for example, the mental. The intuitive idea, I suggest, is simply that, on the naturalist view, the world contains nothing supernatural, that, at the bottom level, there are microphysical phenomena, governed by the laws of microphysics and, at higher levels, phenomena that not only participate in causal interactions describable by scientific laws but also bear the same general metaphysical relationship to microphysical items as do the items falling within the scope of such higher-level laws as those that obtain in, for example, geology and neurophysiology. I want now to say something about what I take this relationship to be.

Consider Mount Everest. Suppose that *t* is one of the chunks of matter Everest would have lost had certain bombs been detonated at its top. Suppose also that the bombs are not in fact detonated. Then it is true that Everest might have existed without *t*. But the same is not true of the aggregate or sum of Everest's material parts. Hence, Everest and the sum differ in a modal property. Hence, Everest is not strictly identical with this sum. Rather, Everest is *constituted* by it. What is true here for Everest is true for other geological objects. A glacier, for example, is constituted by a massive chunk of ice, but it is not strictly identical with it. Indeed the same is true for higher-level natural objects and events generally. Each horse is constituted by a torso, four legs, a head, a tail. Each horse leg is constituted by a thigh, a calf, a hoof. Likewise, a predator's eating its prey is constituted by an action of chewing and swallowing. Each action of chewing is constituted by certain movements of the jaw, and each action of swallowing by certain movements in the throat. In all of these cases, modal considerations show that there is no strict identity.[4]

If higher-level concrete particulars or tokens are viewed in this way, then it must be granted that each such token may vary in its constitution in different possible worlds. Something similar to this is true of higher-level types (properties, types of process, types of state, types of event), I believe, if the naturalist perspective is adopted. Let me explain.

In general, higher-level natural types are not identical with lower-level ones. There are no types from chemistry and physics, for example, with which being a neuron, being a continent, or being an earthquake may plausibly be identified. Likewise, there is no single biochemical property with which the property of aging (in the sense of wear and tear) is identical. Plants and animals all age, and in aging their biochemical properties change. But there is no *shared* biochemical process that always goes along with aging. Similarly, gene types are not identical with chunks of DNA, contrary to what many philosophers have supposed. One and the same gene can be associated with different chunks of DNA. Moreover, some chunks of DNA redundantly repeat others within a single organism.[5]

The general relationship that obtains between higher-level and lower-level natural types is one of *realization*. Higher-level property types have *multiple* lower-level realizations. Consider, for example, the biological property of engaging in a mating ritual. The ritual used by peacocks is dramatically different from the one used by seals. Peacocks spread their tail feathers in a decorative fan, whereas male seals fight it out to demonstrate their dominance. In general, the properties by means of which members of different species engage in mating rituals vary enormously. Engaging in a mating ritual has multiple realizations. Likewise, reproduction is realized in plants and animals by any number of different processes, some sexual and some asexual. Paramecia reproduce by dividing in two; seahorses by the female's laying eggs and placing them in a pouch in the male; humans by bearing live young. To take a well-worn nonbiological example, temperature is realized by mean molecular kinetic energy in a gas and by the blackbody distribution of electromagnetic waves in a vacuum. It has other realizations in solids and plasmas.

The realization relation is not easy to analyze, but it is at least in part one of upward determination or generation: any object that has the higher-level property, or is an instance of the higher-level type, does so *in virtue of simultaneously* having one of the lower-level properties or types that realizes it. A gas has a certain temperature at time t, for example, in virtue of its having a certain mean molecular energy at t.

Box 2.1

In a case of realization, the lower-level type, P, synchronically fixes the higher-level type, Q. If P realizes Q (in objects of kind K [humans, diamonds, etc.]), then the tokening of P at any time t by any object O (that is a member of K) *necessitates* the tokening of Q at t by O but not conversely. What sort of necessity is involved here? It is sometimes supposed that if P realizes Q, then, in all *metaphysically* possible worlds, every instance of P is an instance of Q. However, I shall adopt a much weaker requirement, namely, if P realizes Q (in objects of kind K), then, in all possible worlds sharing our microphysical laws and our microphysical facts, every token of P (in a member of K) is also a token of Q.

Box 2.1 *continued*

> A second aspect to realization, in my view, is that the determination of the higher-level type by the lower-level one is always mediated by an implementing mechanism.[6]

We are now in a position to summarize how naturalistic phenomena in the actual world lying outside the microphysical realm are conceived within the above account:

Higher-level naturalistic phenomena (both token and type) are either ultimately constituted or ultimately realized by microphysical phenomena.

The term 'ultimately' appears here, since, on the naturalist perspective, there is a hierarchy of constitution and realization relationships between higher-level and lower-level natural phenomena whose foundation is the microphysical realm.

If this is how we think of higher-level naturalistic phenomena, we might classify something, above the microphysical level, as physical in a very weak and broad sense of the term 'physical' if and only if it is a higher-level naturalistic phenomenon. Returning now to the case of phenomenal states, the physicalist can say that there is nothing inherently magical or miraculous or supernatural about such states. Phenomenally conscious states like pain or the feeling of depression are found in the natural world, and, like other types of phenomena found there, they are ultimately realized by microphysical phenomena. This is what justifies labeling these states as physical.

On the present understanding of 'physical', then, being objective is not a necessary condition for being physical. Rather, what is crucial in the case of types is that the types have *objective realizations in the microphysical realm*. So phenomenal states can be both subjective (in the perspectival sense) and physical. If this is so, it may be urged, the challenge to physicalism now collapses.

But has the challenge *really* been answered, even given the final very weak and broad elucidation of the physicalist's position? Reflection on the next problem of consciousness—the problem of mechanism—strongly suggests that there is still a serious difficulty. It is to this difficulty that I turn in the next section.

Box 2.2

Summary

Definitions of the term 'physical':
1. Something is physical just in case it lies within the domain of physics.
2. Something is physical just in case it lies within the domain of physics, chemistry, molecular biology, and neurophysiology.
3. Something is physical just in case it is described in some theory adequate for the explanation of nonliving matter.
4. Something is physical just in case it is either ultimately constituted or ultimately realized by something within the domain of microphysics.

The proposal on behalf of the physicalist: phenomenal states are both perspectivally subjective and physical in the last sense.

2.2   Perspectival Subjectivity and the Explanatory Gap

Brain states are not themselves perspectival. But phenomenal states are. How is it that items that are realized by nonperspectival items can be perspectival? What is responsible for the production of states with perspectival subjectivity? How can electrical activity in dull gray matter generate feeling and experience? What is wanted here is the description of a possible *mechanism* that underlies the generation of perspectival entities by nonperspectival ones and that closes the enormous gap we intuitively feel between the two. This is the problem of mechanism.

One response to this problem is simply to deny that there is any mechanism that provides a link between the subjective and the objective. On this view, it is simply a brute fact that certain brain states realize certain phenomenal states. There is no explanation or further account of how the former give rise to the latter.

This seems to be John Searle's position when he claims that there is no link between consciousness and the brain.[7] But is it really consistent with the claim that phenomenal states are *physical*? Searle seems to think so. With no apparent concern for consistency, however, having said that there is no link, he then immediately compares the case of consciousness and the brain with that of liquidity and H_2O molecules, in which there certainly is a mechanism (as I noted earlier).[8] Why does he make the comparison? Because, I suggest, it would be ad hoc (at the very least), from the physicalist/naturalist perspective, to suppose that the realization of the phenomenal by the neural is different in kind from other well-established cases of realization in science. As I illustrated in the last chapter, in such cases there is always a mechanism.

There is also another sort of reason grounded in some more-general metaphysical considerations for insisting that there must be a mechanism. This reason may be brought out as follows: some laws in science are basic and others are nonbasic. This distinction can be drawn in a number of different ways. But it seems to me that one way in which laws can be nonbasic is epistemic. An epistemically basic law is one for which there is no further explanation of *why* it obtains or *how* tokens of the property expressed in its antecedent cause tokens of the property expressed in its consequent.

Consider, as an illustration, the microphysical law that elementary particles of like charge repel. To suppose that this is an epistemically basic law is to suppose that there is no further explanation of why sameness of charge brings about repulsion. Alternatively, consider the neurophysiological law that when a neuron reaches action potential, it fires.[9] This law is epistemically nonbasic. Consequently, there is a mechanism implementing the transaction. In this case, the mechanism is chemical. As positively charged sodium ions flow into the neuron from some prior stimulus, the negative electrical charge inside the neuron diminishes. Action potential is achieved at the base of the neuron at a certain threshold of depolarization. Once this threshold is crossed, certain gates in the adjoining region of the postsynaptic neuron open, allowing further charged sodium ions to flow through. This process of gate opening and ion flow is repeated, region by region, in a chain reaction all the way down the axon, thereby generating an electrical impulse. When the process of conduction reaches the end of the axon, it causes the neuron to fire via the release, into the synaptic gap, of molecules of a neurotransmitter (one of several different chemicals), which have been stored in synaptic vesicles.

What is true for this particular law is true for other special science laws, for example, those of biology and geology. Special science laws are always implemented by lower-level mechanisms. Of course, these mechanisms will themselves be governed by the appropriate laws, and these laws, in turn, if they are special science laws, will require their own mechanisms. It follows that the epistemically basic laws lie outside the special sciences.[10]

Suppose next that the feeling of pain is realized in human beings by brain state *B* so that necessarily whenever a human being is in brain state *B*, he or she feels pain at the same time. Call the bridge law here *PL*. Suppose that for *this* synchronic law, there is *no* mechanism: *PL* is epistemically basic and hence unlike the neurophysiological law cited above. The question that now arises is whether *PL* is metaphysically determined by the microphysical laws and initial microphysical conditions. Is it coherent to suppose that all the microphysical facts down to the smallest detail and all the basic microphysical laws of the actual world obtain and that *PL* fails to obtain? Is there another metaphysically possible world that is *just like* our world with respect to its microphysical facts and laws but in which *PL* is not a law? Is *PL*, in this way, metaphysically basic?

If we think of realization in the way I suggested in the last section, the answer to this question must be no. And that seems to me the only answer it is at all plausible to give, if we are indeed physicalists. The point generalizes to all other synchronic bridge laws. So the idea that, for all we know, there is another possible world with all the same microphysical particles as the actual world, having all the same spatiotemporal locations, and interacting in exactly the same ways, according to the same microphysical laws, and yet having different bridge laws and hence different higher-level special science laws and features—different ways of forming glaciers, different types of plants, different combinations of genes, different weather patterns, and so on—seems fundamentally opposed to the physicalist/naturalist perspective.[11] It also seems to many philosophers counterintuitive. As Jaegwon Kim notes,

we seem to share the conviction that . . . if God were to create a world, all he needs to do is to create the basic particles, their configurations, and the laws that

are to govern the behavior of these basic entities. He need not *also* create tables
and trees and refrigerators ; once the microworld is fixed, the rest will take care
of itself. (Kim 1979, p. 40)

Now if it is true that once the microphysical laws are fixed and all
the particular microphysical facts are in place, *all* the other laws are
metaphysically fixed too, including the bridge laws, then *PL* is not like the
microphysical laws from a metaphysical perspective: *PL* is metaphysically
nonbasic. This disanalogy strongly suggests that *PL* cannot be epistemically basic after all, that it cannot just be a brute epistemic fact that
PL obtains, as it is for the microphysical laws. If *PL* is metaphysically
derivative, then there should be *some* explanation of how brain state *B*
gives rise to the feeling of pain, an explanation that is relevant to the
deeper issue of how *PL* is metaphysically determined by the microphysical
laws and facts. So there must be a specific mechanism that implements
PL. Likewise for all other neural-phenomenal bridge laws, and indeed
all laws above the microphysical level.

The conclusion that there must be a mechanism for *PL* is reinforced
by the specific character of the phenomenal. Phenomenal states are perspectival; brain states are not. There seems an enormous gap between
the two. Does not the fact that *B*—that particular brain state—generates
the feeling of pain call out for explanation? Why *could not B* produce a
state that felt different? Why *could not B* fail to produce any feeling at
all? On the face of it, these questions demand answers. To suppose that
in the case of *PL* there are *no* answers, not just that we do not know
what they are, is to adopt an unstable and very unsatisfying position. If
any bridge law has an explanation, surely *PL* must have one. For it is
only in the case of *PL* and the other bridge laws involving phenomenal
states that the perspectivally subjective enters. But as everyone will agree,
at least some of the other bridge laws do have explanations, indeed
explanations that we know. So *PL* must have an explantion, too.

It appears, then, that the physicalist cannot reasonably deny that there
is a mechanism, or set of mechanisms, that provides an explanatory
link between the phenomenal and the neural. Given that there is such a
mechanism or set of mechanisms, the place of phenomenal states in the
natural, physical world is not threatened. But what could this mechanism

be? We currently have no idea. Moreover, the only general picture we
have for understanding the realization of higher-level types by lower-
level ones seems clearly inappropriate here. This needs a little explanation.

Consider the case of hardness in a diamond. Hardness is a constitu-
tional-dispositional property: something is hard in certain circumstances
just in case it is so constituted that it is disposed to resist penetration in
those circumstances. This disposition is realized in diamonds by a certain
crystalline structure in which the arrangement of crystals maximizes inter-
crystal forces. Given such an arrangement, the crystals are very difficult
to split apart, and diamonds, therefore, resist penetration.

In this case, we understand the mechanism by which hardness is generated as operating in accordance with the following model: the higher-
level property has a certain essence. This essence is of this sort: having
a constitutional property that disposes its possessor to *V* (resist penetration, in the case of hardness). Given that, as a matter of nomological
necessity (the sort of necessity found in laws of nature), the lower-level
property disposes its possessor to *V*, it follows that once any individual
has the lower-level property, it necessarily has *a* constitutional property
that disposes its possessor to *V*, and hence it necessarily has the higher-
level one. Of course, the particular law appealed to here, namely, that
objects having the lower-level property are disposed to *V*, itself demands
explanation if it is not microphysical. Further mechanisms and still-lower-
level laws will be relevant to *this* explanation.

Box 2.3

This model provides an explanatory structure in terms of which the generation of hardness in diamonds can be understood. It should be noted, however, that it is not crucial to our understanding of how hardness is generated
that hardness be taken to have the specified essence. To see this, suppose
that it is merely sufficient, without being necessary, for an object to be
hard in certain circumstances that it be so constituted that it is disposed
to resist penetration in those circumstances. So long as this connection is
a *conceptual* one, that is, one that we can know obtains by reflecting on our
concept of hardness, the explanation goes through in a parallel manner.[12]

Likewise, if the higher-level property has a functional essence, then a similar account can be given. Here the higher-level property is of this general type: having *a* property that plays functional role *R*. So the lower-level property determines the higher-level property in a corresponding manner to the dispositional case.[13]

It appears, then, that if phenomenal states are realized by neural states, their realization should at least conform to one of the above models in the following way: phenomenal states should have *second-order essences,* that is, essences of the type, being *a* state that itself has feature *F* (e.g., plays such and such a functional role).[14] A given neural state *N* will then realize a given phenomenal state *P* by itself having the relevant feature *F*, as a matter of nomological necessity, so that necessarily any instance of *N* is an instance of *a* state's having *F* and hence is necessarily also an instance of *P*. This, it seems plausible to suppose, must still be the case even if—as one well-known philosopher, Colin McGinn, has urged—we are ourselves so constituted that we cannot fully understand the specific mechanisms responsible for producing perspectival states.[15]

According to McGinn, with respect to understanding these mechanisms, we are in the same predicament as small children asked to grasp some abstruse concepts in theoretical physics, or chimpanzees presented with triples of objects of varying size and asked to reliably identify the one intermediate in size. Understanding is beyond our cognitive capacities.

This suggestion initially seems very strange. But McGinn notes that if other creatures in nature can lack the capacity to understand some of the things we understand, surely we too, as products of nature ourselves, *might* not have the power to understand everything. As McGinn puts the point, there could be an explanation that is *cognitively closed* to us of just how phenomenal consciousness is generated. If this is the case, as McGinn believes, then God knows wherein the answer lies, but for *us* the matter must remain an impenetrable puzzle.

But what *exactly* is beyond our cognitive capacities here? McGinn's view is that phenomenal states have essences that we cannot grasp, "hidden" essences, as he calls them.[16] McGinn seems to agree, however, that the realization of phenomenal states by lower-level physical states must conform to the very general picture sketched above (or at least to the essentialist part of it). He writes,

Functionalists claim that the causal role of brain states is what . . . supplies the link to consciousness. But they also hold—what indeed follows—that causal role constitutes the nature or essence of conscious states. Only because conscious states are held to be defined in terms of causal role can functionalists assert that this is the right property of the brain to provide the necessary link. They are thus rightly committed to a thesis about the nature of consciousness itself. And I think that any proposal . . . must take this form. (1991, pp. 68–69)

Perhaps McGinn does not mean here to commit himself to the view that phenomenal states must have second-order essences, as, for example, on the functionalist account, but only to the view that they must have essences of *some* sort, if there is to be any explanation of how they are produced in the brain. But whatever his real view, it certainly seems that *no* appeal to essences is going to close the explanatory gap. For if phenomenal states are perspectival and have essences that define them, as McGinn supposes, then their essences must be perspectival. So how can a comprehension of these *essences* help us, or anyone else, to understand the generation of phenomenal states from brain states?

The main difficulty here is that if the second-order essence, being a state that has feature *F,* is perspectival, then *F* will surely have to be perspectival, too. That is because if *F* is not perspectival, then there seems nothing left in the essence that could account for its being perspectival. But what is the mechanism that explains how *this* perspectival feature is generated in the brain? The gap between the perspectivally subjective and the objective seems as large and inexplicable, at this level, as it did for phenomenal states initially. So no real progress has been made. Talk of a hidden essence appears to be of no assistance.[17]

The overall conclusion to which we seem driven is that phenomenal states really are *not* realized by lower-level physical states at all. But of course if this is the case, then phenomenal states are not themselves physical states, not even in the extremely broad sense elucidated earlier. This is, of course, a very strange view. It requires us to suppose that phenomenal consciousness emerged from the physical world at some stage in the history of evolution without there being any explanation whatsoever of its emergence. It is just a brute fact about the world that certain physical states are associated with certain nonphysical phenomenal states. Phenomenal consciousness, then, is not like life or aging or temperature or any other natural phenomenon. It is something supernatural, something that goes beyond any scientific laws; its existence is magic or a miracle! This is very hard to believe, especially when we reflect on how widespread phenomenal consciousness is within the natural world, being found not only in human beings but also in many nonhuman creatures.

Nonetheless, the conclusion that phenomenal states are nonphysical is reinforced by further examination of the problem of phenomenal causation.

Box 2.4

Summary

If phenomenal states are both perspectivally subjective and physical, then they must be realized by objective, physical states. This realization demands a mechanism, an explanation of how the phenomenal states are generated. Where one state S realizes another T, the explanation fits the following very general model: it is assumed that T is, by its very nature, the state of being a state that has such and such feature F; S is then discovered to have F (not accidentally but with the sort of necessity found in laws). Necessarily, then, anything that is an instance of S is simultaneously an instance of a state having F.

This model provides a framework for understanding how one state S can generate or determine another T at one and the same time. But it appears that the model cannot be used in the case of phenomenal states, because each phenomenal state will have to be supposed to have a nature that incorporates a feature F, which is different for each state and which is itself perspectivally subjective. The question will then arise of how the relevant objective states, the Ss, as it were, in the above model, can each have a perspectivally subjective feature. Unless this question has an answer, no satisfactory explanation will have been given of how the phenomenal states are generated. But the model provides no answer. So the conclusion we are led to is that phenomenal states are not physical after all (assuming that they are perspectivally subjective).

2.3   Physicalism and Phenomenal Causation

Suppose that you are newly arrived in the United States and that you are being driven along a country road with the windows down. As you turn a bend, a dead skunk comes into view and an extremely unpleasant odor fills the air, of a kind you have not smelled before, causing you to hold your nose. This is a simple example of phenomenal causation. There is something it is like for you, as you smell the noisome skunk scent. That phenomenal quality in your experience causes your subsequent behavior.

The neurophysiological story of this causal transaction is, in broad outline, clear. Airborne molecules of skunk scent are picked up by incredibly sensitive receptors in your nose. Transducers then convert this physical input into a neural message that is sent to the olfactory bulbs deep within the brain. Firing patterns there produce other firing patterns, culminating in a sequence of firing patterns on the motor neurons, which, in turn, send electrical messages down the nerves. The result is that your hand moves to your nose and you grasp it between your thumb and first finger.

It is part and parcel of any physicalist view of the world that the story just told can, in principle, be completed without introducing any nonphysical or subjective causes. How, then, can the felt quality of your olfactory experience make any difference? If the objective physical features belonging to the events and processes going on inside you suffice to provide a complete explanation for the kind of arm and hand movements you made, then how can the way your experience feels to you play any causal role at all in the production of those movements?

At the level of concrete particulars, it is evident that the physicalist must hold that your experience, e (that particular experience belonging to you then and there and to no one else), is identical with, or constituted by, one of the firing patterns in your head (call it f). Were this not the case, there would be a nonphysical cause, namely, e. At the level of types, the situation is a little more complicated.

Consider the kind of movement you made. Ex hypothesi, there is a *complete* objective, physical explanation of how f caused you to produce a movement of that kind. So f must have caused a movement of the sort that it did *wholly* because it had such and such objective, physical properties.

Equally, however, there is an explanation of why you moved your arm and hand to your nose that cites the felt quality Q of e. Of course, had you had different beliefs or desires (for example, had you thought that holding your nose would offend your host and had you wanted very strongly not to offend her), then you would have behaved differently. But still, in the circumstances, *e,* because it had quality *Q,* caused your arm and hand to move as they did. Had your experience possessed a different felt quality, had you smelled the sweet fragrance of roses, say, then you would have behaved differently.

Now, given that *e* is *f* (where the 'is' here is either identity or constitution), we seem to face a problem. How can *e* bring about one and the same piece of behavior *both* wholly because it is constituted by an event having certain objective, physical properties, $P_1, P_2, \ldots, P_n$ (both relational and nonrelational) *and* because it has a certain felt quality? There appears to be only one answer available to the physicalist: *e* must have its subjective felt quality because it has some specific objective, physical property, P_k, within the above cluster. If this is the case, then indirectly the felt quality *Q* makes a difference. It is because *e* has *Q* that it causes the movement, but, at a deeper level, *e* has *Q* because it has P_k, and the movement results wholly because *e* has a certain set of objective, physical properties, including P_k.

The idea, then, is that the causal relevance that *Q* has with respect to *e*'s causing the given movement is not intrinsic to *Q.* Rather it is derived from *Q*'s presence in *e* being simultaneously determined or fixed or necessitated by the presence of objective, physical property P_k in *e*. P_k, then, has the real causal power. *Q* inherits its causal power from P_k, the objective, physical property by which it is simultaneously (and nomologically) *necessitated.* Had *Q* been missing, P_k would have been missing, too, and if P_k had been missing, the given movements would not have resulted. You would not then have held your nose. So, indirectly, if *Q* had been missing, you would have behaved differently. Both *Q* and P_k, therefore, are causally efficacious.

But how can *Q* be simultaneously necessitated by P_k? How can it be the case that (at least) in all possible worlds sharing our microphysical facts and laws, at any time at which P_k is present, *Q* is present, too? It cannot be magic, at least not if physicalism is true. There must be some explanation. But if the felt quality *Q* is perspectivally subjective, then it appears that there can be no satisfactory explanation. *Q* cannot be *realized* by any objective, physical property at all. So *Q* itself is not a physical property, not even a subjective one; physicalism about phenomenally conscious states is false.

We have arrived again at the same conclusion we reached in the last section, this time via considerations pertaining to phenomenal causation.

Box 2.5

Summary

If the physicalist view of the world is correct, then the felt qualities of our experiences can make a difference to how we behave in only one way: they must be generated in the experiences from the objective, physical properties of the underlying firing patterns that constitute those experiences. In this way, the felt qualities inherit the causal powers of the lower-level physical properties that generate them. The generation here requires that it be necessary that once the appropriate objective, physical property is present, such and such a felt quality is present, too. But that cannot just be a brute fact. It demands explanation, and no satisfactory explanation seems possible. So physicalism about experience again seems untenable.

2.4 On the Denial of Perspectival Subjectivity

At this stage of our reflections, it is beginning to look as if the only alternative left open to the physicalist is to deny that phenomenal states are perspectivally subjective, contrary to what we supposed earlier. Without this denial, the three problems I have discussed above seem to refute physicalism. But how can perspectival subjectivity be denied? The answer must be that a wedge can be drawn between knowing fully what a phenomenal state is and knowing what it is like to undergo that state. The question we must now face is whether this is really plausible.

Suppose that phenomenal states have lower-level objective natures (neurophysiological ones, let us say) so that for these states the so-called type identity theory is true. Then, for each phenomenal state S, there will be some neural state N that is identical with S. If this is so, then someone might know fully what a certain phenomenal state itself was, namely, such and such a neural state, without ever having actually undergone that neural state and hence without ever having experienced the phenomenal state in question.

Suppose, for example, that I am a scientist and I find out that whenever you eat fudge, you are subject to a certain type of firing pattern K in your brain. This firing pattern is never present when you eat anything else. It goes along with a certain phenomenally distinctive experience you undergo, an experience I shall call 'fudgefeel'. According to the type identity theory, I now know fully what fudgefeel is, namely, K, even if I myself have never tasted fudge and so do not know what it is like to experience it.

The suggestion, then, is that the challenge to physicalism, presented by the earlier problem of perspectival subjectivity, derives its force from conflating knowing fully what a sensation or feeling *is* and knowing what it is *like* to undergo the sensation or feeling. Once this conflation is revealed, the problem is solved. With the rejection of perspectival subjectivity, the challenges posed to physicalism by the subsequent problems of mechanism and phenomenal causation also lose their *immediate* force, because now there is no barrier presented by perspectival subjectivity to the view that phenomenal states have objective physiological or functional natures.

The physicalist is certainly not yet out of the woods, however. For one thing, the problem of duplicates and the problem of the inverted spectrum have not yet been answered, and they both present powerful objections to the thesis that phenomenal states are either physiological or functional. For another, notwithstanding the appeal (at least to physicalists) of the strategy summarized above, the issue of perspectival subjectivity has not really been put to rest. Instead, the strategy is at best only partly effective.

To the extent that the problem allegedly posed by perspectival subjectivity is framed the way opponents of physicalism standardly frame it (and which I myself have followed so far), it seems to me that the response I have briefly described is not unreasonable. However, the problem can be sharpened further in a manner that makes it much harder to suppose that two types of knowledge, which must be kept distinct, are being conflated.

Fudgefeel is an experience defined, I am supposing, by reference to its phenomenal or subjective character. So there is something it is like to undergo fudgefeel. Moreover, by hypothesis, any (actual or possible) particular experience that feels just the way fudgefeel feels will be an instance of fudgefeel. So there is something it is *essentially* like to undergo fudgefeel. That is to say, there is some felt quality such that it is simply incoherent to suppose that fudgefeel is present without it. The state or experience I am calling fudgefeel has this felt quality whenever and wherever it is, or could be, found.

What it is like to undergo fudgefeel, then, is essential to fudgefeel. From this, the following claim surely follows:

(1) Not knowing what it is like to experience fudgefeel entails not knowing something *essential* to fudgefeel (namely, what it is like to experience it).

Given (1), we can infer

(2) Fully understanding the essential nature of fudgefeel requires knowing what it is like to experience fudgefeel.

And, of course,

(3) Knowing what it is like to experience fudgefeel requires adopting a certain experiential point of view (that conferred by eating fudge and having experiences like yours in doing so).

So,

(4) Fully understanding the essential nature of fudgefeel requires adopting a certain experiential point of view.

However,

(5) Fully understanding the essential nature of the objective basis of fudgefeel in you—that is, firing pattern *K*—does *not* require adopting any particular experiential point of view.

The claim in (5), I should emphasize, is a claim at the *type* level. It does not concern tokens of *K*. The point is that creatures with very different ranges of experiences can fully understand the essence of the neurophysiological type *K*. No particular experiential point of view is required.

Finally, from (4) and (5), we reach the conclusion

(6) Fudgefeel is not identical with *K*.

This argument has been stated with specific reference to the type identity theory. But it generalizes to any view that holds that phenomenal states are identical with objective, physical states or properties.

My proposal, then, is that the thesis that phenomenal states are subjective in the perspectival sense is best articulated in the manner of (4) above with the explicitly essentialist qualification, rather than in the somewhat looser way adopted earlier. Given this way of understanding the thesis, the charge that two different sorts of knowledge of phenomenal states are being conflated seems difficult to sustain. So, without much further argument, it is no longer open to us to deny that phenomenal states are perspectival. Physicalism remains in deep trouble.

Box 2.6

Summary

For any experience or feeling, what it is like to undergo it is essential to it. In each case, it is incoherent to suppose that *that very* experience or feeling exists without its actual felt or subjective quality. So fully understanding the essential nature of any given experience or feeling requires knowing what it is like to undergo it (and that, in turn, demands a certain experiential perspective). This is the best way to understand the thesis of perspectival subjectivity with respect to experiences and feelings. Given such an understanding, it is very hard to deny that such states are perspectivally subjective.

2.5   The Paradox of Phenomenal Consciousness

The cumulative effect of the considerations adduced so far is to put intense pressure on the view that phenomenally conscious states are physical, in any sense of the term 'physical', no matter how broad. Suppose now we throw in the towel on behalf of the physicalist and adopt an antiphysicalist stance: experiences and feelings have irreducible, nonphysical, perspectivally subjective features. This position, which is sometimes called *type dualism* or *property dualism,* relieves the pressure from the problems of perspectival subjectivity, mechanism, duplicates, and the inverted spectrum. But it helps not at all with the problem of phenomenal causation.

For we seem now compelled to admit that the felt or experienced qualities of our conscious lives play no causal role at all in producing the behaviors we normally suppose they are responsible for.

Consider again the earlier case of the skunk smell. Given that there is a complete objective physical explanation of why your hand and arm moved as they did, there is simply no room for a nonphysical cause to operate even at the type level. This is what was established by the argument in section 2.3. Subjective felt qualities can make a difference only if they are realized or generated in a nonmagical way by underlying objective physical properties, and hence only if they are themselves physical (in the broad sense I explained earlier). So if the unpleasant quality Q in your experience is not even broadly physical, then it did not have any influence on your hand's going to your nose to block out the smell. Even if Q had been absent, you would have held your nose. Q simply did not make any difference at all.

It might perhaps be tempting to some people to deny that there is a complete physical explanation for the production of the specified behavior. This seems a desperate move, however. Given what we now know about how the brain works, about the billions of neurons interacting with one another in response to the electrical messages they receive, it seems very implausible to suppose that there is no wholly physical story. It also goes against the history of science. The postulation of nonphysical causes in the past has always been a mistake. There has always been a deeper, physical explanation (although one unknown at the time). Think, for example, of epileptic seizures and demonic possession or lightning and Zeus's anger. Why suppose that this case is any different?

We seem compelled to admit that the way things feel and look and taste and sound and smell are causally irrelevant. As Frank Jackson (1982, p. 134) notes, "[T]hey are an excrescence. They *do* nothing. They *explain* nothing, they serve merely to sooothe the intuitions of dualists, and it is left a total mystery how they fit into the world view of science." But phenomenal qualities are *not* an excrescence. We *know* that the phenomenal qualities of our mental states are causally efficacious, just as we *know* that we have hands and legs, that there are rocks and trees.

These things are so basic to our ordinary conception of ourselves and the world we live in that we should never trust a philosophical argument that leads to an opposing conclusion. In any such argument, there must surely be a mistake, even if we cannot say just where the mistake lies. To deny this, in my view, is take a position that is simply not credible. Can anyone *really* believe that no man ever chooses to go out with a woman *because* of the way she looks, or that no one ever eats potato chips *because* of the way they taste? (It surely is not the nutritional value of potato chips that is responsible for their popularity—they have virtually none).

Box 2.7

Consider also how we react to the feelings other people have. Seeing you laugh at a funny film just as I am doing, I believe that you are undergoing an experience similar to mine, that what it is like for you at that moment is akin to what it is like for me. Or seeing you accidentally pour boiling water on your wrist, I believe that you are subject to the kind of feeling I call 'burning pain'. How is it possible for me to have these beliefs if phenomenal qualities are a mere excrescence? How can my beliefs be *about* what it is like for anyone if I am not caused to have those beliefs in part by the presence of the relevant phenomenal qualities?

The same sort of point can be made in connection with memories of past experiences, for example, Marcel Proust's being caused to remember certain experiences in his youth by the way a piece of madeleine cake tasted as he took tea one afternoon much later in his life (Proust 1981). Not only is this false, if the way things taste is nonphysical, but also it appears that he could not have remembered any sort of experience or feeling at all. If no phenomenal quality causes anything, then nothing in Proust's past experience could have caused his present psychological state. How, then, could he have remembered *how* he felt in the past? How could his memory reach out to, or be about, those felt qualities in his past experience?

There is also an insuperable problem of other minds if phenomenal qualities are causally irrelevant.[18] Given epiphenomenalism about how things look and feel, what could possibly count as evidence that anyone other than me ever has any experiences or feelings? The epiphenomenalist must concede that there is a possible world in which everything in the actual world is physically duplicated (including people), there are the same laws of nature operative, the same causal transactions, the same behavior, but in which I am the only person who is phenomenally conscious. What could possibly count as evidence that I am not myself actually in such a world? The worry is not just that a proof cannot be given of the existence of other feelings, on an epiphenomenalist view. That cannot be done for many of the things we all take ourselves to know—for example, that the sun will rise tomorrow, that the earth existed long before we did. The worry, to repeat, is that no satisfactory reason of *any* sort can be given for believing that other people are subject to feelings and experiences.

Inductive generalization from a single instance is patently unacceptable. Inference to the best explanation is no better in the above case. The behavior that we normally explain by reference to the hypothesis that others have experiences too cannot be explained in this way by the epiphenomenalist. You do not cry out because you feel pain. You do not smile because you are happy. You do not scratch your arm because you feel an itch. Your feelings and experiences have no behavioral effects. They make no difference whatsoever. There is, then, *nothing* that they explain. Had they been absent, everything else would have stayed exactly the same.

Box 2.8

Frank Jackson has attempted to defend epiphenomenalism against the above objection (1982, p. 134) by arguing that the proper reasoning involves two different inferences. First, I infer from your behavior that your brain is in such and such a brain state (namely, the state my brain would be in, were I producing the same behavior in comparable circumstances). This is an inference to the best explanation. I then infer from the fact that your brain is in this state, that you are undergoing such and such a feeling. Since your brain state causes both the behavior and the feeling, the two inferences are legitimate. Arguing in this way, according to Jackson, is like arguing that the *Telegraph* has reported that Spurs (an English soccer team) won on the grounds that the *Times* is reporting that Spurs won. The latter report does not cause the former (each newspaper sends its own reporters to the game), but it still provides excellent evidence for the *Telegraph's* report. Jackson comments,

Box 2.8 *continued*

I read in the *Times* that Spurs won. This gives me reason to think that Spurs won because I know that Spurs' winning is the most likely candidate to be what caused the report in the *Times*. But I also know that Spurs' winning would have had many effects, including almost certainly a report in the *Telegraph*. (p. 134)

The trouble with this analogy is that, on the epiphenomenalist's view, I do *not* know that the relevant brain state (call it *B*) causes the given type of feeling. How could I know that? Let us grant (for the moment) that in my own case, I can find out whether the one causes the other by a combination of introspection and cerebroscopic examination. What evidence could I have that would allow me to infer the same for others? How do I know that in you *B* causes the same feeling rather than a radically different one? How do I know that in you *B* causes any feeling at all?

I cannot infer that the felt qualities I experience are present in others because of the overt behavior and then proceed to investigate their brains. The felt qualities do not cause the behavior, according to the epiphenomenalist. So how can I rule out the very real possibility (as likely a priori as its negation) that phenomenal states arise in me as a result of a certain total combination of physical factors that are found together in no-one else? There is no corresponding problem in the case of Spurs's winning and the *Telegraph* report. I have plenty of independent evidence for the claim that a game involving a major soccer team would be reported in the *Telegraph*, and moreover that the result would be reported accurately. No such independent evidence exists in the case of *B* and the relevant feeling. Of course, if I had a twin who was a molecule-by-molecule duplicate of me, then Jackson's defense of epiphenomenalism *for that twin* would go through.[19] But I have no such twin. And even if I did, that would be of no help with respect to the general problem.

Perhaps it will now be said that even if no internalist justification can be given for belief in the existence of feelings and experiences in others, still an externalist approach can be adopted. This is simply not so, however, in the present context. If knowledge is a matter of having an appropriately caused true belief, so that knowledge is possible without the capacity to articulate a relevant reason, still, on the epiphenomenalist view, there can be no knowledge of the experiences of others, no justified belief with respect to how they feel. By hypothesis, there is no causal chain at all: phenomenal states are causally irrelevant.

I conclude that if felt qualities have no effects, then there is *no justification whatsoever* to suppose that other people feel what I feel or that they feel or experience anything at all. The problem of other minds *cannot* be solved.

The situation is even worse than this, on the epiphenomenalist's view. For the epiphenomenalist with respect to experience must admit that there is a possible world W in which I am *exactly* like the way I am in the actual world, except that *I* lack any experiences and feelings, assuming that she is prepared to grant that phenomenal qualities attach only to experiences and feelings. But then what reason could possibly be given for supposing that I am not actually in W? In W, I have exactly the same beliefs as I do in the actual world. After all, if beliefs themselves have no phenomenal character and phenomenal states make no difference at all, then my beliefs will be completely unchanged, if my phenomenal states disappear while all else remains the same. For example, in W I believe that I now feel pain, indeed that my toothache is excruciating; that the warm sun feels good on my skin, that the wine I am drinking tastes wonderful. Since this is just what I actually believe, how do I know that I am not in W? There is surely an insuperable problem here of one's own mind for the epiphenomenalist, which runs parallel to the problem of other minds.

Note that nothing that has been said above counts against the general possibility of zombie replicas. The hypothesis that I might have a molecular duplicate without any experiences does not entail that I do not know that I am not such a duplicate myself. For if epiphenomenalism is false, as I have argued, then felt qualities do make a difference. So I can know that I have experiences via, for example, inference to the best explanation of the contents of my phenomenal beliefs, given that they are true.

For all the reasons given above, we cannot simply embrace the conclusion we have reached, namely, that phenomenal states are causally impotent. And that, I suggest, is the paradox of phenomenal consciousness.

Box 2.9

Summary: The Paradox of Phenomenal Consciousness

(7)   Phenomenal states are perspectivally subjective.[20]

(8)   If phenomenal states are perspectivally subjective, then they are neither identical with, nor realized by, objective physical types.

(9)   If phenomenal states are neither identical with, nor realized by, objective physical types, then they are not even broadly physical states.

(10)   If phenomenal states are not even broadly physical states, then they are causally irrelevant.

Therefore,

(11)   phenomenal states are causally irrelevant.

Unfortunately, (11) is clearly false. What makes for a paradox is that all of the premises seem clearly true, once we reflect on them in the context of the problems presented in this chapter. And (11) follows from (7) through (10) via the rules of formal logic. So, we should be deeply perplexed.

2.6   The Available Strategies

In this section, I want to lay out, and comment on, a number of different strategies that might be adopted in connection with the paradox I have presented. This is intended to provide the reader with a clear idea of the options curently available and the problems they face.

The first strategy is to insist that the conclusion of the paradox is true, notwithstanding the fact that it is wildly counterintuitive. The paradox is really a sound argument. To adopt this strategy is to accept *epiphenomenal type dualism.*[21] Phenomenal properties are causally impotent, nonphysical properties. The major problem this strategy faces is that it goes against what we already know, namely, that phenomenal properties are causally efficacious. It also requires us to believe in magic or miracles with respect to the emergence of phenomenal consciousness in the natural world.

The second strategy is to maintain that phenomenal states are identical with neurophysiological states (or lower-level objective, physical states). This is the *type identity theory.*[22] One major problem here is that the strategy seems committed to denying perspectival subjectivity. Another is that the position cannot allow the metaphysical possibility of philosophical zombies or of microphysical twins having inverted experiences.

A third strategy is to embrace *functionalism* with respect to phenomenal states. On this view, there really is, in the end, no *special* problem presented by phenomenal consciousness. Phenomenal states, like mental states generally, have a functional character.

Within the functionalist strategy, there are two further standard alternatives: *commonsense functionalism* and *scientific* or *psychofunctionalism*.[23] On the former view, we can define each and every phenomenal state in terms of the causal or teleological role it plays, as that role is conceived in everyday life. So, for example, to be in a state with the phenomenal character of normal human experiences of pain is to be in a state that is typically caused by bodily damage and that typically causes the the belief that something undesirable is present, together with the desire that it cease; these states, in turn, typically cause attempts to protect oneself and to move away from the damaging stimulus. Or to be in the above state is to be in a state whose natural purpose is to signal bodily damage and to elicit the appropriate desire and belief.

On the latter view, psychofunctionalism, the proposal is that there is some fine-grained functional role that each phenomenal state occupies, a role that is not specifiable *simply* by armchair reflection on the state and its connections with other things. This role is one that will be discovered a posteriori by a full-grown empirical psychology.

Both of these versions of functionalism seem compelled to deny perspectival subjectivity. They are also committed to rejecting the metaphysical possibility of functional duplicates with inverted experiences or no experiences at all. So the problems are again pressing and similar to those confronting the type identity theory.

A fourth strategy is what we might call *brute nonreductive physicalism*. The claim here is that phenomenal experience is metaphysically determined by objective physical states and properties, so that it is metaphysically impossible for two creatures to be exactly alike in all objective, physical respects and yet phenomenally different, but there is no explanation whatsoever for this determination. So the determination is brute or

basic. Phenomenal states are perspectivally subjective states that are neither identical with lower-level objective, physical states nor realized by
them (in the sense in which I have been using the term). Nonetheless,
since they are metaphysically determined by such states, they may be
classified as physical.

On this view, either it is held that some physical realizations are not
grounded in mechanisms, contrary to my account, in which case premise
(8) of the paradox of phenomenal consciousness can be deemed false (the
premise that asserts that if phenomenal states are perspectivally subjective,
then they are neither identical with, nor realized by, objective physical
types), or it is granted that realizations, where they obtain, require mechanisms, and premise (9) is denied instead (the premise that asserts that if
phenomenal states are neither identical with, nor realized by, objective
physical types, then they are not even broadly physical). The largest
problem here, on which I commented earlier in connection with both the
problem of mechanism and the problem of phenomenal causation, is
that of defending the apparently ad hoc and highly implausible claim
that there is brute, synchronic determination of the phenomenal. There
is also some question as to whether the position is really properly called
a version of *physicalism* at all, and more needs to be said about zombie replicas.

A fifth strategy is to deny that phenomenal states are physical states
in any sense of the term 'physical', no matter how broad, but to insist
that nonetheless they are causally efficacious.[24] On this view, premise
(10) is at fault. This position, *fully interactionist type dualism,* must deny
that the physical world is causally closed, which presents it with a very
serious problem. It also makes the emergence of phenomenal consciousness miraculous. One way to try to deal with the problem of emergence
within a dualist framework is to adopt *panpsychism,* according to which
everything is phenomenally conscious (albeit to varying degrees), even
microphysical entities. This is highly counterintuitive, however, and it
still countenances miracles (boson feelings, for example).

A sixth strategy is to adopt a position I shall call *nonreductive, mechanistic physicalism.* The proposal here is that phenomenal states are perspectivally subjective, physical states that are realized by objective, lower-
level physical states, so that there really is a mechanism that explains
their generation. But we currently have no idea of what this mechanism

is. As far as the paradox goes, then, it is premise (8) that is contested. On one variant of this view, we will never know what the relevant mechanism is; indeed, it is beyond our cognitive capacities to grasp just how phenomenal consciousness is generated.[25] On another variant, we do not now know the mechanism, but there is no good reason to suppose that we *could* not know it, that we are cognitively closed to its operation by our psychological natures.[26] We might call the former variant *deeply pessimistic, nonreductive, mechanistic physicalism* and the latter *open-minded, nonreductive, mechanistic physicalism,* thereby indicating their assessments of our epistemic condition with respect to the relevant mechanism.

One major problem with both of these positions is that it is radically unclear whether it is even intelligible to postulate a mechanism whose operation is as strange and alien as this one must be, if it is to connect the perspectivally subjective and the objective. Certainly, the general picture we have of how higher-level properties are generated by lower-level ones is not appropriate here. As with brute nonreductive physicalism, there is also the question of zombie replicas.

Whichever way we turn, we seem embroiled in difficulties. One final radical response is to adopt *eliminativism* with respect to phenomenal consciousness. On this view, in its most extreme form, there are no states in the world answering to our talk of what it is like. The paradox of phenomenal consciousness is based on a false presupposition.

A less radical version of the thesis is that there are no phenomenal states *insofar* as they are taken to form a separate class of mental items. Instead, phenomenal states should be identified with beliefs or judgments of one sort or another. As such, they exist but are not really perspectivally subjective.[27] This position ultimately becomes a version of *functionalism* if beliefs and judgments are taken to be functional states. But, with or without this further development, the position is committed to dissolving the paradox by denying premise (7). And that, of course, presents it with a severe problem.

Another significant problem the more moderate thesis faces is that it seems so implausible: on the face of it, feelings and experiences can occur without the presence of any (relevant) beliefs. A third is that beliefs and judgments, formed on the basis of sensory input, are limited in a way that phenomenal states are not. This last point needs a little elaboration.

Forming the perceptual belief (or judgment) that something is an F (e.g., a dog, a cat, a red object) necessitates remembering what Fs look like. The perceptual information about Fs is stored in a schema (on the standard psychological model of perceptual memory). Once the sensory input is brought under the appropriate schema, belief formation can take place. Perceptual beliefs, then, are constrained by limitations on memory. If one lacks the appropriate schema, the corresponding belief cannot occur.

Phenomenal experiences, however, are not generally limited in this way.[28] Normal perceivers can distinguish millions of different shades of color, for example, but they have many fewer color schemas (probably a few hundred). Human memory simply is not up to the task of storing a different schema for each of these different shades.[29] This is why I cannot identify red_{28} as such, even though I have no difficulty at all in picking out red things as red: I have a schema in memory for the generic category of redness but not for the specific shade of red_{28}. Nonetheless, there is something it is like for me to experience red_{28}, something that is different from what it is like to experience the other shades of red. How red_{28} looks, the experience involved, is phenomenally distinguishable from the experiences of red_{33}, red_{37}, and the like.

So phenomenal seeming or looking is not essentially schema-dependent or schema-involving. From this it follows that any attempt to identify experience or feeling with belief or judgment will inevitably fail to capture distinctive features of the phenomenal mind.

2.7   The Way Ahead

What is the answer to the paradox of phenomenal consciousness? How are the ten problems adumbrated in chapter 1 to be solved? These are no easy questions. In my view, a new overarching theory of the nature of phenomenal character or "what it is like" is needed. The theory I advocate is presented in the next part of the book. Unlike Athena, who sprang fully formed from the head of Zeus, my account is developed gradually, piece by piece, in the context of the problems.

The position I defend is an *intentionalist* one: phenomenally conscious states are essentially representational states of a certain sort. This claim flies in the face of philosophical tradition, as I noted in the introduction. Surely, many philosophers will respond, it is *obvious* that some feelings are nonrepresentational. Suppose, for example, that I just feel happy, without there being anything in particular about which I am happy. This state has no representational content: it does not itself say how the world is. And what about pains? Pains are not *of* things, like visual experiences, for example. Nor can pains be pains *that* so-and-so is such-and-such in the way that beliefs are always beliefs that something or other is the case. Pains, then, are not representations at all. Claims to the contrary are unintelligible.

I argue in part II that the views just expressed are false. In my view, the only way to solve the problems of transparency, felt location and phenomenal vocabulary, and the alien limb—problems that have not concerned us in the present chapter, since they are not directly implicated in the production of the paradox of phenomenal consciousness—is to appreciate that phenomenal states are all representational, indeed intentional. This stand, of course, raises further questions of its own. What exactly is an intentional state? Just how are phenomenal states intentional? What is their intentional content? Is phenomenal character one and the same as intentional content? In this connection, what is to be said in response to the earlier problem of super blindsight?

I supply answers to these questions, and I argue that the answers provide us with important clues about how to solve the paradox of phenomenal consciousness. So it is to the issue of intentionality and the associated problems I turn before I present any response to the paradox. The first problem I want to take up, however, is the problem of ownership. This is again concerned with subjectivity, but, unlike the problem of perspectival subjectivity, it is focused on concrete phenomenal objects —particular pains, itches, afterimages, and so on—rather than on types of phenomenal states or phenomenal properties.[30] What I argue in the next chapter (and part of the following chapter) is that this problem has a solution, one that provides us with the beginnings of a route through the philosophical jungle that threatens to engulf us as soon as we begin to reflect on the other problems.

II

3

Can Anyone Else Feel My Pains?

The problem of ownership purports to cast a shadow over the view that all mental objects of experience—all pains, itches, tickles, afterimages—are physical, by pointing to certain properties these items have that are not possessed by any physical item. In the one case, the property is that of necessary privacy. My pains, for example, are necessarily private to me. You could not feel any of my pains. Physical things, however, are not necessarily private in this way. Any physical thing that is mine could be yours, my watch, for example, or even my heart.

In the other case, the relevant property is that of necessary ownership by *some creature or other*. There could not be a pain that belonged to no creature at all. An unowned pain is impossible. But again this is not true of anything physical. My watch might have been discarded and left without any owner at all. My heart might have been torn from my chest and placed in a jar.

The kind of necessity at play in this puzzle is very strong. It is simply not coherent to suppose either that someone else feels my pains or that some pains exist without any creature's being in pain. However the laws of nature are varied, whatever else takes place in the world, these things are unimaginable and hence metaphysically impossible. Or so it is claimed.

The physicalist about phenomenal experience has three possible strategies with respect to the problem of ownership. One is to try to show that even though there certainly are pains, itches, afterimages, and other such phenomenal objects, these items do not really have the physically problematic property—in the first case, necessary privacy, and in the second, necessary ownership by some creature. Another strategy is to argue that

[handwritten marginal note: No different from other attributes?]

although it is certainly true that people feel pains and itches and have images, this way of talking is misleading. Really there are no such things as pains, itches, and images. The world itself contains no phenomenal objects. So there is, in reality, nothing to have the physically problematic properties. A final strategy is to accept that there are pains, itches, and the like, and also that these items have the properties of necessary privacy and necessary ownership by some creature, but to challenge the assumption that no physical thing is necessarily private or necessarily owned.

Each physicalist strategy has its virtues. But, as we shall see, there are also a number of problems to be faced along the way. I should perhaps add that there is a variant on the middle ("repudiate and relax") strategy described above, namely, to deny *both* that there are any pains or other phenomenal objects *and* that it is even true that people feel pains or have images. This radical eliminativist (or "take no prisoners") stance certainly brings relaxation for the physicalist in its wake. But it is the sort of relaxation that one gets from curing a headache by cutting off one's head[1] (except that, of course, in this case, nobody ever has a headache to be cured). Happily, as we shall see in this chapter and the next one, aspirin is readily available for the physicalist. No ludicrously counterintuitive elimination is necessary.

3.1   The Repudiation of Phenomenal Objects

How can it be held that it is true that people feel pains, even though there really are no pains for them to feel? The answer, according to the eliminativist with respect to phenomenal *objects* (hereafter, the object eliminativist), is that our ordinary way of expressing ourselves here is deceptive. Grammatical form is sometimes misleading. Just as it can be true that the average family has 1.2 children even though there really are no families with a fraction of a child, so too you can feel an intense pain even though there really are no pains.

But what is it that we are asserting when we say, in ordinary parlance, that someone *has* a blue afterimage or a throbbing pain or a terrible itch? In the case of the claim that the average family has 1.2 children, the answer is reasonably obvious. We are talking about numbers, and what we are really asserting is that the number of children divided by the number of families equals the number 1.2. In the case of phenomenal talk, however, if its grammatical form is indeed misleading, the answer is much less obvious. It is to be found, according to object eliminativists, in our ordinary talk of other things—of smiles and limps, of voices and stutters.

Suppose we ask ourselves whether there really are, in the world, any such things as limps. If we reply "Yes," then we seem to face some puzzling questions just like the ones raised for phenomenal objects. If Patrick has a pronounced limp, then can Paul have that very same limp (the particular, token limp Patrick has, not one just like it but numerically different)? If not, why not? Can Patrick's limp exist without anyone at all having it? "Of course not," you say? But why not? Is this just a brute fact admitting of no explanation? If so, how does the admission of such a brute fact fit in with the conception of nature sketched in the last chapter? Or are limps supernatural phenomena?

One reasonable response to these puzzling questions is to deny that there really are any such things as limps to which people are related by the 'having' relation. On this view, when we say that Patrick has a pronounced limp, what we are really saying is that Patrick *limps* in a pronounced manner. Likewise, smiles, voices, and stutters. If Patrick also has a charming smile, a loud voice, and a noticeable stutter, what is really the case is that he smiles charmingly, speaks loudly, and stutters noticeably. There are no smiles, voices, and stutters, conceived of as things people have.

Analogously, according to the object eliminativist, there are no pains, itches, or visual images, conceived of as objects people have. Instead, to have a terrible itch is to itch terribly; to have an intense pain is to hurt intensely; finally, to have a blue afterimage is to sense bluely or in a blue manner. Now the problem for the physicalist supposedly disappears. There are no phenomenal *objects* as such, and so there is no question of trying to accomodate their necessary privacy and ownership in the physical world.

Unfortunately, life is not that easy. To begin with, talk of people sensing bluely is hardly everyday. It cries out for further explanation. Second, if there are no phenomenal objects, then just what is it that makes phenomenal talk true? If, when I have a terrible itch, it is really true that I itch terribly, then what exactly is it about me that *makes* this true? Some account is needed here in order to show that the possession by me of a terrible itch has really been repudiated and not just hidden under a verbal smoke screen.

At this point, the view I have been developing, which is known for obvious reasons as the adverbial theory of sensation or experience, splits into two theories (see here Chisholm 1957; Ducasse 1942; Sellars 1968; Tye 1984, 1989). Both of these alternatives face very significant problems. Since neither approach is entirely straightforward, I have confined further discussion to the box below.

Box 3.1

To understand the two versions of the adverbial theory and their respective costs and benefits, it is necessary to begin with some brief general remarks about adverbs. There are two major theories of adverbs in the philosophical literature: the predicate operator theory and the event predicate theory. According to the latter view, adverbs, or at least a very wide range of adverbs, are best understood as adjectives that are true of events.[2] Consider, for example,

(1)   Patrick is stuttering noticeably.

If we are to bring out what it is that makes (1) true, we should restate it, on the event predicate theory, as

(1a)   There is an event of stuttering that has Patrick as its subject, and that event is noticeable.

Similarly,

(2)   Patrick is speaking loudly

should be recast as

(2a)   There is an event of speaking that has Patrick as its subject, and that event is loud.

So the adverbs 'noticeably' and 'loudly' are really functioning as adjectives or predicates that apply to events, in the one case, to a stuttering, and in the other, to a speaking. What must exist for Patrick to stutter noticeably or to speak loudly is a noticeable stuttering or a loud speaking of which Patrick is the subject.

This view has a number of virtues, not the least of which is that it requires no alteration, or addition, to the materials available in first-order quantificational logic, as far as the formal evaluation of arguments in which

Box 3.1 *continued*

sentences like (1) and (2) occur.[3] Second, and relatedly, it provides us with a very simple explanation of why (1), for example, entails

(3)   Patrick is stuttering.

(3) is reconstructed as

(3a)   There is an event of stuttering of which Patrick is the subject,

and (3a) follows from (1) via elementary logical rules.

The alternative view takes adverbs to be operators that turn the predicates they modify into more complicated predicates.[4] In (1), for example, 'notice-ably' is held to operate on the predicate preceding it, namely, 'stutters', and to convert that predicate into a syntactically more complicated predicate, namely, 'stutters noticeably'. Metaphysically, the idea is that adverbs stand for functions that map the properties expressed by the properties they modify onto other properties. On this view, what makes (1) true is not the fact that Patrick is the subject of an event, a noticeable stuttering, nor the fact that Patrick owns a special object, a noticeable stutter, but simply the fact that Patrick has a certain property, that of stuttering noticeably. So (1) really is a subject-predicate sentence, just as it appears to be. There is no hidden existential quantification, as, for example, on the event proposal.

This approach requires the admission that the resources of standard logic do not suffice to come to grips with arguments containing adverbs, together with an account of operator detachment that will validate inferences like the one from (1) to (3). So it has significant costs. On the other hand, it allows us to take sentences like (1) and (2) entirely at face value. These sentences certainly look like the straightforward subject-predicate variety, and, by golly, they are, on the predicate operator proposal.

On the event version of the adverbial theory of sensation, statements putatively about phenomenal objects like pains and itches are really about events like hurtings and itchings. So, for example,

(4)   I have a terrible itch

is analyzed as

(4a)   There is an event of itching of which I am the subject, and that event is terrible.

What there must be, then, for (4) to be true is a certain phenomenal *event* of which I am the subject. This event is something that takes place or happens, and hence supposedly belongs to a very different ontological category from the one occupied by phenomenal objects.

By contrast, on the predicate operator version of the adverbial theory, statements putatively about phenomenal objects are really about people or other sentient creatures and the phenomenal properties they instantiate, properties like itching terribly or hurting throbbingly. So (4) requires for

Box 3.1 *continued*

its truth only one concrete item, namely, myself, not two, as on the event theory (myself and an event). What must now be the case is simply that I possess the relevant sensory property.

These two developments of the adverbial theory face serious difficulties, however. First, the predicate operator theory is hard-pressed to account for the truth of ordinary statements putatively about multiple phenomenal objects. Suppose, for example, that after staring at a bright light and turning away, I report the following:

(5)   I have four pink afterimages.

It is not at all easy to provide a plausible account of what in the world makes this true, given only phenomenal properties that I possess. The problem becomes especially difficult once it is appreciated that glibly proposing

(5a)   I sense quadruply pinkly,

or some such contrived statement as the analysis, apparently fails to account for the fact that (5) entails, for example,

(6)   I have at least three afterimages

and

(7)   I have fewer than seven afterimages.

It certainly *looks* here as if, given these entailments, (5) is true if and only if there are four pink afterimages that I have. Another related difficulty arises in connection with the following two statements:

(8)   I have both a red, square afterimage and a blue, round afterimage

and

(9)   I have both a blue, square afterimage and a red, round afterimage.[5]

These statements evidently are not equivalent: one can be true without the other. But if we analyze the former as

(8a)   I sense redly and squarely and bluely and roundly

and the latter as

(9a)   I sense bluely and squarely and redly and roundly,

then the difference between (8) and (9) is lost. For the order of the conjuncts in a conjunction makes no difference to the conditions under which it is true.[6]

These problems, it should be noted, are also challenging for the event version of the adverbial theory. In this case, however, there is a reasonably straightforward reply. Allow there to be as many different sensings as there *appear* to be afterimages referred to in the original statements. Then (5) becomes

Box 3.1 *continued*

(5b) There are four pink sensings of which I am the subject.

Now the entailments to (6) and (7) are easy to explain. Likewise, there is no difficulty in distinguishing (8) and (9). In both cases, there are two sensings, but they have different properties.

Does it really make sense to talk of my undergoing four simultaneous sensings, each with the same property? Some philosophers have certainly thought not (for example, Jackson 1977, pp. 70–71). And it must be admitted that it is not at all easy to find clearcut examples from ordinary life of cases in which a single individual is the subject of multiple simultaneous events of exactly the same sort (and not involving any other objects). I can listen to you with my left ear and also simultaneously listen to you with my right, or I can inhale deeply through my left nostril and at the same time inhale deeply through my right, but in both of these cases other objects are also involved (namely, ears and nostrils). I can simultaneously be the subject of a singing and a walking and a smiling, say, but apparently I cannot simultaneously be the subject of three singings or three walkings or three smilings.

So the event version of the adverbial theory is called into question here too. And there are other problems. What, for example, can it possibly mean to call an event "pink"? Does it make any sense to suppose that there is such a way of sensing as bluely? Is it really intelligible to say that when I have a pain, I am the subject of an event that is a *hurting* but that lacks any further object? This certainly sounds very strange.

A further worry is that the event version of the adverbial theory really does not put to rest the issue we began with, namely, the threat posed to physicalism by the necessary privacy and necessary ownership of phenomenal objects. Of course, it is true that on the event theory there are no phenomenal objects as such, no pains, afterimages, or itches. But there are hurtings, sensings, and itchings. So the event theory simply transfers the problem. Surely, it may be urged, no one else can be the subject of my very hurtings or my very itchings. Other people can hurt or itch in the same way as me, but my hurtings and itchings are mine alone. Furthermore, the idea that there might be an itching, say, without any creature that itched seems just as absurd as the idea that there might be an itch without an owner. So the advocate of the event version of the adverbial theory apparently has not done *enough* repudiating of phenomenal items. Relaxation is not yet in order.

3.2   Publicizing the Phenomenal: Split Brains

In this section, I want to examine a very different physicalist approach to the issue of privacy. Suppose the physicalist takes the view that the maneuvering of the last section will not work, and that pains, itches, afterimages, and the like, are real mental objects. Then an alternative strategy is to challenge the initial assumption that all such objects are necessarily private. This requires the physicalist to adopt a position that seems very counterintuitive. On the face of it, the idea that you could feel my pains or experience the very same, particular appearances things present to me is absurd. So the physicalist has considerable work to do to make such a stance plausible.

What is demanded of the physicalist is that he or she coherently describe a possible case in which two different people have numerically the same pain or other phenomenal object. For example, the physicalist might ask us to imagine that Siamese twins joined at the hip are stung there by a bee, and both simultaneously feel pain. The trouble with this case, of course, is that it illicitly argues from sameness of cause (a single bee sting at the hip) to sameness of effect (a single pain). Here surely there are two numerically different pains, one experienced by each twin. So any plausible hypothetical case that the physicalist dreams up will have to be a good deal more far-fetched than this. What is needed, it appears, is not a pair of people joined at the hip but a pair who share a brain, or part of a brain. An imaginary case of this sort has been described by Arnold Zuboff and re-presented by Peter Unger. Let us begin, then, with Zuboff's example.[7]

Suppose that I am sitting in a room, undergoing a variety of perceptual experiences and bodily sensations. In an adjacent room, a person who is a molecule-by-molecule duplicate of me (my identical double) is undergoing phenomenally identical experiences and feelings. At this stage, there are clearly two sets of particular, datable visual experiences, pains, itches, and the like—one for me and one for him—but the members of these sets have exactly the same phenomenal or experiential features.

Suppose now that the left and right halves of my brain are slowly separated and that, as the nerves connecting the two halves are severed one by one, they are each immediately replaced by a pair of radio communicators, or transceivers, one for each half brain, so that communications between the two sides of the brain continue as before. This procedure—"zippering," as Unger has called it—is also used to introduce communicating transceivers in place of the nerves connecting the two half brains and my body.

Eventually, all the nerves are removed and replaced by transceivers, so that in place of the original electrical impulses along the nerves, there are now radio signals. Since my brain is in other respects just as it was before, it seems coherent to suppose that my experiences will continue just as they did before. An identical zippering procedure is also performed on my identical double.

Next suppose that I am separated into three parts in three different rooms. My debrained body is sitting in the original room, my left half brain (left brain) is in a second room, kept alive in a vat, and my right half brain (right brain) is in another vat in a third room. Both during the separation and afterward, radio communications continue between the three parts of exactly the same sort as would have occurred had the three parts been joined in close proximity in the original room. As a consequence of this, my experiences are still just as they would have been, had none of this happened. For me, phenomenally, it is as if I were still in the chair in the room in which I started.

My identical twin undergoes an identical separation procedure at the same time. At every point in the separation, it is ensured that his three parts communicate in exactly the same ways as my three parts, so that at the end of the procedure, he and I are still undergoing experiences and feelings that are qualitatively identical.

Now suppose that a switch is flipped so that my double's left brain suddenly starts to communicate with my right brain and body in exactly the same way as my own left brain. It is ensured that both bodies receive identical sensory inputs throughout, so that there is always a precise symmetry in these two sets of communications. Meanwhile, my left brain communicates with his right brain and body in a manner that exactly duplicates the communications between his own left brain and them. After five minutes, another switch is thrown, and the new communications stop while the original communications continue.

Unger and Zuboff (according to Unger) claim that, during the five minutes, I and my identical double undergo experiences and feelings that are not just qualitatively identical but also numerically identical. If, say, thirty seconds into the period, I experience a pain, my double also has that very same token experience. Moreover, given that, when I experience a pain, there is a pain that I experience, my double experiences that phenomenal object of experience, too.

Of course, the case just described is a fantastic one. Perhaps we could ourselves never produce the biotechnology that would be needed to perform the operations involved. This is of little consequence, however. For the claim need be only that the case is *metaphysically* possible. After all, it is the metaphysical privacy of phenomenal objects (and experiences) that the case is intended to challenge.

It is also worth noting that even if my physical constitution is such that *were* the procedure performed on me, my experiences *would* change radically, contrary to what is being supposed, this does not undercut the example. My physical constitution might have been different in various ways, so my experiences might not have changed dramatically. Alternatively, imagine that the example is described with respect to possible creatures whose experiences would not be altered by such a procedure. Is it not metaphysically possible that there are such creatures? If it is, then phenomenal items are not metaphysically private: it is metaphysically possible for one and the same phenomenal token (e.g., a particular pain or image or auditory experience) to belong to two different creatures.

Another reply that might be made to the case is that for the relevant five minutes, my double and I merge and become one, so that there is really only a single person in the situation. This reply is not very plausible. To begin with, there is really no such thing as numerical identity at a time. The claim that I am identical with my double for the crucial five minutes, insofar as it is a claim of *identity* at all, is best understood to assert that I exist for the five minutes, as does my double, and he and I are strictly identical. The final part of this assertion is false, however. If my double and I are strictly identical, then every property I have my double has, and conversely. Since I have the property of having been in room *A* at the beginning, whereas my twin does not (he was in a different room), my twin and I are not strictly identical. So my twin and I are not identical for the crucial five minutes.

Second, it is intuitively very plausible to suppose that during the middle five minutes, I am where my three original parts are located (assuming I exist at all). This is why it is natural to grant that if these parts are destroyed, I no longer exist. My twin, however, is where his original three parts are located. Intuitively, he survives the destruction of my original parts. As Unger notes, the theoretical reason at play here is one of assimilation among parts. Given only five minutes of communication, my parts and my twin's parts have not become properly absorbed into a single system. But if my twin and I occupy different locations for the five minutes, then we are certainly not identical for that period of time. And this is the case, even if it is supposed that claims of identity at a time are not to be analyzed in the way suggested in the last paragraph.

So, the Zuboffian case still stands. There is one further response that is worth exploring. Why suppose that during the critical five minutes my twin and I undergo *numerically identical* experiences rather than just qualitatively identical ones (that is, experiences that feel the same to both of us even though they are really numerically distinct)? After all, as Unger grants, it seems plausible to maintain that I am then where my original parts are. It seems to me equally plausible to maintain that the experiences I undergo are somewhere within where my two half brains are, or at least where I am. Likewise for my twin. So my experiences occur in a different place from his. It follows that my experiences and his are *not* numerically identical.

This conclusion is reinforced by the observation that, as far as my brain is concerned and its interactions within its two halves and also with my body, nothing changes during the five minutes. All that happens is that new duplicate communications are established between it and a second brain. It seems to me very odd to suppose that the location of the experiences I undergo shifts after the switch is flipped.

Where, then, do these reflections leave us? The Zuboffian case seems initially to provide the physicalist with a response to the privacy part of the problem of ownership, one that allows him to hold that, notwithstanding the highly plausible character of the claim that phenomenal objects are metaphysically private, a clear imaginary counterexample can be produced. But the Zuboffian case, it now turns out, is not really compelling: there are two competing descriptions, only one of which makes the case a counterexample. Still, it might be urged, the description adopted by Unger and Zuboff is at least *permissible,* even if it is not *obligatory.* And that is all the physicalist requires.

Unfortunately, this assessment seems to me incorrect. If the physicalist is to undermine fully the challenge privacy presents to her position, it does not suffice to present a case that cannot be proven *not* to be a counterexample and is, in that sense, permissible. Instead, she must invent a case that is intuitively a clear counterexample, one that intuitively has only one description. This does not rule out fantastic cases, of course, but it does demand that we have clear intutions about what is going on in them. Not enough has been done yet, I suggest, to secure the physicalist's position. Moreover, nothing in the case provides any reason to deny that phenomenal objects are necessarily owned by some creature or other. So one aspect of the problem of ownership has not been addressed. Physicalism, then, is still not wholly out of trouble.

Box 3.2

There is one further imaginary case described by Unger (again, based on unpublished work by Zuboff) that is worth briefly taking up.[8] As in Unger's discussion of the case above, the focus is on particular phenomenal experiences rather than phenomenal objects. But it applies mutatis mutandis to the latter. For ease of exposition here, I shall follow the example, which again concerns the issue of privacy for phenomenal experiences, just as Unger presents it.

My brain again is split into two halves by a zippering procedure that does not adversely affect communications between the two halves. The left half is placed in room 1 in a supportive vat; the right in room 2. As this takes place, I continuously have a visual experience of blue throughout my visual field.

In rooms 3 and 4 there are duplicates of my left and right half brains in their own respective vats. These duplicates have just come into existence. They are in *exactly* the same physical states as my two half brains, and they are equipped to communicate by transceivers (although they are not yet doing so). A switch is flipped, and the left brain in room 3 starts to communicate with my original right in parallel with my original left for one minute. Then another switch is flipped. This stops all communication with my original left brain, so that for one further minute, my original right only communicates with the left in room 3.

Next, another switch is thrown. This time, my original right together with the right in room 4 both communicate in parallel with the left in room 3. This again continues for one minute, at which time yet another

Box 3.2 *continued*

switch is flipped, breaking any communication between my original right and the duplicate left. Only the brain halves in rooms 3 and 4 are now communicating.

The two half brains in Rooms 3 and 4 are taken and placed in a body that is a duplicate of mine, while their communications continue uninterrupted. By another zippering procedure, the transceiver connections are replaced by neural connections. The person at the end of all this has a visual experience of blue throughout his visual field. Meanwhile, my two brain halves have been put back in my body, and I am in another room playing table tennis.

Unger claims that it is correct to say that, in the above case, a particular experience of blue, which began as my experience and lasted for quite a few minutes, ended as the experience of someone else. I am inclined to disagree.

Consider the minute during which both the left brain in room 3 and my original left brain communicate with my right brain. It seems to me very plausible to hold that the introduction of identical communications between the new left brain and my original right creates a *new* token experience, so that there are, for that minute, *two* particular experiences of blue. After all, surely adding the new communications, while leaving the original communications intact, does not destroy the old experience or change its location. The old experience is located wherever it was originally—somewhere within the place I am located. And I am located where my original parts are, so I am the subject of only one of these experiences. The other experience is undergone by a duplicate person, who comes into existence when the left brain in room 3 and my original right brain start communications. Once communications cease between my two original half brains, the particular experience I undergo is extinguished, leaving only the duplicate's experience. Similarly, when the half brains in rooms 3 and 4 communicate, there is a further duplicate created who undergoes *another* qualitatively identical experience. So again for a minute there are *two* experiences of blue. This new duplicate is the one who survives the experiment, and the token experience left at the end is the one that he, and only he, ever undergoes.

Unger suggests that what the example shows is that experiences might be physical things like colds. Just as you can come to have a cold that was initially mine, just as my cold might flow from me to you, so my experiences might flow through various combinations of half brains from me to you. But the analogy is not evidently appropriate. In the envisaged scenario, my experiences do not clearly flow anywhere. Instead, they are duplicated. My experiences overlap for a minute with the duplicate experiences, and they

Box 3.2 *continued*

arguably cease to exist when my two half brains cease communication. The duplicate experiences are then duplicated by still further experiences with which they also overlap. Then the initial duplicates cease to exist. It is not at all clear that there is a single token or instance of the experience of blue. Again, in my view, the example cannot do the work that is asked of it.

The upshot, I suggest, is that the fantastic thought experiments considered above do not undermine the initial intuition that phenomenal objects are necessarily private. The physicalist has not yet fully solved the problem of ownership.

3.3   Phenomenal Objects as Events

Suppose we grant that pains and indeed all other phenomenal items are necessarily private. Any given pain necessarily belongs to its owner and no one else. What about the claim that physical things are *not* necessarily private in this way? Clearly, some physical things are not—for example, my car or my house. But are *all* physical things like this?

Consider my laugh as I read a funny cartoon, or my scream as I am drenched with cold water. These are uncontroversial examples of physical things. Could anyone else have had any of them? Obviously other people might have laughs or screams just like mine. But intuitively they could not have *my* laugh or *my* scream. These facts about screams and laughs (assuming we agree they are facts) derive, I suggest, from their being *events* rather than *objects*.[9] It is a fundamental feature of our ordinary conception of the world that there are such items as events as well as objects, and events are generally individuated in part via the items that undergo them.[10] My laughing essentially involves me. The eruption of Vesuvius essentially involves Vesuvius. No event that is undergone by a given item could have been undergone by any other item. In this way, each event is necessarily private to its subject or owner.

Events are items that occur or take place; they have beginnings and ends; they are sudden, active changes; they stand in causal relations. One common way of referring to events is by means of descriptions of the type "x's F'ing at t," for example, "my yawning at 4:00 p.m.," "your speaking at noon," but there are, of course, other shorter ways of picking out events, for example, "my yawn," "your speech." And many events are undergone by more than one object, for example, Stravinski's lowering the baton, Julian's painting his Jaguar. For present purposes, however, the events that matter are those involving a single subject (monadic events, as I shall call them).

Items that meet the above criteria but that are not normally thought of as involving a sudden, active change are typically classified as states (to be precise, state tokens). For example, my weighing 160 pounds and my being tall are both state tokens. But sometimes the terms 'state' (or 'state token') and 'event' are used interchangeably. On either usage, you cannot undergo my token states. In general, token states, like events, are necessarily private to their subjects.

One way, therefore, in which the physicalist can attempt to meet the threat posed by privacy is to argue that *all* phenomenal entities, including pains, itches, afterimages, and the like, are identical with monadic events or state tokens undergone by their owners. If this is the case, then the necessary privacy of pains and other phenomenal particulars is no reason to think that they are not physical.

Perhaps it will be replied that necessary privacy, as it applies to phenomenal objects, is more than just necessary ownership by the actual owner. The point is not just that you cannot have my pains or afterimages. More significantly, you cannot *feel* my pains or *experience* my afterimages. My phenomenal objects are essentially experienced by me alone.[11] This has yet to be accounted for.

I concede this criticism of my proposal so far, and I shall amplify it shortly to meet the objection. First, however, I want to show how the above strategy can be put to work in connection with the second part of the problem of ownership.

Any pain is always *some sentient creature's* pain. Pains necessarily have some owner or other. As I observed earlier, pains in this respect are not like dogs or even legs. But laughs cannot exist unowned, and neither can screams. Likewise, killings, births, and explosions. In each of these cases, there must be a subject for the event: a killer, a creature that is born, an object that explodes. So there certainly are concrete physical entities that are necessarily owned by something or other, even though these entities are not physical *objects*, namely, physical events and state tokens.[12]

That some phenomenal items are events seems undeniable. Consider, for example, my experiencing pain at midnight. This is something that happens. It has a subject; it involves a sudden change. But what about the particular pain I have at midnight? It seems to me not in the least counterintuitive to claim that *that* very pain is one and the same as the event of my experiencing pain at midnight. After all, to have a pain is to feel a pain. And to feel a pain is to experience pain. So, I have a pain just in case I undergo a token (particular instance) of experiencing pain. But there seems to me no clear reason to deny that the "having" relation adverted to here is any different from the relation of undergoing. I undergo (am the subject of) a pain just in case I undergo (am the subject of) a token of experiencing pain. Therefore, my pain is identical with the event of my experiencing pain. In general, I suggest, pains just are token experiences of a certain sort.

The same seems to me true for itches, tickles, and other felt objects. For exactly the same reasons, it seems to me plausible to hold that these items just are token (that is, particular) experiences or feelings. What about general moods, for example, the feeling of depression? Well, if I have this feeling, I undergo, or am the subject of, a certain feeling. The feeling I have just is an event or, perhaps better, a token state of which I am the subject.

Consider next the case of afterimages. It seems to me not to strain ordinary thought greatly to hold that afterimages are one and the same as visual experiences caused in certain characteristic ways (for example, by staring at a bright light and turning away). After all, I have an afterimage if and only if I have a visual experience caused in the right manner. Why not then identify the afterimage and the experience? But the experience is an event or state token that has me as its subject. Likewise, so is the afterimage.

If all phenomenal objects are really token experiences, then the points made above about having pains can also be made with respect to experiencing pains. No one else can *experience* my pains, just as no one else can *laugh* my laughs or *scream* my screams. Similarly no pain can be *un*experienced, just as no laugh can be *un*laughed and no scream *un*screamed.

This proposal—that we *identify* phenomenal objects with phenomenal events or state tokens—faces three main objections. The first of these is that it erroneously conflates experiences with the objects that they are experiences *of*. For example, if I have a blue afterimage, the object of my experience is a blue image. So, the image cannot be identical with the experience. Second, it entails that experiences themselves are sometimes blue or square or stinging or burning, since afterimages and pains have such properties. But this has no clear sense. Finally, it cannot account for cases of phenomenal experience in which multiple phenomenal objects are present. For example, if I have three blue afterimages, the proposal must say that I am the subject of three visual experiences. That seems highly counterintuitive. The last two difficulties are not new ones: they also arose earlier for the event version of the adverbial theory.

I might add here that the present proposal is, of course, very similar to the earlier event view. However, it avoids the introduction of artificial adverbs; it does not deny that there really are pains and afterimages that people have, but instead explicitly identifies them, from the start, with phenomenal events or state tokens; and it is complete in a way that the event version of the adverbial theory is not. In particular, it does not simply transfer the threat posed to physicalism from phenomenal objects to phenomenal events.

I think that the above objections can be satisfactorily answered within the context of the present proposal. However, in my view, the answers require considerable stage setting, and in particular a detailed examination of the question of whether phenomenal states and events are, by their very nature, intentional. It is to this question that I turn in the next chapter. The conclusion I draw now is a conditional one: *if* the above three objections can be overcome, then the physicalist has solved the problem of ownership.

3.4   A Closer Look at Events

There remain two further issues I want to take up in this chapter to complete the present discussion. First, the proposal I have made with respect to the problem of ownership assumes that events (and state tokens) are necessarily undergone by some subject or other, and moreover necessarily undergone by their actual owners. Are there any clear counterexamples to this claim? If there are, then the conditional conclusion I claimed to have established above appears seriously threatened. Second, how should events (and state tokens) themselves to be conceived? Just what sort of an item is an event (or a state token)? This issue needs to be addressed, because it is relevant to our understanding of phenomenal objects themselves. Let us begin with some possible counterexamples.[13]

Consider a flash of light. This is an event, but what is its owner? Apparently there is none. Or consider a football game. What is the relevant subject or subjects here? The football players? But surely if one particular player had not played at all, it would (or certainly could) have been the same *game*. What about the case of the firing squad and its shooting of a condemned man? If one member of the squad had been replaced by another who duplicated the physical movements of the person he replaced down to the smallest details, the same shooting would have taken place (assuming all else remained the same). Indeed, if the whole squad had been replaced, the very same shooting would still have occurred, if the new members had pointed and aimed and fired in just the right ways. Or so it might be supposed.

I find none of these cases very compelling. Events, as I noted earlier, are sudden active changes occurring at particular times. If there is a change —an eruption, a death, a chiming—something changes.[14] A volcano erupts, a king dies, a bell chimes. Our very concept of an event, I suggest, is the concept of a sudden active change in something or other (paradigmatically, a physical object). This is why the canonical description for an event is "x's Fing at time t." In the case of a flash of light, there is likewise a change. What changes? Well, intuitively, when there is a flash of light, light itself flashes. A certain quantity of light is suddenly emitted or given off by some source, and it streams across some region of space. The flash is located where the light streams. It seems to me plausible to hold that the flash of light—that event—is one and the same as the light's flashing. So, there really is a subject here for the event, namely, the emitted light itself. In this way, a flash of light is like a spray of water. With a spray of water, there is a quantity of water that sprays across a certain region of space. The spray is an event, which has the water as its subject.

In the case of the football game, the relevant subjects, I suggest, are the two football teams involved. The game is one and the same as the one team's playing the other. Each team consists of, or is constituted by, a certain group of players. But neither team is one and the same as the aggregate of its constituent players. Teams do not cease to exist when players are traded or become hurt. Substituting one player for another does not destroy the team. So if one player who in fact participated in the match had not played, there would still have been the same two teams opposing one another. On the view that the objects undergoing events are essential to them, it does not follow that the same match would not have taken place.

Likewise, in the case of the firing squad, the squad is made up of a number of men. But it can survive the loss of a member. The squad simply becomes a little smaller if the lost man is not replaced. The same shooting can occur even if not all the same fingers are on the triggers. The object involved in the event is the squad as a whole. The shooting is one and the same as the squad's shooting the prisoner.

What about the case in which all the members of the squad are replaced? In this case, it seems to me plausible to say that there is now a different squad. But is the event of the squad's shooting the prisoner, in this situation, intuitively the same event as the actual one? The counterfactual shooting duplicated the actual one, and the prisoner died in the same way (assuming the individual movements of the squad did not change), but did the very same token shooting take place? I think not. The event of the one firing squad's shooting the man is, in my view, a numerically different event from the event of the other squad's shooting him even though they are qualitatively identical, since the squads are different. Some philosophers may want to deny this, of course, but, at a minimum, there is here no clear counterexample.

So, the above cases do not seem to me to undermine my position. Let us turn next to the question of how to conceive of events generally.

On one view of events—the conception associated most notably with Donald Davidson (1969)—events are ontologically basic particulars that enter into causal relations. To say that they are ontologically basic is to say that are not ontologically constructed out of more basic *kinds* of entities that do not themselves fall into the event category. In particular, they do not have the physical objects or people that undergo them as constituents. Sebastian is not a constituent of the event of Sebastian's strolling, for example. This view of events provides no immediate explanation as to why events are necessarily owned by someone or other and necessarily private to their owners.

On an alternative approach to events—the conception elaborated by Alvin Goldman (1970) and Jaegwon Kim (1976)—events are complex entities consisting of objects having properties at times. As originally developed by Goldman and Kim, this approach assumes that any description of the type "x's Fing at t" picks out an event or state token consisting of the object denoted by 'x', the time denoted by 't', and the property expressed by 'F'. The event or state token is supposed to take place wherever the object undergoing the event is located. On this view, events and state tokens literally have objects as constituents. Sebastian is a part of the event of his strolling.

It might be supposed that there is an immediate straightforward explanation, on the Goldman/Kim view, as to why events are necessarily private to their owners: change the owner, and you change a constituent of the event; what you now have is a different event. This would be a little too hasty, however. It is consistent with the claim that Sebastian is a constituent of his strolling to hold nonetheless that Sebastian is only a contingent constituent, that the event of Sebastian's strolling might have been undergone by someone else, and hence might have had someone else as a constituent. It appears, then, that necessary privacy requires that events, on the above account, have their actual object constituents as *essential* constituents—as constituents, that is, in all possible worlds in which they exist. The Goldman/Kim view, in and of itself, apparently offers no explanation of this fact. So as far as necessary privacy goes, no advantage apparently accrues to the Goldman/Kim approach over the Davidsonian one. Both approaches must take the fact that no event could be undergone by a different item from the one that actually undergoes it as an ontologically basic fact about the nature of events.

What about the issue of necessary ownership by something or other? Here it may seem that the Goldman/Kim view does rather better than the Davidsonian account. After all, on the former view, events are meta-physically complex items, partly constituted by objects. So events cannot be entirely unowned by *any* object without ceasing to be events. Similarly for state tokens. This again yields no clear advantage, however, since the Davidsonian can reply that necessary ownership is conceptually induced. Events, in and of themselves, are not metaphysically derivative items. They do not have objects as constituents. Rather, as I suggested earlier, our concept of an event is the concept of a sudden active change in something or other. We can tell by armchair reflection alone that we would not count something as an event unless it had an owner, just as we can tell in like fashion that we would not count someone a bachelor who was married. This need not be to hold that the concept of an object is prior to the concept of an event. For one thing, the Davidsonian view can allow that some events have items other than objects as owners (for example, spatial regions).[15] For another, our concept of an object is (at least in part) the concept of something that persists through change.

Which of the above two approaches to events is to be preferred? One very serious difficulty the Goldman/Kim conception faces is that of individuating events too finely. In particular, this view entails that the event of a's Fing at t_k is identical with the event of b's Ging at t_l if and only if $a = b$, Fness = Gness, and $t_k = t_l$. If I talk loudly at midnight, the event of my talking at midnight is not identical with the event of my talking loudly at midnight, since the property of talking is not identical with the property of talking loudly (often people talk without talking loudly). Similarly, if Stravinski signals the cellos by lowering the baton, the event of his signaling the cellos is not the same as the event of his lowering the baton, since again the constituent properties are not the same. Intuitively, however, there is a single event, a single action, which has been described in two different ways.[16]

Another difficulty for the Goldman/Kim approach concerns event location. If events are complexes of objects exemplifying properties at times, then where are events located? The only plausible answer seems to be wherever the objects are located. This was the answer Kim gave (1976). But there is an objection to this suggestion, as far as the physicalist is concerned. Where are mental events located? Intuitively, if such events are anywhere at all, they are in the brain. But I am not in my brain, even if my mental events are. A second problem is that if afterimages are token experiences, as I have proposed, and token experiences are mental events, then people are themselves constituents of their own afterimages. That is very hard to swallow.

For these reasons, I prefer the Davidsonian approach, and I shall assume, for the rest of my discussion, that pains and other phenomenal objects are ontologically basic particulars.

Box 3.3

Summary

Particular pains, itches, afterimages, and the like—phenomenal objects generally—are to be identified with individual experiences. Experiences belong to the general metaphysical category of event or state. It is required of all members of this category that they cannot exist without some subject or other, and moreover that their actual subjects are essential to them. So we need not suppose that pains and other phenomenal objects are peculiar nonphysical items in order to account for their necessary privacy and necessary ownership. On the contrary, we can take them to be ordinary physical events. The fact that you cannot undergo my pains and the fact that there cannot be a pain without a creature that has it, are no more mysterious or supernatural than the fact that you cannot undergo my death and the fact that there can be no death without something that dies. Events and states are themselves best taken to be ontologically basic particulars, as, for example, on the view of Donald Davidson.

Three remaining objections to the above approach will be dealt with in the next chapter.

4
The Intentionality of Feelings and Experiences

Philosophers usually agree that the sensations and experiences involved in perception have a representational aspect. Consider, for example, the visual sensations I undergo as I watch a distant plane make its way across a clear sky. These sensations represent to me that there is a silver spot moving in a certain direction and producing a white trail against a bright blue background. It also seems evident that some feelings have representational content, in particular, certain emotions and moods, for example, feeling annoyed that the train is late or feeling happy that the book is written at last. But it is frequently denied that bodily sensations are representational. And it is almost universally denied that all feelings are representational. Here are some typical remarks (by Colin McGinn, John Searle, and Ned Block, respectively):

By sensations, we shall mean bodily feelings . . . as well as perceptual experiences. These differ in an important respect, which calls for a subdivision within the class of what we are calling sensations: bodily sensations do not have an intentional object in the way that perceptual experiences do. We distinguish between a visual experience and what it is an experience of; but we do not make this distinction in respect of pains. Or again, visual experiences represent the world as being a certain way, but pains have no such representational content. (McGinn 1982, p. 8)

Many conscious states are not Intentional, e.g., a sudden sense of elation. (Searle 1983, p. 2)

Note . . . that phenomenal content need not be representational at all (my favorite example is the phenomenal content of orgasm). (Block 1995, p. 234)

In my view, these claims are mistaken. *All* states that are phenomenally conscious—*all* feelings and experiences—have intentional content.

I begin by explaining what I mean by saying that a state is an intentional state, a state having intentional content. I then make some general remarks, which are relevant to my overall position, about the way in which simple perceptual sensations represent. Once this is done, I turn to specific problem cases. I first argue that afterimages have intentional content, contrary to the standard view. Next I take up the case of pains and other bodily sensations. Then I consider background feelings, emotions, and moods. The picture that emerges from my discussion is one of experiences and feelings as *sensory representations* either of the outside world or of certain sorts of internal, bodily changes. Moods, emotions, and bodily sensations, in my view, are importantly like maps of our own internal physical workings, guides to our inner body states, graphic representations of what is going on inside (and to) our skins. Perceptual experiences are representations of the same sort, but their focus is the outside world, the external terrain.

The theory developed in this chapter solves both the problem of felt location and phenomenal vocabulary and the problem of the alien limb. It also permits me to complete my response to the problem of ownership. In particular, it affords replies to the three objections that had been left unanswered at the end of the last chapter.

4.1   Intentional States and Intentional Content

It is generally agreed that at least some mental states can represent or be about things that do not exist. For example, I can hope for a life that lasts two hundred years, want a blue emerald, think that there are golden mountains, wonder whether unicorns ever have two horns, believe that Santa Claus lives at the North Pole, and seem to see a pink elephant, even though there are, in reality, no human lives of two centuries, no blue emeralds, no golden mountains, no unicorns, no Santa Claus, and no pink elephants.

The Austrian philosopher Franz Brentano believed that in each of these cases, although the relevant objects do not really exist, they nonetheless are presented in the mental states themselves. He called this presentation "intentional inexistence." In Brentano's view, *every* mental state has its own intentionally inexistent object or objects, whatever reality itself is like. This, according to Brentano, is the basis of intentionality. It is found, he claimed, only in mental states and never in anything physical. He comments,

> Every mental phenomenon is characterized by what the Scholastics of the Middle Ages called the intentional (or mental) inexistence of an object, and what we might call, though not wholly unambiguously, reference to a content, direction toward an object (which is not to be understood here as meaning a thing), or immanent objectivity. Every mental phenomenon includes something as object within itself, although they do not all do so in the same way. In presentation something is presented, in judgement something is affirmed or denied, in love loved, in hate hated, in desire desired and so on. This intentional in-existence is characteristic exclusively of mental phenomena. (Brentano 1874/1973, p. 88)

Brentano's doctrine of intentional inexistence is deeply obscure. Brentano's student Alexius Meinong took Brentano here to be supposing that the objects of mental states have a special sort of existence, or subsistence, quite apart from their being in the real world.[1] Thus, on Meinong's interpretation, a thought about golden mountains is one that relates its subject to subsistent golden mountains. Regrettably, this amounts to explaining the obscure by the still more obscure. The idea of a realm of objects that do not exist and yet that have being seems unintelligible.[2] Moreover, if intentional inexistence is the mark of the mind, then mental states are not, as we normally suppose, about real objects in the world. For example, my wish that I could afford a particular Ferrari I saw for sale yesterday is not really about a real Ferrari at all but rather concerns a subsistent one. That, however, is not what I wish I could afford. Probably I can already afford one of *those*. It is the real thing that is beyond my means.

Brentano himself disavowed the interpretation Meinong adopted, seeing perhaps the difficulties mentioned above. But he offered no alternative characterization of intentional inexistence. So his own view remains obscure. Still, Brentano did succeed in drawing to our attention an extremely interesting fact about a wide range of our mental states (whether or not they are all ultimately like this), namely, their capacity to represent or be about things that do not exist.

There are two other features of mental representation that have been much discussed by philosophers and that are also typically taken to be part and parcel of intentionality. The first of these features is closely related to the capacity to represent mentally what does not exist. We can, it seems, think about or imagine or desire or hope for a yacht or a house in the country, say, without there being any particular yacht or house that is being thought about or imagined or desired or hoped for.

By contrast, we can sometimes adopt these very same attitudes with respect to particular real things in the world. There may be some particular yacht that I am thinking about or want. In some cases, then, the mind seems to "reach out" into the world and "latch onto" specific real objects.

Mental representation is also fine-grained. We have the capacity to think that all humans have hearts without thinking that all humans have at least one kidney, even though the property of having a heart is co-instantiated with the property of having one or more kidneys (i.e., every instance of the one is an instance of the other and vice versa). This is true, moreover, even in those cases in which the properties are *necessarily* co-instantiated. Thus, I can believe that some closed figure has three sides without believing that it has interior angles totaling 180 degrees. What is still more astonishing is the fact that we can, it seems, believe that P without believing that Q, even when 'P' and 'Q' have the same meaning. For example, if I erroneously think that a dozen is ten of a kind, and I believe that Tom gave Jane a dozen roses, I will not believe that Tom has given Jane twelve roses, even though the predicates "has given a dozen roses" and "has given twelve roses" are synonyms.

I shall say that an *intentional* mental state is a state that (a) can represent or be about an F without there being any particular F that it represents or is about, indeed without there really existing any Fs at all, and (b) is fine-grained in at least one of the ways specified above with respect to the manner of its representation. Uncontroversial examples of such states are hoping, believing, desiring, thinking, wondering, intending. The *intentional content* of any particular instance of one of these states is what is hoped for, believed, desired, and so on. In the case of beliefs, the content is expressed in the "that-clause" used to specify the particular belief. Thus, if I believe that snow is white, what I believe, namely, that snow is white, is the intentional content of my belief.

Reflection on the cases mentioned above in connection with the fine-grained character of mental representation shows that we cannot simply identify the intentional content of a belief with its truth conditions (conditions that obtain if and only if the belief is true). Beliefs that differ in content can have the same truth conditions. I should stress that I am not claiming here that there is *no* established use of the term 'content', in connection with beliefs, according to which the intentional content of a belief is the truth conditions of the sentence embedded in its that-clause. Clearly, some writers do think of content in this way. I am adopting a broader usage, one that also has wide currency, according to which belief content is what is ascribed to a belief state via its that-clause. Given this usage, same truth conditions do not entail same content.

How, then, are states with intentional content generated? This is a large question that I cannot pursue fully here. But I would like to make some pertinent remarks. Many philosophers maintain that intentional mental states have a fundamentally *linguistic* structure. The "language of thought" hypothesis is an empirical hypothesis about how mental states are actually stuctured. It is not an a priori philosophical analysis. So it is not intended to cover the (intentional) mental states of all actual and possible creatures. In its most general form, it concerns *all* actual representational mental states. The basic thesis, stemming from the computer model of mind, is that such states are encoded in symbol structures in an inner language.

In the case of the propositional attitudes—that is, those mental states, like belief, whose contents are standardly expressed in that-clauses—it has typically been supposed that the relevant symbol structures are sentences.[3] The apparent need to acknowledge inner sentences in an account of the propositional attitudes (hereafter, the *PA*s) derives from several different sources.

To begin with, the *PA*s are systematic: there are intrinsic connections between certain thoughts. Consider, for example, the thought that the boy is chasing the dog and the thought that the dog is chasing the boy. Anyone who has the capacity to think the former thought also has the capacity to think the latter and vice versa. Second, the *PA*s are productive: we have the capacity, it seems, to think indefinitely many thoughts and to think thoughts we have never thought before. The *PA*s are also fine-grained, as I noted earlier: I can think that you know something important without thinking that you justifiably and truly believe something important, even if "justifiably and truly believe" is the correct analysis of "know." Finally, the *PA*s have truth values: my belief that the English pound is worth fewer American dollars than it was two years ago is either true or false.

Facts exactly parallel to these obtain in the case of sentences in public languages. There are intrinsic connections between certain sentences (for example, "The boy kissed the girl" and "The girl kissed the boy"); we produce new sentences all the time (indeed, except in special cases, we rarely utter the same sentence on different occasions); in writing down or uttering a sentence *S* that means the same as another sentence *T*, we still have not thereby written or uttered *T*; finally, sentences can be true or false.

According to adherents to the language of thought hypothesis, these parallels are best explained by supposing that the *PA*s themselves have a sentence-like structure.[4] Thus, believing that lemons are bitter, say, is a matter of producing internally, in one's belief compartment (see below), a token of a sentence that means or represents that lemons are bitter. This sentence is not usually supposed to be a sentence in any public, natural language, but rather a sentence in a special, inner language that the brain has been wired to use by evolution (just as artificial computers are wired to use binary). The inner language is shared by all creatures capable of thought, belief, and other *PA*s, not just those human beings who have mastered a public language.

Box 4.1

Talk of a belief compartment is not intended to presuppose that there is a special, spatially discrete region of the brain dedicated to beliefs, any more than talk of the memory space of a computer demands that there be some single, contiguous physical region within the machine in which information is stored. Rather, the idea is that there is a *functionally* discrete region. Sentences that are tokened in this functional belief space are alike in that they play a common functional role with respect to other mental sentences, sensory inputs, and behavioral outputs. Beliefs, on this view, are states that function in a distinctive way with respect to perceptual information, desires, and behavior. Any sentence token that occupies a role of the sort that is distinctive to beliefs belongs in the belief compartment.

The linguistic view of *PA*s naturally leads to the following proposal about intentional content, for the case of belief. The belief that *P* represents the external state of affairs of *P*'s being the case. The belief is true if, and only if, this state of affairs actually obtains. The content of the belief is a joint product of the relevant state of affairs and its manner of linguistic encoding in the belief. States of affairs are complex items into which real objects, properties, and relations enter, but no representational or conceptual items. So, for example, having a belief about golden mountains involves representing a state of affairs into which the real property of being a golden mountain enters (though no particular golden mountain, for there are no such things). The property of being a golden mountain is itself constituted by the properties of being golden and being a mountain. The content of the belief is given by the relevant state of affairs (for example, the state of affairs of there being golden mountains in Mexico, or that of all golden mountains' being unclimbable) *and* the sentence tokened in the belief. Likewise, believing that this is a popular place to eat is a matter of having a belief that represents a certain worldly state of affairs in the appropriate manner or under the appropriate (partly indexical) sentence. This belief is different from the belief that Le Tour D'Argent is a popular place to eat, even if this is Le Tour D'Argent, since the constitutive sentences, and in particular the linguistic representations of Le Tour D'Argent, in the two cases are different. The one uses an indexical, the other a name.

This approach can be extended to other intentional mental states. But it is not necessary to suppose that all such states are just like the *PA*s. In particular, it need not be supposed that sentences are present in the head (or soul) in each and every such case. That would be much too quick. A commitment to an inner symbol system within which mental representation occurs is not a commitment to *sentences* in each and every case. After all, computers—symbol manipulators par excellence—operate on all sorts of symbol structures (for example, lists, sentences, arrays); to mention one example, there are well-known theories of mental imagery that fall within the computational approach but reject the thesis that images are sentences.[5] I shall return to this point later.

This still leaves us with one very large question. How is it possible for a state in the head—a belief, hope, desire, or whatever—to represent an external state of affairs? More generally, how can any state in nature represent anything at all? Here is not the place to try to present a fully general response to these questions (and hence a solution to the problem of intentionality), but, in the next section, I sketch out one approach, which seems to me promising in the context of sensory experience.

Box 4.2

Summary

Intentional mental states are states that can represent, or be about, things of a certain sort without there being any particular real things of that sort that they are about, indeed without there being any real things of that sort at all. Moreover, intentional mental states are states that can represent in a fine-grained way (so that, for example, such a state can represent only one of two properties that are necessarily always present in objects together). Intentional states are plausibly taken to have a symbolic structure, and their intentional contents are plausibly viewed as the joint product of their symbolic features and what it is that the symbols represent. In the case of beliefs, the symbol structures are sentences, but not, I claim, in the case of sensations (see section 4.7).

4.2   How Perceptual Sensations Represent

Consider the case of tree rings. Intuitively, the number of rings on a cross section of a tree trunk *represents* something about the tree, namely, how old it is. This is not a matter of our knowing anything about tree rings or of our inspecting the rings. Rather it is an objective, observer-independent fact, or so it seems plausible to suppose. Before any human ever noticed any rings inside trees, the number of rings represented the age of the tree, just as it does now.

How should we think of natural representation of this sort? Well, different numbers of rings are correlated with different ages; moreover, in any given case, a certain number of rings are present *because* the tree is a certain age. But what about odd climatic conditions? Or a disease infecting the tree? Surely, the number of tree rings will not *always* correlate with the tree age.

What really matters, it appears, is correlation, or more accurately, causal covariation, *under optimal conditions* (Stampe 1977; Stalnaker 1984). The general suggestion, then, is that for each state S of object x, within the relevant set of alternative states of x, we may define what the state represents as follows:

S represents that P = df If optimal conditions obtain, S is tokened in x if and only if P and because P.[6]

When optimal conditions do not obtain, there is *mis*representation. The state of having N rings represents that the age of the tree is N years by causally correlating with that age under optimal conditions, but if, in reality, the conditions are not optimal, then the tree age will not match the number of rings.

This proposal about representation applies straightforwardly to simple artificial or conventional examples. Consider the height of the mercury column in a thermometer. It represents the temperature of the surrounding air. Different heights causally correlate with different temperatures under optimal conditions and thereby represent those temperatures. In this case, the correlation is artificially induced by the designer of the thermometer. If the device malfunctions, conditions are not optimal and there is misrepresentation. Likewise in the case of a speedometer and the position of the needle. Here it is speed that is represented.

The key idea, then, is that representation is a matter of causal covariation or correlation (*tracking*, as I shall often call it) under optimal conditions. If there are no distorting factors, no anomalies or abnormalities, the number of tree rings tracks age, the height of the mercury column tracks temperature, the position of the speedometer needle tracks speed, and so on. Thereby, age, temperature, speed, and the like, are represented.

Obviously, this approach needs further amplification; but I have said enough to comment on the question of whether it can be used to understand *mental* representation generally. Clearly, there are difficulties. In particular, the account is not straightforwardly applicable to beliefs across the board. Take, for example, the belief that the Devil is an angel who fell from grace. What are the relevant optimal conditions here? And what about mathematical beliefs, the belief that $2 + 2 = 4$, say? Again, the proposal does not seem applicable. There are no states in human

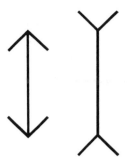

Figure 4.1
The Muller-Lyer diagram

heads that are tokened *because* 2 + 2 = 4. That abstract mathematical fact has no causal power.

In the case of simple perceptual sensations, however, the causal covariation approach seems to be very promising. For these sensations, in my view, are normally mechanically produced by external stimuli. Let me explain.

It is a well-known fact that the Muller-Lyer and other familiar visual illusions do not alter with alterations in beliefs about what the seen properties of the object really are. For example, in the case of the Muller-Lyer diagram, knowing that the two lines are really of the same length has no tendency at all to make the lines *look* the same length.

The same sort of thing is true with the figure below. Knowing that the two lines are parallel does not make them look parallel. On the contrary, they continue to look bowed.

Why should this be? One plausible hypothesis is that vision is modular in the sense that it generates representations of a certain class of properties of distal stimuli via perceptual processes that operate on the retinal input in a largely fixed, autonomous manner.

On the standard computational approach, the receptor cells on the retina are taken to be transducers. They have, as input, physical energy in the form of light, and they convert it immediately into symbolic representations of light intensity and wavelength. These representations are themselves made up of active nerve cells. Hence, they are physical. And they are symbolic, since they are the objects of computational procedures. Moreover, they represent light intensity and wavelength, since that is

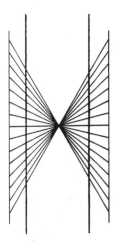

Figure 4.2
The Hering figure

what they reliably track, assuming the system is functioning properly. The computational procedures operating on these representations generate further symbolic representations first of intensity and wavelength changes in the light, then of lines of such changes, then of edges, ridges, and surfaces, together with representations of local surface features, for example, color, orientation, and distance away. The salient procedures operate mechanically. At these early stages, the visual system is much like a calculator that has been hardwired to perform addition. There are no stored representations in memory, whose retrieval and manipulation govern the behavior of the system.

So representations are built up of distal features of the surfaces of external objects in mechanical fashion by computational processes. The initial, or input, representations for the visual module track light intensity and wavelength, assuming nothing is malfunctioning. The output representations track features of distal stimuli under optimal or ideal perceptual conditions. Thereby, it seems plausible to suppose, they represent those features, they become sensations *of* edges, ridges, colors, shapes, and so on.[7] Likewise for the other senses.

The broad picture I have here of perceptual sensations draws a sharp distinction between these states and beliefs or other conceptual states. Perceptual sensations, in my view, form the outputs of specialized sensory modules and stand ready to produce conceptual responses via the action of higher-level cognitive processing of one sort or another.[8] So perceptual sensations feed into the conceptual system, without themselves being a part of that system. They are nondoxastic or nonconceptual states. This, I want to stress, does not mean that perceptual sensations are not symbolic states. But, in my view, they are symbolic states very different from beliefs. I shall elaborate on this point later.

It is important to realize that just as perceptual sensations are not to be conflated with thoughts or beliefs elicited by the appropriate sensory stimulations, so too they cannot simply be identified with (or modeled on) episodes of seeing-as or seeing- that. Seeing something as an *F* necessitates remembering what *F*s look like. The perceptual information about *F*s is stored in a schema (on the standard psychological model of perceptual memory). Seeing-as demands bringing the sensory input under the appropriate schema. So seeing-as is constrained by limitations on memory.

Perceptual sensations, however, can, and often do, occur without corresponding schemas. Color sensations, to take one obvious case already mentioned in chapter 2, subjectively vary in ways that far outstrip our color schemas.[9] The experience or sensation of the determinate shade red_{29} is phenomenally different from that of the shade red_{32}. But normal perceivers typically have no schema in memory for red_{29} or red_{32}. I myself, for example, do not know what red_{29} looks like. So I cannot see something as red_{29} or recognize that specific shade as such; if I go into a paint store and look at a chart of reds, I cannot pick out red_{29}. The same is true for our sensory experiences of sounds, to mention another obvious example. They too admit of many more fine-grained distinctions than our stored representations of sounds in memory.

There are, of course, good architectural reasons why human memory is thus limited. Were all the things we can discriminate retained in memory, we would quickly suffer unmanageable information overload. Limitations on memory are necessary for information reduction.

I might add finally that the picture I have presented above can allow that processing in the conceptual arena can feed back down into the sensory modules, and sometimes influence *certain* parts of the processing that goes on there. In this way, beliefs and thoughts can affect how things appear.[10] But, in my view, there are many aspects of appearances that cannot be influenced in this way.

That, then, is one way of thinking of perceptual sensations and how they represent. What I shall try to show in the following sections of this chapter is that the above approach may be extended to sensory objects and experiences that seem initially to have no representational content at all. I turn first to the case of afterimages.

Box 4.3

Summary

There are many different theories about the nature of representation, but one approach that seems well suited to sensory representations (although not to beliefs) is the causal covariation view.[11] On this view, if optimal or ideal perceptual conditions obtain, sensory states of the sort found in perception track the presence of certain external features; they thereby represent those features.

4.3 Afterimages

Afterimages can be produced in a number of different ways. Turning the light on and off, after a long period in the dark, generates an afterimage with the color of the light. Looking quickly at the setting sun often results in a relatively sharp image. Staring at a colored light or surface and then turning one's gaze on a white surface produces an image with the complementary color.

One well-known objection to the view that afterimages are brain processes was first raised by J. J. C. Smart in the fifties. The objection, which is very simple indeed, goes as follows: afterimages are sometimes yellowy-orange; brain processes cannot be yellowy-orange.[12] So afterimages are not brain processes.

This objection is often presented as a reason for denying that afterimages are *literally* yellowy-orange or any other real-world color. So it forms part of the background for the problem of phenomenal vocabulary.

The reply that Smart himself made to the objection was to deny that afterimages exist, there really being, in Smart's view, only experiences of *having* afterimages, which are not themselves yellowy-orange. I have already rejected this reply. In my view, afterimages are visual experiences. Hence, if afterimages are yellowy-orange, so too are certain experiences. But what can this mean? If, in predicating color words of images, we are not attributing to them the very same properties we attribute to external objects via our use of color language, then what properties are we attributing? Indeed, how is it that color vocabulary is applied at all to afterimages, given that they do not really have the appropriate colors?

One solution proposed by Ned Block is to say that color words are used elliptically for expressions like 'real-blue-representing', 'real-green-representing', and so on, in connection with images generally.[13] In my view, this solution has a number of important virtues.[14] For one thing, brain processes can certainly represent colors. So the identity theory is no longer threatened. For another, as Block has noted,[15] terms like 'loud' and 'high-pitched' are standardly applied directly to oscilloscope readings used in connection with the graphical representations of sounds. In this context, these terms evidently do not name real sounds made by the readings. One possibility, then, is that they pick out representational properties, such as loud-representing and high-pitched-representing. If this is so, then there already exists an established usage of terms that conforms to the one alleged to obtain in the case of color terms and afterimages.

There is a serious difficulty, however. Mental images are not literally square any more than they are literally blue. Extending the above proposal to shape, we get that a blue, square afterimage is simply one that is square-representing and also blue-representing. Intuitively, this seems too weak. Surely, a blue, square image cannot represent different things as blue *and* square. Unfortunately, nothing in the above proposal rules this out. 'Blue', then, in application to afterimages, does not mean blue-representing. Likewise 'square'.

This difficulty is not peculiar to images. Precisely the same problem can be raised in connection with oscilloscope readings. The way out, I suggest, is to appreciate that there is nothing elliptical about the meanings of terms like 'blue' or 'loud' in the above contexts. Instead, it is the contexts themselves that need further examination. Let me explain.

The contexts "Hopes for an *F*" and "Hallucinates a *G*" are typically *intensional*. For example, I can hope for eternal life and hallucinate a pink elephant, even though there are no such things. Similarly, I can hope for eternal life without hoping for eternal boredom, even if in reality the two are the same. It seems evident that the terms substituting for '*F*' and '*G*' in these contexts retain their usual meanings. The above peculiarities are due to the fact that hoping and hallucinating are intentional states, and to the special character of intentionality.

Now precisely the same peculiarities are present in the case of the context "an *F* image," where '*F*' is a color or shape term. Thus, in a world in which nothing is really triangular, I can still have a triangular image. Also, if I have a red image, intuitively, it does not follow that I have an image the color of most fire engines, even given that most fire engines are red. The explanation, I suggest, is straightforward: an *F* image is an image that *represents that something* is *F*.[16]

Likewise, where '*F*' is a color term and '*G*' a shape term, an *F, G* image is an image *that represents that something* is both *F* and *G*. In the case of an afterimage, what is represented is that there is something perpendicular to the line of sight that is *F* and *G*, typically, something that has a dim and hazy character. My suggestion, then, is that there is nothing elliptical or peculiar about the meanings of the terms '*F*' and '*G*' in the context "an *F, G* image." Rather, the context itself is an intensional one, having a logical structure that reflects the intentional character of images generally.

It may still be wondered why we *say* that the image itself is *F* and *G*, for example, blue and square. This is, I suggest, part of a much broader usage. Frequently, when we talk of representations, both mental and nonmental, within science and in ordinary life, we save breath by speaking as if the representations themselves have the properties of the things they represent. In such cases, in saying of a representation that it is *F*, what we mean is that it represents that something is *F*. So, when it is said of some given oscilloscope reading that it is loud and high-pitched, what is being claimed is that the reading represents some sound as being loud and high-pitched. 'Loud' and 'high-pitched' mean what they normally do here. The context itself is intensional.

The above proposal solves the problem of the blue, square image. Here the image represents that something is both blue and square, not merely that something is blue *and* that something is square.[17]

The claim that afterimages are representational, I might add, does not entail or presuppose that creatures cannot have afterimages unless they also have the appropriate concepts (at least as 'concept' is frequently understood). Having the concept *F* requires, on some accounts, having the ability to use the linguistic term '*F*' correctly. On other accounts, concept possession requires the ability to represent in thought and belief that something falls under the concept. But afterimages, like other perceptual sensations, are not themselves thoughts or beliefs; and they certainly do not demand a public language. They are nondoxastic or nonconceptual representations.[18]

In admitting that afterimages are nonconceptual or nondoxastic representations, I am not thereby granting that they do not really have *intentional* content, that they are representations of a nonintentional sort. As I observed in the last section, intentionality, as I view it, does not require concepts. As I use the term 'intentionality', the key feature is fine-grained representation of the real and nonreal. This feature, I have argued, is present in the case of afterimages. So afterimages are intentional. Those philosophers who want to insist that there cannot be full-blooded intentionality without concepts (or that intentionality is restricted to the central executive) are entitled to their use of the term. But any disagreement here is, I suggest, purely verbal. Nothing of substance hangs on which usage is adopted.

Box 4.4

Summary

An afterimage is a sensory experience, typically produced by staring at a bright light and looking away, that represents that something is present with a certain two-dimensional shape and color, something that is usually

Box 4.4 *continued*

> somewhat dim and fuzzy. Since there really is no such item, an afterimage is a misrepresentation: the subject of such an experience is undergoing a sort of illusion. The illusion is created by the abnormal state of the person's sensory apparatus induced by the bright light.

4.4 The Problem of Ownership Revisited

We are now in a position to return to the three unanswered objections to the solution I had offered in the last chapter to the problem of ownership. The first of these was that if afterimages are literally identified with certain visual experiences, then the objects of those experiences are erroneously conflated with the experiences themselves. For example, if I have a blue afterimage, the object of my experience is a blue image. So the image cannot be identical with the experience.

My reply to this objection is to deny that afterimages really are objects of experiences at all. In having a blue image, I certainly experience something. What I experience is that something (or other) is blue. In one broad sense, an object of experience is simply the intentional content of the experience—in this case, that something is blue. Afterimages are clearly not objects of experience in this sense. In another closely related but narrower sense, an object of experience is a real, concrete thing that enters into the content of the experience (for example, a particular tree). Afterimages, on the view presented above, are not objects of experience in this sense either.

Afterimages, I suggest, are mental objects that people *have* when they undergo certain sorts of sensory experiences. But they are not themselves the objects *of* those experiences. They are objects that people have by being things that people undergo, namely, events. To have an afterimage is to undergo a mental event of a particular type. Afterimages are, in one sense, *what* people sometimes experience, just as deaths are what people die and laughs are what people laugh. For trivially, experiences are what people experience. But there is no substantive sense in which afterimages are objects of experience.

The second objection was that the proposed identification of phenomenal objects with experiences entails that experiences are sometimes stinging (as in the case of pains) or square or yellow (as in the case of afterimages), and that has no clear sense. My reply, of course, is that such claims make perfectly good sense. They are to be understood in the manner explained above in connection with afterimages (and shortly to be generalized to pains), as describing properties that enter into the representational contents of the experiences.

The third objection was that if phenomenal objects are experiences, then when multiple phenomenal objects are present, a red afterimage to the left of a green one, say, multiple different visual experiences must be undergone simultaneously, one for each image. But that seems very odd or counterintuitive. Surely, even if I have two afterimages, I only have one visual experience.

It is certainly true that if I have a red afterimage to the left of a green one, overall I have only a single visual experience. My experience represents that something red is to the left of something green. But this can still be held to be a *composite* experience, having as components a token experience of something red and also a token experience of something green.

Consider, for example, the case of a picture of a square object next to a round one. There is only one picture, but it contains within itself a picture of a square object and a picture of a round object. That is to say, within the picture as a whole, there is a part pictorially representing something square and a part pictorially representing something round. The same is true for maps. In my view, visual experience is similar.

What is true here for pictures and maps is not true for sentences. A sentence describing a square and a circle need not have a sentence describing a square and a sentence describing a circle as components. This is one of the reasons why I remarked earlier that perceptual sensations do not have a sentence-like structure.

Perhaps it will be objected that pictures and maps are objects, and experiences, on my proposal, are events or state tokens. So the parallel is not really appropriate. But this difference seems to me not to make a difference in the present context. In each case, there is a complex representational token of a certain type (experiential or pictorial or topographic). This token contains other representational tokens of that same type. Whether the tokens are objects or states is of no consequence.

That completes my discussion of the problem of ownership. I want next to turn to pains.

4.5 Pains

It is often supposed that terms applied to pain that also apply to physical objects do not have their ordinary meanings. Ned Block, who takes this view, says,

There is some reason to think that there is a systematic difference in meaning between certain predicates applied to physical objects and the same predicates applied to mental particulars. Consider a nonimagery example: the predicate '_____ in _____ '. This predicate appears in each premise and the conclusion of this argument:

The pain is in my fingertip.
The fingertip is in my mouth.
Therefore, the pain is in my mouth.

This argument is valid for the "in" of spatial enclosure . . . , since "in" in this sense is transitive. But suppose that the two premises are true in their *ordinary* meanings. . . . The conclusion obviously does not follow, so we must conclude that "in" is not used in the spatial enclosure sense in all three statements. It certainly seems plausible that "in" as applied in locating pains differs in meaning systematically from the standard spatial enclosure sense. (Block 1983, p. 517; see also Jackson 1977, p. 76)

This seems to me quite wrong. There is no more reason to adopt the strange position that 'in' has a special meaning in connection with pain than there is to say that 'orange' has a special meaning in connection with images. The inference Block cites certainly does *not* establish his claim. To see this, consider the following inference:

I want to be in City Hall.
City Hall is in a ghetto.
Therefore, I want to be in a ghetto.

The term 'in' has the same meaning in both premises and the conclusion. But the argument is invalid: I might want to be in City Hall to listen to a particular speech, say, without thereby wanting to be in a ghetto. The same is true, I suggest, in the case of Block's example, and the explanation is the same. In both the first premise and the conclusion, the term 'in' appears in an intensional context. Just as when we say that an image is blue, we are saying that it represents that something is blue, so when we say that a pain is in my fingertip, we are saying that it represents that something is in my fingertip.

It is perhaps worth noting here that the invalidity of the inference involving pain has nothing to do with the fact that the mouth is a cavity of a certain sort, and hence an item whose ontological status might itself be questioned. If I have a pain in my fingertip and I slit open a small portion of my leg, into which I then thrust my finger, still it does not follow that I have a pain in my leg. Suppose, for example, that my leg has been anesthetized. In this case, I feel a pain in my finger, but not in my leg.[19]

That there is a hidden intensionality in statements of pain location is confirmed by our talk of pains in phantom limbs. We allow it to be true on occasion that people are subject to pains in limbs that no longer exist. For example, a patient who has had his leg amputated may report feeling pains in the leg in places where he had experienced pain previously. Pains are also sometimes felt in phantoms of other body parts. For example, one man, who underwent amputation of his penis, felt severe pain in the phantom penis. Another, I might add, reported feeling a painless, but continually erect penis for a four-year period following the amputation (see Melzack 1990).

How can pains be felt in phantom limbs? Answer: You can have a pain in your left leg even though you have no left leg, just as you can search for the Fountain of Youth. Again the context is intensional: specifically, you have a pain that represents that something is in your left leg.[20]

Of course, there is some temptation to say that if you do not have a left leg, then you cannot really have a pain in it. But that is no problem for my proposal. For there is an alternative (de re) reading of the context, namely, that to have a pain in your left leg is for your left leg to be such that you have a pain in *it*. Now a left leg *is* required.

But does not a pain in the leg represent more than just that something is in the leg? Why, yes. To have a pain is to feel a pain, and to feel a pain is to experience pain. Thus, if I have a pain, I undergo a token experience of a certain sort. This token experience is the particular pain

I have. Now in optimal conditions, sensory experiences of the pain sort track certain sorts of disturbances in the body, paradigmatically, bodily damage. So pains represent such disturbances.

For example, a twinge of pain represents a mild, brief disturbance. A throbbing pain represents a rapidly pulsing disturbance. Aches represent disorders that occur *inside* the body rather than on the surface. These disorders are represented as having volume, as gradually beginning and ending, as increasing in severity and then slowly fading away.[21] The volumes so represented are not represented as precise or sharply bounded. This is why aches are not felt to have precise locations, unlike pricking pains, for example. A stabbing pain is one that represents sudden damage over a particular well-defined bodily region. This region is represented as having volume (rather than being two-dimensional), as being the shape of something sharp-edged and pointed (like that of a dagger).[22] In the case of a pricking pain, the relevant damage is represented as having a sudden beginning and ending on the surface or just below, and as covering a very tiny area. A racking pain is one that represents that the damage involves the stretching of internal body parts (e.g., muscles).

In each of the above cases, the subject of the pain undergoes a sensory representation of a certain sort of bodily disturbance. The disturbances vary with the pains. Consider, for example, a pricking pain in the leg. Here, it seems phenomenologically undeniable that pricking is experienced *as* a feature tokened within the leg, and not as an intrinsic feature of the experience itself. What is experienced as being pricked is a part of the surface of the leg. This is nicely accounted for by the above proposal. It should also be noted that since pricking pains do not represent pins, my account does not have the implausible consequence that creatures who live in worlds without pins cannot have pricking sensations or that in these worlds creatures undergoing such sensations are misrepresenting what is going on in them.

My proposal, then, is that pains are sensory representations of bodily damage or disorder. More fully, they are mechanical responses to the relevant bodily changes in the same way that basic visual sensations are mechanical responses to proximate visual stimuli. In the case of pain, the receptors (known as nociceptors) are distributed throughout the body. These receptors function analogously to the receptors on the retina. They are transducers. They are sensitive only to certain changes in the tissue to which they are directly connected (typically, damage), and they convert this input immediately into symbols. Representations are then built up mechanically of internal bodily changes, just as representations are built up of external surfaces in the case of vision. These representations, to repeat, are sensory. They involve no concepts. One does not need to be able to conceptualize a given bodily disturbance in order to feel pain. And even if one can, it is not relevant, because feeling pain demands the sensory experience of that disturbance.

It is interesting to note that there are circumstances in which people cannot tell whether they are feeling pressure or pain, for example, during dental drilling under partial anesthetic. This has a simple explanation on the above account. Both sensations involve the representation of a bodily disturbance. Some disturbances—tissue distortions of certain sorts—fall on the border between those paradigmatic of pain and those paradigmatic of pressure. Sensory representations of such disturbances are neither clearly pain experiences nor clearly pressure experiences.

Perhaps it will now be said that it is not clear how the above proposal accomodates the well-established fact that pain is susceptible to top-down influences. For example, in one experiment, joggers were found to run faster in a lovely wooded area than on a track. Apparently, they experienced less pain in their arms and legs while viewing the trees and flowers and, as a result, ran at a quicker pace.[23] There is also the interesting case of some Scottish terriers raised in restricted environments. When released, Melzack tells us, they behaved as follows:

They were so frisky and rambunctious that inevitably someone would accidentally step on their tails. But we didn't hear a squeak from them. In their excitement, they would also bang their heads with a resounding smack on the building's low water pipes and just walk away. I was curious, and lit a match to see how they would respond to the flame. They kept sticking their noses in it, and though they would back off as if from a funny smell, they did not react as if hurt. (Melzack, quoted in Warga 1987, p. 52)

Anxiety, by contrast, increases the experience of pain, as, for example, when one compares a present injury to some past one.

These facts, if indeed they are facts (see below), about pain are no threat to my position. They may be explained by supposing that the pain receptor pathway in the spinal column leading to the somatosensory cortex (the primary center of pain) has a gate in it that is controlled by input from the higher brain centers (the gate control theory).[24] When this gate is partly closed, less information gets through, and the feeling of pain diminishes. As it opens further, more information is enabled to pass. Anxiety, excitement, joy, concentration, and other higher-level activities affect the orientation of the gate. So, the fact that the experience of pain is, *in the above sense,* cognitively penetrable presents no real difficulty for my proposal. What happens is simply that one's cognitive assessment of the situation feeds back down into the sensory module for the experience of pain and affects how much information gets through about bodily damage.

I might add that it is also not obvious to what degree the experience of pain itself, considered as a sensory state, really can be changed by the cognitive centers. What seems undeniable is that cognitive reactions can affect one's *awareness* of pain experiences. But awareness of a pain experience is itself a cognitive state. It involves bringing the experience under concepts. These concepts are what allow us to form conceptions through introspection of what it is like for us to undergo the experiences.

Unless we apply such concepts, we are oblivious to our experiences. We are like the distracted driver who is lost in thought for several miles as he drives along. During this time he keeps the car on the road and perhaps changes gears. So he certainly sees the road and other cars.[25] But he is not aware of his visual sensations. He is not paying any attention to them. In short, he has no thoughts about his perceptions—his thoughts lie elsewhere.

Consciousness of the sort the driver lacks is not phenomenal consciousness. Rather it is what I called in chapter 1 higher-order consciousness. Consciousness, in this sense, is consciousness of one's own mental states. For that, concepts *are* required.

This point—that sensory experiences demand concepts in order for their subjects to be aware of them—is a significant one, to which I shall return later. My present interest in the point pertains only to the issue of evidence for cognitive penetrability.

So far I have said nothing directly about the painfulness of pains. How is this feature of pains to be accounted for within the above proposal?

To begin with, it should be noted that we often speak of bodily damage as painful. When it is said that a cut or a burn or a bruise is painful or hurts, what is meant is (roughly) that it is *causing* a feeling, namely, the very feeling the person is undergoing, and that this feeling elicits an immediate dislike for itself together with anxiety about, or concern for, the state of the bodily region where the disturbance feels located.

Now pains do not themselves cause feelings that cause dislike: they *are* such feelings, at least in typical cases. So pains are not painful in the above sense. Still, they are painful in a slightly weaker sense: they typically elicit the *cognitive* reactions described above. Moreover, when we introspect our pains, we are aware of their sensory contents as painful. This is why, if I have a pain in my leg, intuitively, I am aware of something in my leg (and not in my head, which is where the experience itself is) as painful. My pain represents damage in my leg, and I then cognitively classify that damage as painful (via the application of the concept *painful* in introspection).

In normal circumstances, a person who has a pain in a leg and who reports that something in her leg is painful is not under any sort of illusion. But a man who reports to his doctor that he has a pain in his left arm is in a different situation if it is discovered that the real cause of his pain lies in his heart. Such a man has a pain in his left arm—he undergoes a sensory experience that represents to him damage there—but there really is nothing *in his left arm* that is painful. What is painful is something happening in his heart.

Pains, I conclude, like afterimages, have representational content. Unlike images, however, they have bodily locations (in the representational sense I have elucidated).[26] So although pains are really constituted by physical processes in the head, it is also true to say that they can occur anywhere in the body.[27]

4.6   Other Bodily Sensations

The intentionalist approach to pain extends in a natural way to all bodily sensations. To have a tickle in a toe is to undergo a certain sort of experience. What experiences of the tickle sort track (in optimal conditions) is the presence of something lightly touching or brushing against the surface of the body. So that is what they represent. Tickles are sensory representations of bodily disturbances, just as pains are. Tickles also have a standard reactive component (like pains in normal cases): they cause an impulse to break contact with the object brushing lightly against the skin, together with a further desire to rub or scratch the affected bodily region, if contact continues.

Itches also represent surface disturbances, though not ones of the same sort as tickles. In addition, itches cause in their owners reactions of dislike (less intense than for pains) plus the impulse to rub or scratch the relevant bodily part.[28]

Tingling sensations represent patterns of bodily disturbance that consist of a large number of tiny distinct parts, each of which is quickly varying or pulsating. The feeling of thirst represents dryness in the throat and mouth. Feeling hot is a state that represents an increase in body temperature above the normal one. Hunger pangs represent contractions of the stomach walls when the stomach is empty.[29] In these cases, the representations themselves are sensory experiences, not conceptual states. So the fact that for some bodily sensations—for example, the feeling of hunger—the person in the street may not be able to say just which bodily state is represented has no significance. Whereof you cannot speak (or think), thereof you can still sense.

Box 4.5

That the experience of hunger pangs tracks contractions of the stomach walls, all being well (and hence, on my account, represents those contractions), was first established by W. Cannon and A. Washburn in 1912. Washburn inserted a tube ino his stomach for several hours each day. At the end of the tube was a balloon that was inflated to fit the stomach walls. The stomach tube was attached to a manometer (which measured sudden pressure changes). A pneumograph was also connected to the waist with the aim of registering movements in the abdominal muscles. Washburn pressed a button whenever he felt pangs of hunger. These pangs were found to correlate perfectly with strong stomach contractions. As the psychologist Frank Geldard notes in his discussion of hunger,

The simple conclusion would seem to be indicated that feelings of hunger are caused by stomach contractions and thus are kinesthetic sensations of a certain pattern. (1953, pp. 244–45)

Box 4.5 *continued*

> This is not to deny that hunger, in the sense of desire for food (or appetite)
> may not often be present without stomach contractions. Indeed, in one
> extreme case, a patient, who had his stomach taken out and his esophagus
> connected directly to his intestines, still had a normal desire to eat (Wangen-
> steen and Carlson 1931).

What about Block's example of the sensations involved in orgasm? In this case, one undergoes sensory representations of certain physical changes in the genital region. These changes quickly undulate in their intensity. Furthermore, they are highly pleasing. They elicit an immediate and strong positive reaction.

It is important to stress again that the representations of bodily changes involved in orgasms are nonconceptual. This is why if I see that my partner is having an orgasm, it does not follow that I am having one myself. Seeing-that is conceptual. It involves believing-that together with associated visual sensations. Feeling an orgasm requires nonconceptual sensory experience of the pertinent bodily changes, not conceptual representation of the generic state. No belief about myself or my partner is necessary. Furthermore, my orgasms represent physical changes in *my* body, not in my partner. But what I see, if I see that she is having an orgasm, is something about *her*.

Bodily sensations besides pains are common in phantom limbs. There are feelings of warmth, pressure (for example, the tightness of a wedding band on a phantom finger), itches, tickles. Phantom bladders even feel like the real thing. Sometimes, after a bladder removal, patients report that their bladders feel uncomfortably full or that they feel themselves urinating. In all of these cases, the people are undergoing sensory representations of bodily states or changes that do not really exist.

If the above reflections and those of the last section are correct, then the problem of felt location and phenomenal vocabulary has been solved. There is nothing very strange or peculiar about the meaning of physical-object vocabulary, as it applies to pains or itches or afterimages. Terms like 'stinging', 'intense', 'yellow', and 'in' mean what they normally mean.

The contexts in which these terms are applied, however, are intensional. It is the intensionality of the contexts that is responsible for the peculiarities on which the problem is founded. This intensionality is itself a reflection of the representational character of pains, itches, afterimages, and other phenomenal items.

This view seems to me intuitively very appealing. And it fits in well with our talk of experiences and feelings generally. A burning smell is surely a smell that represents that something is burning. A drowning feeling is a feeling that represents that someone, namely, the owner of the feeling, is drowning. An out-of-body experience is an experience that represents that its owner is out of his body. The terms 'burning', 'drowning', and 'out of body' do not change their meanings in these contexts. The contexts are intensional.

Box 4.6

Summary

Bodily sensations generally are generated in a mechanical fashion from information contained in receptors distributed throughout our bodies. These receptors respond to proximate stimuli of various sorts. Computational processes transform the initial highly localized representations into more general representations of bodily changes, together with their locations (leg, arm, stomache, etc.). We are hardwired by evolution to undergo these computations (although, as noted earlier, there can be some cognitive feedback). So there are specialized sensory modules for bodily sensations, just as there are for perceptual sensations connected with the five senses.[30] The output representations of these modules are the sensory representations to which I have been referring. These representations, which are themselves nonconceptual, serve as the inputs for cognitive processing. They supply information directly to a cognitive, reasoning system. Representations produced earlier on within the modules supply information we (and other creatures) need to construct or generate the sensory representations, but they are not themselves sensory (as I am using the term). It is at the level of the inputs to the cognitive arena that bodily sensations (pains, itches, feelings of hunger, thirst, etc.) are first found.

4.7   The Format of Sensory Representations

Sensory representations, on the story I have told so far, represent either internal or external physical states. But what exactly is the format of these representations? How is information coded in them? What sort of symbol structure constitutes a sensory representation?

Consider again the case of pains. The considerations mentioned in section 4.1 in support of the view that beliefs and other propositional attitudes have a sentence-like structure do not justify a sentential view of pains. There are no general systematic connections between pains of the sort found in thoughts (connections like the one obtaining between the thought that the boy is kissing the girl and the thought that the girl is kissing the boy). And pain is not productive; we cannot generate endlessly many new kinds of pain in the way that we can generate endlessly many new thoughts.

There is also some scientific evidence that counts against a purely sententialist view of pain. We know that in visual perception, the retinal image is reconstructed in the visual cortex, so that in a quite literal sense adjacent parts of the cortex represent adjacent parts of the retinal image. There is, then, an orderly topographic projection of the retinal image onto the brain. This has been established from experiments in which a recording electrode is placed inside the visual cortex. Greater neural activity is picked up by the electrode when light is shone onto a particular spot on the retina. Moving the electrode a little results in the continued registration of greater activity only if light is directed onto an adjacent part of the retina.

Topographic organization of this sort is also found in the somatosensory cortex. There is, for example, an orderly topographic representation of the surface of the human body that is dedicated to touch. Here adjacent regions of the body surface are projected onto adjacent regions of the cortex. Enhanced activity in one of the relevant cortical regions represents that the region of body surface projected onto it is being touched. Some relatively small portions of the body, for example, the hands and face, provide input to more neurons than do some relatively large portions, for example, the trunk. This is why when people are asked to say whether there are two separate points that are both being touched on their faces or just one, the smallest distance between the points at which both can be felt is much less than when the points are located on the trunk.

There are further representations of the human body in the somatosensory cortex that are similarly structured. It has been established that the experience of pain is associated with activity in this cortex.[31] Now the fact that the somatosensory cortex is topographically organized and that it is the primary locus of pain raises doubts about the sentential view of pain, because sentences do not have the requisite maplike representational structure.[32]

The obvious suggestion, then, is that pains themselves have a topographic or maplike structure. Likewise other bodily sensations and perceptual sensations.

Box 4.7

More precisely, my proposal is that pains qua sensory representations are patterns of active (or filled) cells occurring in topographically structured three-dimensional arrays or matrices to which descriptive labels are attached. This proposal may be unpacked as follows.

For each pain, there is an array or matrix made up of cells corresponding to irregular-sized portions of the body, with adjacent cells representing adjacent body regions.[33] Activity in any given cell may be conceived of as representing (in the manner of a simple symbol) that there is tissue damage at the body region to which the cell is dedicated. The irregularity of the grain in the array is partly responsible, I suggest, for variations in our experience of pain when the same degree of damage occurs in different bodily regions of the same size (for example, the face versus the torso).

Since the cells within the pain array itself are individually concerned only with arbitrary, small body regions, there is no representation in the array of natural body parts. Segmentation of the body regions into such parts occurs via processes that examine patterns of active cells in the array and assess them, on the basis of their location, as pains in arms, legs, and so on. It is here that descriptive labels that represent the relevant body parts are appended to the array. I speculate that further labels are introduced for global features of the represented damage via further routines that mechanically work over the array and extract at least *some* of the relevant information from its contents. For example, in the case of stabbing pains, we may suppose that there is a sudden pattern of activity in the array, beginning at a part of the array representing a narrow region of body surface and extending in the proper temporal sequence to cells representing

Box 4.7 *continued*

adjacent deeper internal regions. The relevant computational routines process this activity and assign an appropriate descriptive term.[34] In the case
of stinging pains, we may suppose that certain cells in the array representing
contiguous regions of body surface along a narrow band are strongly
activated, more or less simultaneously, for a brief period of time. This
activity generates a computational response, and some relevant term is
again affixed. Whether these suppositions are along the right lines is a
matter for investigation by cognitive psychology.

This crude model is, of course, very sketchy indeed. What it gives us, I
suggest, is an alternative way of thinking about pains as representations,
one that seems to me much more promising than the purely sentential
view. Pains, I believe, represent similarly to maps that contain additional
descriptive information for salient items ("treasure buried here," "highest
mountain on island"). In this respect, they are like mental images, as I
conceive them.

There is strong evidence that images and visual percepts share a medium
that has been called the "visual buffer."[35] This medium is functional: it
consists of a large number of cells, each of which is dedicated to representing,
when filled, a tiny patch of surface at a particular location in the visual
field. For visual percepts and afterimages, the visual buffer is normally
filled by processes that operate on information contained in the light striking
the eyes. For mental images (other than afterimages), the visual buffer is
filled by generational processes that act on information stored in long-term
memory about the appearances of objects and their spatial structure.

Images and percepts, I have argued elsewhere, are interpreted, symbol-
filled patterns of cells in the visual buffer. One model for conceiving of the
visual buffer is that of a very large matrix drawn on a sheet of paper, some
of whose cells contain written symbols. The symbols represent at least
some of the following *local* features: presence of a tiny patch of surface,
orientation of the patch of surface, determinate shade of color, texture,
and so on.[36] Interpretations are affixed to the patterns of filled cells in the
form of descriptions that provide a more specific content, for example,
whether the imaged object is a circle or a square or, in more complex cases,
a duck or a rabbit. I have elaborated this view in detail in another work,[37]
so I shall not pursue it here. I maintain that bodily sensations generally,
perceptual experiences, and imagistic experiences all have their contents
encoded in arrays or matrices functionally like the sort I have described.

I should perhaps emphasize here a point I made earlier in connection
with afterimages. On my view, although the processes responsible for filling
the arrays in both bodily and perceptual sensation do not essentially require
belief or thought, they certainly involve mechanical categorization. Consider, for example, the sorts of categorization that go on in very early

Box 4.7 *continued*

vision, for example, the detection of edges and the computation of distance—categorizations that are relevant to how the visual buffer is filled. These categorizations are automatic. They do not demand that the creature have beliefs or thoughts about the properties of visual stimuli that are represented in such categorizations. Nor, at this very early stage, do stored data structures pertaining to the categories in question play any role. The system is simply hardwired to perform the relevant categorizations. Much the same is true, I maintain, in the case of bodily sensations. So nothing in the proposed account entails that a very small child or an animal could not feel pain. Their relative conceptual impoverishment does not preclude them from undergoing processing and representations of the sort necessary to fill some portion of the appropriate array.

What about the descriptive labels that are appended to the arrays? Is thought or belief involved here? Consider, for example, simple shapes in perceptual experience. Nothing looks square to me unless the appropriate processes have operated on the filled cells in the visual buffer and categorized them as representing a square shape.[38] But it is not necessary that I think (or believe) that the object I am seeing is square. Indeed, I need not have any thought (or belief) at all about the real or apparent features of the seen object.

In many cases, the descriptive labels utilized in sensory representations do not demand thought or belief. The categorizations are performed mechanically at a nonconceptual level. This is not true for all categorizations involved in experience, of course. One cannot see something as a duck or form an image of an elephant without bringing to bear the pertinent concepts from memory. But it is true for sensory representations of the sort I am concerned with in this chapter.

4.8 Background Feelings

So far I have said nothing about background feelings. These are what we feel from moment to moment when we are not gripped by any particular emotion or mood. As I write, I am not especially happy or unhappy; I am not angry or sad or fearful. Nothing out of the ordinary is happening, feeling-wise. But it would be a serious mistake to infer from this that there is no feeling going on at all. I am constantly feeling all sorts of things pertaining to my body, for example, where all my limbs are, and how they are connected to one another, even though I rarely attend to these feelings.

The importance of background feelings to our mental lives is difficult to overstate. Think about lying motionless in bed in the dark, breathing rhythmically, and yet being unable to fall asleep. Imagine that you are focusing on your breathing. Still, you can feel all your limbs and where they are in the bed. Now imagine losing those feelings of your body, going completely numb all over. Would you still have a clear sense of yourself? Imagine that you even lose any feeling with respect to your own head, your own breathing, the pressure of the pillow on your head. It seems to me that if this situation were to continue your sense of yourself would, at best, be seriously threatened.

Here is another example. Anosognosics are people who have had serious strokes resulting in brain damage, are typically partly paralyzed, but do not know that anything is wrong. When their attention is drawn to their paralyzed parts, they acknowledge that those parts will not move, but they then ignore the problem and act as if nothing is amiss. They are also rather emotionless and unconcerned about the future.

Anosognosics have lost full sensory access to their *present* overall body state. Not only do they lack the normal current sensory representations of their bodies but also they fail to respond cognitively to the sensory representations they do have. Their responses are based on *past* sensory input, on images they retain in their minds of how their body used to feel. So they are not concerned about their condition. They used to feel whole, normal, in good health, and, as far as they know, that is how they now feel.[39]

These people, in lacking sensory access to their present body states, are living in the past. They are only partly with us when we speak to them. Background feelings tracking their current overall body states are missing.

So background feelings, I maintain, are representations that fit into the general category of bodily sensations, although they are not confined in their contents to single, discrete bodily regions like pains. They are constantly present in normal persons, anchoring them in their bodies.

We are now in a position to present a solution (in general terms) to the problem of the alien limb. It will be recalled that, to the man who fell out of bed, the alien leg did not feel to be *his* leg. By contrast, if I have a pain in a leg, there seems to be a sense in which I experience pain as being in one of *my* legs. This is once again strong evidence for the intentionality of sensations and, in particular, background feelings. The man who fell out of bed did not experience the alien leg *as* his leg. He no longer had any sensory representation of the sort found in general bodily feeling, which linked that leg with the rest of his body. He lacked an overall representation of his body within which a representation of that leg was an integral part. So he rejected the leg. He viewed it as alien, as counterfeit. He believed that it did not belong to *him*.

In my own case, if I have a pain in a leg, I simultaneously feel that I have a leg belonging to me within which the pain is occurring. This is because I have an overall sensory representation of my body, which connects the relevant leg to the rest of me, and a further sensory representation of tissue damage in part of that leg.

So the answer to the question, "How do I get to be involved in my own feelings?" is this: I am continuously subject to background feelings that represent my overall background body state. These background feelings make possible the sense of continuity I have with respect to discrete bodily sensations (for example, pains and itches) and emotions (see below), the sense that they are all mine. Discrete bodily sensations represent particular physical changes occurring at particular bodily locations. These locations are connected to me by being represented in relation to other parts of my body via simultaneous (and continuing) background feelings.

4.9 Emotions

I come finally to the case of emotions and moods. Some felt moods and emotions obviously have intentional content. Feeling elated that an exam has been passed or feeling angry that it is raining yet again are two straightforward examples. These states are plausibly taken to be compound, however, having a belief and a simple mood or emotion as a component. In the one case, there is the belief that an exam has been passed, which elicits the feeling of elation, and, in the other, the belief that it is raining yet again, which causes the feeling of anger. The beliefs here are certainly intentional, but the simple feelings of elation and of depression do not themselves seem to be intentional at all. Or so it is widely supposed.

This view is much too hasty. Simple felt moods and emotions are sensory representations similar in their intentional character to background feelings and bodily sensations like pain. Let me begin with some comments on the emotions.

Suppose you suddenly feel extremely angry. Your body will change in all sorts of ways: for example, your blood pressure will rise, your nostrils will flare, your face will flush, your chest will heave as the pattern of your breathing alters, your voice will become louder, you will clench your teeth and hands, the muscles in your cheeks will become more tense, your immune system will alter rapidly. These physical changes are registered in the sensory receptors distributed throughout your body. In response to the activity in your receptors, you will mechanically build up a complex sensory representation of how your body has changed, of the new body state you are in. In this way, you will *feel* the physical changes. The feeling you undergo consists in the complex sensory representation of these changes.

In different circumstances, you might still feel very angry without feeling *just* the way you do above. For your body might change in somewhat different ways. The felt difference arises because of the different body state that is sensorily represented. You might even feel anger if you lose your body altogether and you are kept alive as a brain in a vat, stimulated to undergo the very brain states you do when you are angry in normal circumstances, via instructions from a computer. This is because you need not actually undergo changes like those I have described. It suffices that you undergo a sensory *representation* of those changes. Where there is representation, there can be misrepresentation. And misrepresentation, or illusion, is what is going on in the case of the brain in the vat.

Here is another example. Suppose you think that you are about to be robbed, and you feel very scared. Again, assuming circumstances are normal, your body will change both internally and externally. For example, your face will go white, your stomach will turn, your heart rate will speed up, your lips will tremble, your legs will go weak.[40] There are sensory states in your head that track all these changes and others. So you will sense the changes and, sensing them, will feel great fear.

Why accept this view? For one thing, it comports very nicely with the views expressed in the earlier sections on bodily sensations and background feelings. For another, consider what it would be like to feel angry if you felt *no changes at all* of the sort specified above in connection with anger. I myself can form no clear conception of what is being asked. Take away the sensations of all such changes, and there seems to me no feeling of anger left. Likewise fear.

It is worth noting that there is also some empirical data that can be brought to bear on the issue. In an experiment conducted by Paul Ekman (1992), subjects were instructed to move their facial muscles in certain ways, so that they looked as if they were undergoing a specific emotion (anger or elation, for example). The subjects were told nothing of the emotion itself in the instructions. They were then asked how they felt. The subjects reported feeling qualified emotions, corresponding to the facial expressions. For example, subjects asked to generate an angry look (without realizing at the time what they were doing) reported feeling something like anger without *really* being angry.

Given that the subjects were only sensing in themselves a very small subset of the physical changes that are relevant to experiencing the emotions and given further that the relevant cognitive reactions were missing (see below), this is a suggestive result. I might add that even the facial changes induced by the instructions were only partly appropriate to the corresponding emotions. In the case of a smile of real happiness, for example, it has been established that one of the facial muscles involved (the orbicularis oculi) cannot be moved simply by the action of the will.[41] This is another reason why the emotions are not really fully felt.

To claim that emotions are sensory representations need not be to claim that they *only* have sensory aspects. In fact, I reject the latter position. Part of what makes a given state an instance of anger is its effects on what the person wants and/or believes, and relatedly on how he or she behaves. Anger, for example, normally causes the desire or urge to act violently with respect to the perceived cause. Fear normally causes the impulse to flee. Any sensory state that did not play causal roles like these would not be classified as an instance of anger or fear. So cognitive reaction is undoubtedly an important factor in each emotion.

Furthermore, emotions are often triggered by cognitive assessments. My thinking that I am about to be robbed causes various physical reactions in my body of the sort described earlier. These reactions activate sensory receptors located throughout my body, and a complex sensory representation is then generated of the physical changes that have occurred in me. This representation tracks those changes (in optimal conditions). In turn, it causes certain cognitive reactions, for example, the desire to run and the belief that the best way out is to my left, which may themselves produce further bodily changes that are also sensorily registered.

Emotions are not always produced by cognitive states, however. Some very basic emotions, which are universally felt, are often produced by noncognitive stimuli. In these cases, we are wired to experience the emotions in response to the stimuli. Consider, for example, the sensations of chest pain and pressure involved in a heart attack. These stimuli elicit the feelings of anxiety and fear. Arguably, we are innately built to respond mechanically to activity in the relevant nociceptors first by generating the nonconceptual pain and pressure experiences and then, in reaction to those experiences, by generating the feelings of anxiety and fear. It does seem plausible to suppose that it is not necessary to *think* to oneself that one is about to die or that danger is present in order to feel fear in these circumstances. Of course, not all felt emotions are like this. Many require a cognitive cause. Think, for example, of the feeling of embarrassment or gratitude or indignation.

4.10 Moods

The view I have taken of emotions and background feelings can be extended to moods. We think of moods as descending on us, as filling us up, as coming over us. As John Haugeland (1985, p. 235) has noted, moods are like "vapors that seep into and infect everything we are about." Moreover, this is what our experience of moods tells us. We experience moods *as* descending on us, *as* being located where we are, *as* taking us over.

Mood experiences, I maintain, like emotions, are sensory representations. What exactly they represent is not easy to pin down, but the general picture I have is as follows: For each of us, there is at any given time a range of physical states constituting functional equilibrium. Which states these are might vary from time to time. But when functional equilibrium is present, we operate in a balanced, normal way without feeling any particular mood. When moods descend on us, we are responding in a sensory way to a *departure* from the pertinent range of physical states. We are sensing physical changes in our "body landscapes" (as Damasio [1994] puts it). Again, this is not to say that a full body is needed to experience what normally embodied people experience when they are subject to a particular mood, sadness, say. For the experience consists in the sensory representation of the physical states, and the existence of the representation does not demand the existence of the states.

So moods, like emotions, are intentional states; and like emotions, moods also have certain standard cognitive effects that are partly definitive of their presence. These effects, however, are not as straightforward to specify as they are in the case of emotions. For depression or anxiety, there is no characteristic activity standardly caused by them as in the case of fear or anger. Rather, there is a characteristic style or manner of behavior. Depression is a state that causes people who are subject to it to behave in a depressed manner, whatever they may be doing. Similarly, anxiety causes people to behave anxiously.

It is often argued that moods are not intentional, since the 'of' in the context "feeling (or experience) of *M*," where *M* is a mood, is not intentional. John Searle, for example, says,

> [W]hen I have a conscious experience of anxiety, there is indeed something my experience is an experience of, namely anxiety, but this sense of "of" is quite different from the "of" of Intentionality, which occurs, for example, in the statement that I have a conscious fear of snakes; for in the case of anxiety, the experience of anxiety and the anxiety are identical; but the fear of snakes is not identical with snakes. It is characteristic of Intentional states, as I use the notion, that there is a distinction between the state and what that state is directed at or about or of. . . . On my account the "of" in the expression "the experience of anxiety" cannot be the "of" of Intentionality because the experience and anxiety are identical. . . . [M]y aim now is just to make clear that, as I use the term, the class of conscious states and the class of intentional states overlap but they are not identical. (1983, p. 2)

It is not evident that Searle's premise here is true. In my view, one might conceivably feel just what normal people feel when they are anxious and yet not be anxious oneself, if, for example, one's state has no tendency at all to cause one to behave or to react anxiously (due to very odd inner wiring). But arguably the feeling then would not be the feeling *of anxiety*. So let us be charitable and grant Searle's premise: anxiety and the experience of anxiety (at least as Searle is presumably understanding the latter) are one and the same.

Now we should agree with Searle that it follows, from the identity, that the 'of' in 'experience of anxiety' is not the 'of' of intentionality. But this certainly does *not* show that the experience of anxiety is not an intentional state, any more than the parallel points about belief and the state *of* belief show that belief is not an intentional state. Rather, all we are entitled to infer is that the use of the 'of' in this context is not a good reason to suppose that the experience of anxiety is an intentional state.

To make this point clearer, consider again the case of pain. Intuitively, pain is a feeling; pain and the feeling of pain are identical. So the 'of' in 'feeling of pain' is not intentional. So, we cannot yet conclude that pain is intentional. But, as my earlier discussion is intended to show, there are other reasons for drawing this conclusion.

Box 4.8

Summary

Emotions are complex sensory representations of bodily changes that trigger characteristic cognitive reactions and behavior. Moods are similar except that they trigger certain *styles* of reaction and behavior. The felt character of moods and emotions may be traced to the sensory representation. Moods and emotions vary in how they feel in virtue of differences in the body states represented (see the next chapter). Noncognitive stimuli sometimes elicit felt emotions and moods (for example, anger or happiness), but often these states are cognitively produced. In the latter case, cognitive assessments elicit bodily reactions, which are registered in sensory receptors, thereby providing the input for the mechanical construction of a complex

Box 4.8 *continued*

sensory representation of the pertinent body states. Representation here is again a matter of tracking in optimal conditions, and the construction of the final sensory state a matter of computing that state from the information supplied by the receptors.

The overall conclusion I draw is that feelings and experiences generally have intentional content. Philosophical orthodoxy on this topic is just plain wrong. The issue we must now address is that of how the phenomenal character of feelings and experiences is related to their intentional contents. In what *exactly* does the phenomenal character of pain or anxiety or the visual experience of red consist? I have made a number of brief remarks in connection with this question already. In the next chapter, I address it at some length.

5
What What It's Like Is Really Like

As I write, I have a backache. There is something it is like for me to be the subject of this backache. But what it is like to be the subject of this backache is not the same as what it is like to be me, even though I am the subject of this backache. Why not?

What it is like to be the butt of Raucous Roger's jokes is acutely embarrassing. But what it is like to be Friendly Fred is not acutely embarrassing, even though Friendly Fred is the butt of Raucous Roger's jokes. Why not?

There is, on occasion, something it is like to be a creature with a heart. Characteristic beating sensations are felt in the chest. There is also, on occasion, something it is like to be a creature with kidneys. Here too there are characteristic bodily sensations (for example, soreness in the back immediately above the hips). But there are two things it is like here, not one. And they typically do not go together. How can there be something it is like for me to be a creature with a heart at time t without there being something it is like for me to be a creature with kidneys at t, given that all and only creatures with a heart are creatures with kidneys?

As I stare across from me, I see some square tiles. Square is also the shape of the picture on the wall above the tiles. The light is playing strange tricks. The tiles look square to me, but they do not look to me the shape of the picture. How can this be, given that square *is* the shape of the picture?

The answer to these questions is that the above contexts are intensional. Predicates that are true of the same things and singular terms that refer to the same things cannot always be safely substituted without change of truth value. What creates the intensional contexts is the representational nature of phenomenal character or "feel." How the tiles look, what it is like to undergo a particular headache or to be the butt of someone's jokes or to have a heart, how that feels, are themselves intentional matters.[1]

In this chapter, I elaborate an intentional view of phenomenal character. I begin by supplying some further motivations for an intentional approach.

5.1   Why Be an Intentionalist?

Consider the overall conclusion of the last chapter, that all feelings and experiences are intentional. Is this necessary connection between phenomenal consciousness and intentionality a brute fact, admitting of no further explanation? Surely not. The *simplest* explanation is that the phenomenal character of a state is itself intentional.

Consider also my earlier comments on how specific pains differ. Twinges of pain represent mild, brief disturbances; throbbing pains represent rapidly pulsing disturbances; aches represent disturbances inside the body, ones that have imprecise volumes, beginnings, and ends; pricking pains represent sudden, short-lived disturbances covering a tiny area on the surface or just below. These differences are paired with felt differences, according to the view developed in the last chapter. More generally, my claim is that experiences and feelings are sensory representations that elicit various sorts of cognitive reactions, and that differences in what the sensory representations represent go along with differences in what it is like to undergo the experiences and feelings. Again, the simplest explanation for this pairing is that differences in what it is like are simply intentional differences.

Perhaps it will be objected that what it is like for the masochist is different from what it is like for me, even if we are subject to sensory representations of exactly the same sort of tissue damage. The fact that the masochist responds positively to his sensation, whereas I am overcome with an immediate reaction of dislike, is itself phenomenally relevant.

My reply is that the felt quality of the *pain* is the same for both of us. I find the felt quality horrible and I react accordingly. He has a different reaction. Our reactions involve further feelings, however. I feel anxiety and concern. He does not. Here there is a phenomenal difference.

Box 5.1

Some unfortunate people have a condition known as intractable neuralgia. They suffer very frequent, excruciating pains. When the pains strike, they report the sensation of knives ripping their flesh. During these attacks, they are completely unable to function. Not surprisingly, they become obsessed with their pains. Neurosurgical intervention can help. In particular, prefrontal leukotomies (that is, surgical severing of the neural connections in the deep white matter of both frontal lobes of the brain) can make a dramatic difference. Patients who undergo such a procedure are typically relaxed and cheerful afterward (in sharp contrast to their state before). They report that they still feel pains, but they no longer mind them. Their *suffering* is either gone or greatly diminished.

The way to understand what is going on here is to draw a distinction between what one senses or feels in having a pain and how one reacts to it. The above patients feel or sense much of what they felt before, but they no longer dislike the sensation. Their pains are no longer painful to them.[2]

Perhaps it will be objected that, after the operation, what it is like for these patients to feel pain is not the same as what it was like for them to feel pain before. This, I am prepared to concede, may well be the case. But it is no threat to my position. Disliking something intensely has all sorts of effects, both physical and psychological. The disappearance of the reaction of dislike in the patients after the operation may well feed back down and affect the sensory experience of pain in the way I described in chapter 4. So the phenomenal character of the patients' pains may change somewhat. It is also worth noting that the patients no longer feel anxious or concerned, and further they pay much less attention to their pains (so their *awareness* of how the pains feel diminishes).

Consider finally the problem of transparency. Why is it that perceptual experiences are transparent? When you turn your gaze inward and try to focus your attention on intrinsic features of these experiences, why do you always seem to end up attending to what the experiences are *of*? Suppose you have a visual experience of a shiny, blood-soaked dagger. Whether, like Macbeth, you are hallucinating or whether you are seeing a real dagger, you experience redness and shininess as outside you, as covering the surface of a dagger. Now try to become aware of your experience itself, inside you, apart from its objects. Try to focus your attention on some intrinsic feature of the experience that distinguishes it from other experiences, something other than what it is an experience *of*. The task seems impossible: one's awareness seems always to slip through the experience to the redness and shininess, *as instantiated together externally*. In turning one's mind inward to attend to the experience, one seems to end up scrutinizing *external* features or properties.

Generalizing, introspection of your perceptual experiences seems to reveal only aspects of *what* you experience, further aspects of the scenes, as represented. Why? The answer, I suggest, is that your perceptual experiences have no *introspectible* features over and above those implicated in their intentional contents. So the phenomenal character of such experiences—itself something that is introspectibly accessible, assuming the appropriate concepts are possessed and there is no cognitive malfunction—is identical with, or contained within, their intentional contents.

The same is true for bodily sensations. Suppose you have a pain in your toe. Then your toe is where you feel the painful disturbance to be. Now try to turn your attention away from what you are experiencing in your toe to your experience itself apart from that. Again, inevitably what you end up focusing on is simply what is going on *in your toe,* or rather what your experience represents is going on there. The phenomenal character of your experience—certainly something you are introspectively aware of on such an occasion—must itself be representational.

Even in the case of general moods, transparency exists. Suppose you suddenly feel elated. It is hard to put into words what you experience. The mood simply comes on you and fills you up. You feel full of energy, disposed to smile easily, quick to respond. You sense or experience a whole host of subtle changes in yourself. Now turn your attention away from these things that you are feeling to the feeling or experience itself apart from them. Try to focus on *that* alone. I submit, again, that it is not possible. In attending to the feeling, inevitably you find yourself focusing again on *what* you are feeling, on its content, even though you may not be able to articulate clearly to yourself or to others just what this involves.

Still, if phenomenal character is best understood in terms of intentional content, just how is it to be further elucidated? What is *phenomenal content,* as I call it?

Box 5.2

Summary

Phenomenal character (or what it is like) is one and the same as a certain sort of intentional content. This is the most straightforward explanation of the fact that "what it is like" linguistic contexts are intensional, of the fact that all experiences and feelings have intentional content, of the pairing of felt differences and intentional differences, and of the phenomenon of transparency.

5.2   Phenomenal Content: The PANIC Theory

Sensory representations serve as inputs for a number of systems of higher-level cognitive processing. They are themselves outputs of specialized sensory modules (for perceptual experiences, bodily sensations, primary emotions, and moods).[3] Representations occurring within the modules supply information the creature needs to construct or generate sensory representations, but they are not themselves sensory. Phenomenal content, in my view, is not a feature of any of the representations occurring *within* the sensory modules. As I noted in the last chapter, experience and feeling arise at the level of the outputs from the sensory modules and the inputs to a cognitive system. It is here that phenomenal content is found.

Sensory representations (viewed in the above way) represent either internal or external physical items. Bodily sensations represent internal bodily changes. They are directly tuned to such changes (in optimal conditions). Likewise emotions and moods. In the case of perceptual experiences, the items sensorily represented are external environmental states or features.

Phenomenal content, I maintain, is content that is appropriately poised for use by the cognitive system, content that is abstract and nonconceptual. I call this the PANIC theory of phenomenal character: phenomenal character is one and the same as Poised Abstract Nonconceptual Intentional Content. I hope that this will not be taken as a literal indication of the state of mind to which I have been driven by the problems of consciousness! It follows that representations that differ in their

PANICs differ in their phenomenal character, and representations that are alike with respect to their PANICs are alike in their phenomenal character.

The claim that the contents relevant to phenomenal character must be *poised* is to be understood as requiring that these contents attach to the (fundamentally) maplike output representations of the relevant sensory modules and stand ready and in position to make a direct impact on the belief/desire system. To say that the contents stand ready in this way is not to say that they always do have such an impact. The idea is rather that they supply the inputs for certain cognitive processes whose job it is to produce beliefs (or desires) directly from the appropriate nonconceptual representations, *if* attention is properly focused and the appropriate concepts are possessed. So, attentional deficits can preclude belief formation as can conceptual deficiencies.[4]

The relevant sensory modules vary, of course. In the case of vision, the pertinent module is the one that has as its output a unified representation of the entire visual field (of the sort described earlier). This is served by more specialized visual modules. Their outputs (for surface color or distance away, for example) provide inputs to the more generalized module, within which integration occurs and the final overall nonconceptual representation of surfaces and their features is constructed.

The PANIC theory entails that no belief could have phenomenal character. A content is classified as phenomenal only if it is nonconceptual and poised. Beliefs are not nonconceptual, and they are not appropriately poised. They lie within the cognitive system, rather than providing inputs to it. Beliefs are not sensory representations at all.

The claim that the contents relevant to phenomenal character must be *abstract* is to be understood as demanding that no particular concrete objects enter into these contents (except for the subjects of experiences in some cases). Since different concrete objects can look or feel exactly alike phenomenally, one can be substituted for the other without any phenomenal change. Which particular object is present, then, does not matter. Nor does it matter if *any* concrete object is present to the subject at all. Whether or not you have a left leg, for example, you can feel a pain in your left leg; in both cases, the phenomenal character of your experience can be exactly the same. So the existence of that particular leg is not required for the given phenomenal character. What is crucial to phenomenal character is the representation of general features or properties. Experiences nonconceptually represent that there is *a* surface or *an* internal region having so-and-so features at such-and-such locations, and thereby they acquire their phenomenal character.

The claim that the contents relevant to phenomenal character must be *nonconceptual* is to be understood as saying that the general features entering into these contents need not be ones for which their subjects possess matching concepts. I made some remarks pertinent to this requirement in the last chapter, but some additional comments may be useful.

Consider again the case of color. The *Dictionary of Color*, by Maerz and Paul (1950), contains 7,056 color samples and 4,000 color names. Most of us have a *much* more limited color vocabulary, but even Maerz and Paul have no names for many of their samples. And humans can discriminate many, many more colors than those presented in Maerz and Paul, something on the order of ten million, according to some estimates. So we have names for only a few of the colors we can discriminate, and we also have no stored representations in memory for most colors either. There simply is not enough room.

Beliefs and thoughts involve the application of concepts. One cannot believe that a given animal is a horse, for example, unless one has the concept *horse*. At a minimum, this demands that one has the stored memory representation *horse*, which one brings to bear in an appropriate manner (by, for example, activating the representation and applying it to the sensory input). However, as noted above (and in the last chapter), phenomenal seemings or experiences are *not* limited in this way. My experience of red_{19}, for example, is phenomenally different from my experience of red_{21}, even though I have no stored memory representations of these specific hues and hence no such concepts as the concepts red_{21} and red_{19}. These points generalize to the other senses. Phenomenal character, and hence phenomenal content, on my view, is nonconceptual.

Sensory experiences, then, are *determinate* in a way that our stored memory representations are not. We have general concepts for the determinables but not for their determinate values. I do not deny, of course, that we can represent the determinables via indexical concepts when we focus our cognitive gaze upon them. But experience outstrips such acts of noticing (and can occur without them altogether). Indexical concepts do not enter into phenomenal character any more than general concepts. Phenomenal character, I claim, is wholly nonconceptual.

Box 5.3

On the PANIC conception, the phenomenal character of sensory representations is very rich. Consider the case of visual sensations. As I explained in
the last chapter, these states represent in the manner of maps or, more
precisely, matrices, within whose cells are symbols for determinate surface
features at particular viewer-centered locations to which the cells are
dedicated.

One way to picture this idea is to imagine a large, transparent matrix
placed over the visual field. Each cell in the matrix covers a tiny portion
of the field; within each cell, there is an ordered sequence of symbols for
various features of any surface at that location in the field (for example,
distance away, orientation, determinate color, texture, etc.).

So there is a level of phenomenal content for visual sensations into which
a myriad of local surface features enters. But there is also a further level.
Imposed over the matrix, in standard cases, are more general descriptions
that are attached to groups of cells and that involve symbols for nonlocal
spatial features and shapes, for example, 'edge' and 'square'. Where a figure
has an ambiguous decomposition into spatial parts, concepts can influence
which decomposition occurs. This is one way in which top-down processing
can make a phenomenal difference. But once a particular decomposition
is in place, the way in which an ambiguous figure phenomenally appears
is fixed.[5]

It is at this nonlocal level of content that a distinction can be drawn
between the phenomenal character of the experience one undergoes when
one sees the figure below as two faces and the experience one undergoes
when one sees it as a vase. In the former case, one segments the figure into
spatial parts corresponding to the foreheads, the noses, the lips, the chins.
In the latter case, the parts are drawn differently, corresponding to the
bowl, the stem, the base (Jackendoff 1989, p. 336). These segmentations
are no doubt conceptually influenced, but the resulting representations of
spatial parts are not themselves automatically conceptual. What it is like
to experience the vase base, for example, is not something into which the
concept of a vase base or the concept of that particular shape enters.

I should add here that I do not wish to deny that concepts can enter into
some experiential episodes, broadly construed. One cannot see something as
a rabbit, for example, unless one has the concept rabbit. Likewise, it cannot
appear to one that there is a rabbit by the hat unless one has the concepts
rabbit and hat. What happens in cases like these is that one has a sensory
representation whose phenomenal content is then brought under the given
concepts. Still, the concepts do not enter into the content of the sensory
representation, and they are not themselves phenomenally relevant.

Box 5.3 *continued*

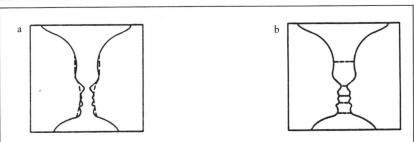

Figure 5.1
The part boundaries of the faces (*a*) and the part boundaries of the vase (*b*) occupy different locations. Reprinted with permission from Ray Jackendoff 1989, *Consciousness and the Computational Mind,* Cambridge, Mass.: MIT Press, p. 336.

Which features involved in bodily and environmental states are elements of phenomenal contents? There is no a priori answer. Empirical research is necessary. The relevant features will be the ones represented in the output representations of the sensory modules. I call these features, whatever they might be, *observational* features. They are the features our sensory states track in optimal conditions. Since the receptors associated with the various sensory modules and the processing that goes on within them vary, features that are observational for one module need not be observational for another. What gets outputted obviously depends on what gets inputted and how the module operates. I conjecture that for perceptual experience, the observational features will include properties like being an edge, being a corner, being square, being red_{29}.

In classifying being square as observational, I am not supposing that it has that status for all possible species of creatures. Observationality, in my view, is relative to creatures with a certain sort of sensory equipment. Thus, some features that are observational for us might not be for other possible creatures (and vice versa).

Suppose, for example, it looks to me that there is a tiger present. It seems plausible to suppose that the property of being a tiger is not itself a feature represented by the outputs of the sensory modules associated with vision. Our sensory states do not track *this* feature. There might conceivably be creatures other than tigers that look to us phenomenally just like tigers. Still, perhaps the property of being a tiger *could* have been sensorily represented by some creatures. Perhaps we can imagine that there are alien creatures with microscope eyes whose visual sensory states are tuned to the genetic essence of tigers. If so, what it is like for these creatures, when they view tigers, will be very different from what it is like for us. The phenomenal contents of their states will be very different from ours. What will it be like for them? We cannot say (or think): we lack the right sensory perspective.

We are now in a position to solve another problem of consciousness, the problem of super blindsight. Blindsight subjects are people who can issue accurate statements about the presence of certain basic sorts of stimuli in areas of their visual fields with respect to which they have no phenomenal consciousness. These people have brain damage that makes them phenomenally blind to these areas, and yet, amazingly, if forced to guess what is in them, they do so correctly more often than not.[6]

Super-blindsight subjects are people with blindsight who have been trained to elicit guesses in themselves by acts of will, and who, through time, come to believe the reports they spontaneously make about their blind fields. To my knowledge, there are no such people, but there might have been. What exactly is the difference between these people believing that such and such stimuli are present and normally sighted people experiencing those stimuli? Is the difference ultimately just one of the richness of the content of their mental states?

According to the PANIC theory, the difference consists in four things. First, there is an enormous difference in content. The experiences represent determinate features; the beliefs do not. The experiences represent the presence of local surface features throughout the field; the beliefs do not. Second, and relatedly, there is an important difference in the vehicles involved. The experiences represent in the manner of maps or matrices; the beliefs represent in the manner of sentences. Third, there is a difference with respect to the role that stored representations play. The experiences do not draw on memory representations, or at least need not do so (see box above). The beliefs must draw on such representations. Fourth, the experiences are appropriately poised for use by the cognitive system; the beliefs are already a part of that system.

More generally, super-blindsight subjects lack any states with *PANIC* pertaining to the blind field. For these people, there is no complete, unified, nonconceptual representation of the visual field, the content of which is poised to make a direct difference in their beliefs. Their visual systems, unlike ours, do not output (at any given time) a full, integrated, maplike representation for processing by the cognitive centers.[7] Moreover, the partial nonconceptual representations pertinent to the blind field that are available to serve as inputs to the conceptual domain have an effect on the beliefs of super-blindsight subjects only via their willing themselves to guess. Without such acts of will, there would not be any beliefs about the contents of the blind field. So the impact on the belief system here is both anomalous and indirect. First, an act of will is required; then a guess is generated; then the guess comes to be believed.

The cognitive processes that are operative, then, are not ones whose job it is to generate beliefs (or desires) directly from nonconceptual representations found at the interface with the conceptual realm. Indeed, there are really two different types of cognitive processes at play: first, ones that draw on nonconceptual representations and that issue in guesses, given the act of willing, and then ones that are belief-forming but that take conceptual representations, namely, the guesses, as inputs. So there are no nonconceptual contents (pertaining to the blind field) that are appropriately poised in super-blindsight subjects any more than there are in ordinary blindsight subjects. This is why, according to the *PANIC* theory, experience is lacking in both.

So that is what what it is like is really like. It is *PANIC*. Philosophers who have attempted to draw a sharp distinction between the representational aspects of our mental lives and their phenomenal or subjective or felt aspects are mistaken. The latter form a subclass of the former, like it is not.

Box 5.4

Summary

Phenomenal character is one and the same as phenomenal content. The latter is intentional content that is abstract, nonconceptual, and appropriately poised. It attaches to the output representations of the relevant sensory modules, and it stands ready and available to make a direct impact on

Box 5.4 *continued*

> beliefs and/or desires. Phenomenal states lie at the interface of the nonconceptual and conceptual domains. It follows that systems that altogether lack the capacity for beliefs and desires cannot undergo phenomenally conscious states. For systems that have such a capacity, the sensory or phenomenal states differ from the beliefs in their functional role, their intentional contents, and their internal structure. This approach solves the problem of super blindsight.

5.3   Colors and Other "Secondary Qualities"

On the face of it, colors and other "secondary qualities" (smells, tastes, and sounds, for example) pose a special difficulty for the theory I have been developing. If these qualities are subjective, or defined in part by their phenomenal character, then what it is like to undergo the experiences of such qualities cannot itself be understood in terms of the experiences' representing them. That would create an immediate vicious circle.

Consider, for example, the view of color inspired by John Locke. On the Lockean approach, as it is usually understood, the claim that something, X, is red is analyzed as saying that X is disposed to look red to normal perceivers in standard conditions. This approach has several virtues. Nonetheless, there is an obvious difficulty. 'Red' appears in the analysis as well as in the claim to be analyzed. So there appears to be a simple circle.

One response to this charge is to maintain that, once the Lockean thesis is properly elucidated, the circle is not vicious. There is something it is like to experience red, just as there is something it is like to taste a lemon or to smell a skunk. We all know what these experiences are like from introspective awareness. Each experience has a distinctive, introspectively accessible phenomenal character (or, better, a range of such characters). Let us label the relevant character 'P_k' in the case of the experience of hue, red$_k$. The Lockean position can now be stated in the following a priori definition:

For any k, X is red$_k$ if and only if X is disposed to produce experiences having P_k in normal perceivers in standard circumstances.

This is an improvement. However, on the PANIC theory, P_k itself involves the representation of red$_k$. There is certainly still a damaging circle. Something has to go: either the phenomenal character of color experiences is not to be understood in the way I am proposing or partly subjectivist approaches to color must be rejected. Not surprisingly, I favor the latter alternative.

What, then, are colors, smells, sounds, tastes, and the like? Here is not the place to attempt to articulate a full-blown theory of these qualities. Nonetheless, I would like to make some general remarks about the lines I favor, beginning with the case of color.

The obvious view, suggested by our color experiences (and compatible with my position), is that the colors we see objects and surfaces to have are simply intrinsic, observer-independent properties of those objects and surfaces. We think of colors as inhering in the surfaces of the objects and sometimes throughout the objects (as, for example, in the case of a red crayon). We also think of objects as retaining their colors when they are not seen, thereby helping us to re-identify the objects.

Certainly, we do not experience colors as perceiver-relative. When, for example, a ripe tomato looks red to me, I experience redness all over the facing surface of the tomato. Each perceptible part of the surface looks red to me. None of these parts, in looking red, look to me to have a perceiver-relative property. I do not experience any part of the surface as producing a certain sort of response in me or anyone else. On the contrary, I surely experience redness as intrinsic to the surface, just as I experience the shape of the surface as intrinsic to it. This simple fact is one that Lockean approaches to color cannot accomodate without supposing there is a basic illusion involved in normal experiences of color, that colors are really (response-dependent) relational properties even though we experience them as nonrelational. That, it seems to me, is just not credible.

There are other reasons to adopt a perceiver-independent view of object colors. Consider some facts about the human visual system. The cones in the retina respond to the wavelength of the light. Nonetheless, we do not see the color of the light striking our eyes. Our experiences of color are typically indicative of the real colors of object surfaces away from us. Moreover, even when the light reflected from surfaces is exactly the same, we retain the ability to tell that surfaces differ in color, according to some color scientists (see the experiments described in Land and McCann [1971]).[8]

In general, colors are not as variable as many philosophers have supposed. The colors of objects typically do not change when they are moved from outdoors to a setting illuminated by incandescent lamps, for example. And wearing sunglasses has little effect on the colors objects appear to have (Hilbert 1987). Why should this be?

Surely, the most straightforward answer is that the human visual system has, as one of its functions, to detect the real, objective colors of surfaces. Somehow, the visual system manages to ascertain what colors objects really have, even though the only information immediately available to it concerns light wavelengths. It does this initially, according to the theory developed by Land (1977), by identifying brightness gradients on the retina. Where there are sudden changes in brightness, the visual system assumes that there are changes in surface color. Where there are gradual changes, the illumination conditions are taken to have changed. These assumptions are wired into our visual systems, and they provide the link with surface color. Once each tiny surface patch that is visible in the scene is assigned a color gradient, absolute colors are then computed by a further process.

The parallels here between color and shape should be obvious to anyone familiar with Marr's theory of shape recognition (Marr 1982). In each case, the visual system solves a complicated computational problem and delivers a representation of a distal property on the basis of information about proximal stimuli. But if surface color is an objective property like shape, just which property is it?

There are three sorts of cone cells on the retina. They respond to light of three bands of wavelengths: short, medium, and long. The color of the light incident on the eye is a function of the color of the object surface and the color of the light striking it. It is natural, then, to suppose that the color of a surface is an ordered triple of the *reflectances* of the surface with respect to light in these three wavelength bands (Matthen 1988; Hilbert 1987), where the reflectance of a surface at a given wavelength is its disposition to reflect a certain percentage of the light at that wavelength.[9] On this view, our visual systems are designed to detect certain ranges of spectral reflectances, just as they are designed to identify certain ranges of shapes.

There are two main objections to an objectivist theory of color. First, it is claimed that there are no properties of the surfaces of colored objects with which colors may reasonably be identified. Spectral reflectances, it has been suggested, can vary without any variation in the perceived color of objects. Second, it is argued that there are many facts about the relations between colors, whose explanation seems to require reference to facts about perceivers.

Neither of these objections seem to me very damaging to the objectivist approach. The well-known fact that spectral reflectances can change without any change in perceived color, in and of itself, does not directly show anything very significant. For one thing, the relevant triples of reflectances involve wavebands. There is plenty of room for differences of wavelengths within these bands from object to object without any change in real color. For another, the shape of an object can vary without any variation in perceived shape. All that entitles us to infer is that perceived shape is not always the same as real shape. Similarly, sometimes object surfaces do not actually have the reflectance triples our experiences represent them as having. So what?

There is a further point worth making here. The expression 'the color of an object' is vague. A single object can be red, vermilion, a highly saturated vermilion, vermilion$_{23}$, and so on. This fact is captured nicely by the view of colors as triples of spectral reflectances. The more determinate the color is, the narrower the pertinent wavebands.

Still, it might be argued, there are serious difficulties lurking in the background. Metamers are stimuli that have different spectral reflectance distributions but are exactly the same in their experienced color. In some cases, metamers can have very different spectral reflectance distributions and yet look exactly alike, even when viewed in normal circumstances by normal perceivers. This fact refutes the claim that the color of a surface is one and the same as its reflectance at all wavelengths of all light to which humans are sensitive. But it can be accommodated by the view that colors are triples of reflectances, because this allows wide variations of reflectances at many wavelengths. And metamers have the same, or very similar, surface reflectances within the three pertinent wavebands.

There are also cases of color that seem to have nothing to do with reflectance. Intuitively, the summer sky is blue. But supposedly it is not blue in virtue of reflectance (Campbell 1969). One way to deal with this case is to say that we are deluded when we look at the sky, that we *mis*perceive it as blue. A better response is to say that the sky has numerous particles of dust and moisture in it and that the reflectance properties of these particles is responsible for the blueness of the sky.

Consider next the claim that there are facts about the relations between colors that undercut objectivist theories. Let me mention the two most commonly cited of these "facts." First, there is the fact that the hues form a circle, even though the light frequencies do not (Teller 1991). Second, there is the distinction between the four primary or unitary colors, red, green, blue, and yellow, and the secondary or binary ones (Hardin 1993). Orange, for example, *is* reddish-yellow. Red, however, is *not* orangish-purple. What explains these facts? Nothing in the account of colors as ordered triples of spectral reflectances explains the binary-unitary distinction and why red is a unitary color whereas orange is a binary one. Here, it is sometimes suggested, is another reason for rejecting objectivism about color.

The fact that the hues form a circle is easy to explain on the proposed view. Think of color space as a three-dimensional space, with each dimension corresponding to the surface reflectances at one of the three wavelength bands. Then think of the relevant triples of reflectances as coordinates in this space. The hues may now be seen to mark out a closed circular loop in color space.

As for the binary-unitary distinction, it can be preserved as a basic truth about color mixing. Orange, for example, is the color you get when you mix red and yellow pigments; but red is not the color that results when you mix purple and yellow pigments. These facts are arguably facts we have learned from training, not facts given to us in our color experiences and extractable from them without any basic lessons or art classes on the various colors and their relationships. So in one sense, orange is reddish-yellow, a sense that is comparable to that in which a mule is an equine ass. In each case, you get the one by mixing the others (though the sorts of mixing are obviously different).

This approach to colors extends naturally to the other "secondary qualities." Consider smells, for example. Smells seem patently objective. They have locatable origins; they move through space. Indeed, they spread out and fill volumes of space. The receptors for the olfactory system are now thought to be of a sizeable number of different types, perhaps as many as twenty or thirty.[10] Molecules of odorants come into contact with these receptors and stimulate them. The mechanism by which odorous molecules stimulate receptor cells is a matter of dispute. According to some theories, molecular shape is the primary factor.[11] According to others, the vibratory motion of molecules is also important. With little agreement about the exact nature of olfactory transduction, any definite proposal about the nature of smells would be highly speculative. But the form of such a suggestion would not: the smells humans can discriminate should be identified with ordered n-tuples (where n is between twenty and thirty) of the relevant external property of the odorous molecules (the counterpart for smell to spectral reflectance).

In the case of taste, there are four basic kinds of receptor cells, corresponding to the four primary taste qualities (sweet, salty, bitter, and sour). The taste receptors are not restricted to the tongue, as is often supposed. They are also to be found elsewhere in the mouth, for example, on its roof. This is why patients who have been fitted with a full denture plate that covers the whole roof of the mouth frequently complain of diminished taste.

Each of the four types of taste receptor in humans is sensitive to the action of a certain sort (or range of sorts) of molecules. For example, the sour receptor seems to respond primarily to hydrogen ion concentration. The overall taste of an item has an effect, to varying degrees, on each of the receptors and may plausibly be identified with an ordered quadruple of molecular characteristics. Exactly which characteristics are pertinent to tastes is still a matter of dispute.

Sounds, like smells, have objective locations, and they travel through space. The receptor cells, in this case, are hair cells located within a coiled bony structure, known as the cochlea, inside the ear. There are two sorts of hair cells, inner and outer. Sensations of pitch and loudness seem tied to the frequency and intensity of sound, but the connection is complex.

For example, at a given sound pressure, the loudness of a sound can be altered markedly by altering only frequency, even though loudness also varies most notably with variations in pressure. The hair cells respond to these physical features of sound waves, and (in first approximation) the sounds humans discriminate depend on the number and type of cell responding. So it seems plausible to suppose that an objectivist treatment can be developed for sounds, broadly similar to those for colors, smells, and tastes (even though the details may well be very complicated).

I hope that I have now said enough to indicate how, in my view, the so-called secondary qualities are best handled. I want next to consider the dependence of phenomenal character on brain processes.

Box 5.5

Summary

Colors are objective, physical features of objects and surfaces. Our visual systems have evolved to detect a range of these features, but those to which we are sensitive are indirecty dependent on facts about us. In particular, there are three types of receptor in the retina, each of which responds to a particular waveband of light, and the spectral reflectances of surfaces at these wavebands (that is, their disposition to reflect a certain percentage of the incident light within each of the three bands) together determine the colors we see. So the colors themselves may be identified with ordered triples of spectral reflectances. An account of the same general sort may be given for smells, tastes, sounds, and so on.

5.4   Can Duplicate Brains Differ Phenomenally?

Over 95 percent of amputees who have an arm or leg removed report phantom limbs. The limbs feel to the amputees very like their real limbs. They say that they can move them in a normal way and that they have the same size and shape as before. For example, a patient with a phantom hand may try to reach for objects with it just as he would with a real hand. Through time, the phantom limbs become smaller and often fade away altogether (Melzak 1990).

Interestingly, children who are born without a limb or part of one often feel vivid phantoms. One child reported feeling the palm and middle finger of a phantom hand; another the upper calf and two toes of a phantom leg (Weinstein 1964; Poeck 1964). So it is not necessary to have had a real limb in order to feel a phantom one.

In general, phantom limbs seem intensely real to their subjects, at least initially. Why should this be? One obvious answer is that the experience of a phantom limb is the same as the experience of a real limb because the underlying brain process in the two cases is the same. This leads to the philosophical thought that *necessarily* same brain processes, same phenomenal experiences.

The thought is not obviously correct, however. Consider again the case of the children who are born without certain limbs but who nonetheless feel phantoms. Granted they undergo similar brain processes to those other, fully endowed humans undergo with respect to the corresponding real limbs; still, it does not follow from this that any creature whatsoever, regardless of its setting or evolutionary history, would *have* to feel what the children feel if it were subject to the same brain processes. For there is no guarantee that those brain processes, wherever they occur, must represent the same limbs, any more than there is a guarantee that the sign design 'tumbler' must always mean acrobat (or anything at all, for that matter). And representational content, I claim, is at the heart of phenomenal feel.

The lesson of the problem of transparency is that *phenomenology ain't in the head.* Just as you cannot read semantics out of syntax, so you cannot read phenomenology out of physiology. This is why you cannot find any technicolor qualia, any raw feels, by peering around inside the brain (with or without a flashlight). They simply are not in there. To discover what it's like, you need to look outside the head to what the brain states represent. Phenomenology is, in this way, externally based. So systems that are internally physically identical do not *have* to be phenomenally identical.

Still, it cannot be denied that many philosophers accept the thesis that the internal microphysical facts *metaphysically* fix the phenomenal facts, that brains identical in all microphysical respects *must* support phenomenally identical states of consciousness, whatever the external environment may be like. Call this view *supervenience.*[12]

If empirical facts like the ones adduced above do not establish supervenience, why is it so widely accepted? It seems to me that imaginary cases like the one described below play a large role in many philosophers' thinking.

"Change and decay in all around I see," sings Uncle Theodore each morning, as he surveys the family estate, in Evelyn Waugh's book *Scoop.* The physical processes involved in seeing are, in outline, well known. Light is reflected from the surfaces of objects. It reaches the eye and excites cells on the retina. These cells then stimulate the optic nerve, which, in turn, leads to neuron firings in the visual cortex of the brain. Finally, a visual experience is produced. Uncle Theodore, as he moves his gaze from the diseased trees to the decaying buildings, is subject to a sequence of visual experiences produced in this manner, each with its own phenomenological flavor.

Suppose that one morning crazed scientists intervene in the processes culminating in Theodore's visual experiences, unknown to Theodore. The scientists briefly render him unconscious. When he comes to, all the objective physical events and interactions occurring in his cortex are just as they would have been had the scientists not intervened, but the causes of those firing patterns have changed. No longer is light reflected into Theodore's eyes from aging trees and decrepit buildings. Instead, the scientists themselves are directly stimulating the relevant portions of Theodore's brain via probes, in a laboratory to which they have taken him. Utterly fantastic, of course, but if the scientists are knowledgeable enough, remotely possible. In these circumstances, it seems highly plausible to maintain that, so long as exactly the same internal microphysical processes are present throughout the cortex, Theodore will be oblivious to the intervention: his experiences will have the same phenomenological character as before. What it is like for Theodore is now just what it would have been like for him had the scientists not stepped in. Although Theodore is no longer really seeing the same old familiar things, he cannot tell from his experience that there has been any change.

Now suppose that the scientists' intervention is still more extreme. Not only are they presently stimulating Theodore's brain, but they have been doing so for Theodore's entire life. Theodore has never really seen a tree or a building. Immediately after he was born, he was whisked away to the laboratory, and, ever since, the scientists (assisted by banks of computers) have been directly stimulating Theodore's brain in just the ways that it would have been stimulated, had he grown up in the normal environmental setting. The case is now fantastic in the extreme. But still, it seems plausible to suppose that with the right internal stimulations, what it is like for Theodore at any given time t will be the same as what it would have been like for him at t, had the scientists left him alone.

Does the case of Uncle Theodore demonstrate that *supervenience* is true? No, it does not. Theodore does at least have an evolutionary history. Theodore is a member of the species *homo sapiens,* a species that has evolved from other species. It has not been shown that facts pertaining to evolutionary history are not relevant to the phenomenal character of states of living creatures. It is still *possible* that two different organisms that evolved in different ways, while nonetheless sharing the same internal microphysical states (at some given time t), differ in their phenomenal states at t.

This suggestion might seem strange. But why exactly? If phenomenology is tied to representational content, and content is understood in terms of causal covariation under optimal conditions, then external facts can make a difference to how things feel or seem. And in the case of living biological creatures, it is natural to suppose that the pertinent optimal conditions are ones in which the sensory mechanisms are discharging their biological functions. So it is possible that, with variations in biological function across environments, phenomenally relevant representational differences arise without any internal physical difference. This, I concede, is very hard to envisage for creatures as sophisticated as human beings, but it does seem conceivable for much simpler creatures.[13]

Note that I am categorically *not* claiming here that beings who lack an evolutionary history (artificially created beings, for example, or accidental creations of various sorts) *cannot* be subject to experiences and feelings. That strikes me as highly counterintuitive. Consider, for example, the following cases.

Imagine that a lightning bolt hits a log in a swamp and that, in the ensuing chemical reaction, something emerges from the swamp that is a *molecule-by-molecule* duplicate of some actual human being—me, say.[14] Extraordinarily unlikely, of course, but still metaphysically possible: the idea is surely a coherent one, however bizarre. Alternatively, imagine that a molecule-by-molecule duplicate of me is deliberately created by means of something like the Transporter device on the television series *Star Trek* and that this duplicate is brought into existence on an unexplored planet, while I continue my life on earth.[15]

Is there anything it is like for Swampman or for my transported double? If Swampman is hit in the leg by a spray of bullets as he emerges from the swamp, does he feel anything as he howls loudly? Does he have any perceptual experiences? Does he see anything—for example, the tree root he carefully steps over as he climbs out of the swamp? If he happens to emerge as a murder is taking place next to the swamp, can he be called on as an eyewitness at the trial (Brown 1993)? After all, he will provide as good a description (or sounding description) of the event as I would have done in the same circumstances—indeed the very same description (or sounding description), given that he and I are complete physical duplicates.

If Swampman meets Swampwoman whom he later marries and they have children, do the children have any experiences or feelings? If all your grandparents turn out to be Swamppeople, do *you* have any experiences or feelings? If my transported double is formed on a planet with a temperature of 100 degrees Fahrenheit and he starts to sweat profusely, does he feel very hot, irritable, and breathless, just as I would? If my double materializes face to face with a tiger, does he feel sensations of fright that are phenomenally the same as those I would feel in the same circumstances?

In neither of the two cases is there any evolutionary history. But, intuitively, that does not prove that Swampman and my transported double *cannot* feel anything. Indeed, the intuitive answer to *all* the above questions is surely an unequivocal "Yes."

It should be noted that, on the causal covariation model of representation, no obvious difficulty arises for the claim that some of Swampman's inner states represent things. States in his head certainly track various external environmental states, just as mine do. Moreover, given that there are no distorting mirrors, no special peculiarities in his environment, his behavior is entirely appropriate to the states that are tracked. When he trains his eyes on a square object, for example, and he is asked to trace out its apparent shape, he moves his arm just as I would, in a square-wise manner. So it is natural to suppose that, for a being of his sort, without any evolutionary history to weigh, optimal conditions obtain and hence that there is sensory representation of those external states.

Nor does my transported double present any problem. Given his causal connection with me, the relevant tracking, intuitively, is the tracking that would occur in an ordinary environment like the one *I* live in, not the tracking that obtains in the alien environment (if it is very different from the one on earth). So, his sensory states represent their earthly causal correlates.[16]

It seems to me, then, that we should resist the idea that phenomenal content is *narrow*, if by that is meant the claim that phenomenal content is ultimately metaphysically fixed by what goes on physically inside the brain independently of everything else. It is not *metaphysically necessary* that microphysical duplicates are in states with the same phenomenal character, regardless of their external environments or histories.

5.5   Some Putative Counterexamples

In this section, I want to consider a number of objections that may still be raised to my general thesis that phenomenal character is one and the same as phenomenal content.

A number of years ago, Chris Peacocke described several cases in which, he claimed, visual experiences have identical representational contents and yet are nonetheless phenomenally different.[17] I responded to these cases in earlier work by arguing that the cited visual experiences have representational differences that Peacocke failed to notice.[18] I shall not restate Peacocke's original cases or the earlier replies. Instead, I want to focus on some further problem cases that have been adduced in the more recent literature.

Suppose that you are located in a very dark tunnel, viewing a brightly lit scene at the end. Ned Block (1993, p. 183) has claimed that there will be a phenomenal difference in your visual experience if you go from having both eyes open to closing one of them. But, he asserts, the representational content will remain constant: the same objects and properties will be represented.

This is a variant on one of Peacocke's original cases (as Block acknowledges), and I find it no more compelling than the original one. It seems to me that if there is a genuine phenomenal difference here at all, it *will* be accompanied by a representational difference. In general, using two eyes increases the size of the visual field slightly and hence increases representational content: a slightly larger array of items is represented. Hence the joke by Al Gore that one of the ten best things about being vice president is that if you close your left eye, the seal on the podium in the Senate reads "President of the United States." Using two eyes also improves the perception of depth.

Now if the tunnel is sufficiently long and dark, there may well be no difference in the representation of depth. In both cases, all the objects in the scene may appear equally distant. But there may still be a small difference in the representation of the periphery of the far end of the tunnel in the two cases or in where the objects are represented as being, relative to one's viewing point in the two cases (they may appear to shift in their relative position a little to the left or right). If the viewing situation is such that there are no changes in what is represented, then I simply deny that there is any phenomenal change.

Block has also suggested to me the following problem (in correspondence; see also Block 1995). Consider the olfactory, auditory, and visual representations of a dog. They all represent a dog, or dogginess. There is, then, a common representational part but no corresponding common phenomenal part. Suppose we grant that this is true. Still, it is no difficulty for the thesis that the phenomenal character of a perceptual experience is its phenomenal content. Rather, it is a difficulty for the stronger thesis that, for perceptual experiences, phenomenal character is representational content simpliciter. And this I deny. As I noted earlier, perceptual experiences *can* have both conceptual and nonconceptual contents. The common representational part of the above experiences is part of their conceptual contents. Their phenomenal character is dictated by their nonconceptual phenomenal contents.

Here is another example, again due to Block. Suppose you see something as coming from above. Phenomenally, this is very different from hearing something as coming from above. Arguably, there is no phenomenal overlap between the two experiences. But there is certainly some representational overlap, namely, that something is coming from above. Block (1995) says that, in the case he has in mind, one only catches a glimpse, so that "the (phenomenal) difference cannot be ascribed to further representational differences" (section 4.2, paragraph 7). But even if one has no visual experience as of a specific color or shape, there will inevitably be other features one does experience, in addition to relative spatial position, that are not represented in the auditory experience. For example, one is bound to have some visual impression of the thing's size (tiny as a speck, large as a nearby bird, etc.). Likewise, in the case of the auditory experience, one is bound to have some impression of how loud the sound is. And that will not be represented in the visual experience. So there seems to me to be no serious trouble for representationalists about phenomenal experience, whatever their stripe.

The same points can be made with respect to the case of seeing something square (as square) versus feeling the same square thing by touch. Here there is evidently a phenomenally relevant representational difference. In seeing the square, one experiences its squareness, its color, the color of the background, its position in space, and many other visually accessible features. Not all of these are experienced in the case of feeling the square by touch, for example, its color.

Here is another case.[19] Suppose I have poor eyesight. When I take my eyeglasses off, the world is a bit blurry to me. Or suppose I stare at a bright light and look away. I have a blurry, pink afterimage. Blurriness, it might be claimed, is an aspect of the phenomenal character of my visual experiences in both of these examples. But is it really an aspect of the representational content of the experiences?

Consider a cloud. Clouds, in my view, are vague objects.[20] They have very fuzzy boundaries. When we see clouds in the sky, they often appear to us to have vague boundaries. Our visual experiences represent them as being vague in this way. Blurriness, I suggest, can be taken to be the same as *appearing* to have very fuzzy boundaries. So in the case in which I remove my spectacles and the world *is* blurry to me, I undergo visual experiences that represent to me that all the things I see have very fuzzy boundaries. In fact, the things I see, or many of them, are not very fuzzy—their boundaries are much sharper than clouds (although still not absolutely precise). I am subject to a kind of illusion. Correspondingly, in the case of the afterimage, what I experience is that something with ill-defined boundaries is pink. Again, my experience is delusive.

There is an alternative response that is worth mentioning. It might be supposed that our visual experiences do not represent things as having fuzzy boundaries in the above cases, but instead they leave open the question of where exactly the boundaries of the seen objects are. For a range of locations in the field of view, the experiences neither determinately represent that the boundaries lie on those locations nor determinately represent that the boundaries do not lie there. The problem for this view is that the world is *experienced* as fuzzy in the given cases. What I experience when I remove my eyeglasses is *that* things have fuzzy boundaries. So fuzziness really does enter into the content of the experience and thereby, on my view, into its phenomenal character.

Chris Peacocke has recently suggested that a serious difficulty is created for the representationalist by the case of visual experiences "such as those experienced when your eyes, closed, are directed toward the sun, and swirling shapes are experienced. In these and other visual experiences, it does not really look as if there are shapes in your environment" (1993, p. 675).

I find this unconvincing. Representations are typically indeterminate with respect to some aspects of the things they represent. If I say to you, "There's a tall man at the door," my assertion leaves open whether he is wearing a hat, the look on his face, whether he is overweight, and many other features. It simply does not comment on these matters. Likewise, if I draw a picture of the man, I may well leave unspecified how many stripes there are on his shirt, the color of his cheeks, whether he is wearing a belt.

In the case in which I experience swirling shapes, the situation is similar. I have visual sensations of various shapes occupying certain moving, two-dimensional locations relative to my point of view. I experience a square shape, say, *as* being on my left, next to an oval shape a little to its right and moving away from it. My experience represents these shapes and spatial relations. What it does not do is represent the locations of the shapes in the third dimension either relative to one another or relative to anything in the environment. Nor does it represent the shapes in two dimensions relative to items in the environment. My experience does not comment on these matters. It leaves them open, or at least it does so as long as it is agreed that I do not undergo any sensory representation of the spatial relations just mentioned.[21]

So the PANIC theory seems to me to have the resources to handle some rather subtle phenomenal differences. In the next chapter, I return to the paradox of phenomenal consciousness and the issue of perspectival subjectivity.

6

The Tale of Mary and Mechanism:
A Theory of Perspectival Subjectivity

We come now to what is perhaps more puzzling about phenomenal consciousness than anything else: perspectival subjectivity. I suggested in chapter 2 that denying that phenomenal states are perspectival—that we can fully comprehend their essential nature without knowing what it is like to undergo them (and hence adopting a particular experiential perspective on them)—not only flies in the face of what we intuitively think but also is open to further philosophical objection. On the other hand, admitting that the phenomenal is perspectival seems equally problematic. For phenomenal states cannot be counted as physical states in any sense, I have argued, unless there is an appropriate mechanism for perspectival subjectivity. And what sort of mechanism could possibly explain the generation of perspectival states from nonperspectival ones? Nor does it help to concede that phenomenal states are not physical at all (i.e., not even realized by objective microphysical states). For this concession leads inexorably to the final conclusion of the paradox of phenomenal consciousness, namely, that nothing we ever phenomenally experience or feel has any effect on our behavior. And that we know to be false.

In this chapter, I propose an account of perspectival subjectivity that brings with it a solution to the paradox. I begin my discussion with a broadly physicalist account of the essential nature of phenomenal states. I then go on to explain how phenomenal states can be both broadly physical and perspectival. I call the view that emerges here *perspectival physicalism*. The next two sections are devoted to a consideration of several philosophical thought experiments, including Frank Jackson's

(1982) tale of Mary, the brilliant scientist. The final section takes up the issue of the explanatory gap.

6.1   The Real Nature of the Phenomenal

The received view among philosophers who are sympathetic to broadly physicalist approaches is that we simply do not know enough to be able to say whether phenomenal 'feels' are physiological or functional. Brian Loar comments,

It is possible that phenomenal qualities are psychofunctional; and yet again for all philosophers know it is possible that, say, biochemical properties are essential to their individuation. (1990, p. 101)

This, I maintain, is false.

To begin with, phenomenal character is not neurophysiological or biochemical. Peer as hard as you like at the neurons. Probe deeper and deeper into the structure of the brain. According to the PANIC theory, you will not find any phenomenology. It simply is not in there. This, it seems to me, is the root of the intuition that the more developed our neurophysiological and chemical theories of brain processes, the further away we are getting from phenomenal consciousness itself, from the vivid purples and oranges of our color experiences, the smell of rotten eggs, the felt qualities of the sensations of pain and anger. As neurophysiology advances, we learn much, to be sure. But the gap between its subject matter and consciousness seems wider, if anything, than it did before we started.

Phenomenal character is also not psychofunctional. There is no hidden scientific essence to phenomenal consciousness that an ideal, universal psychology (if such there could be) will one day reveal. Peer as long as you like at the detailed functioning of the brain. Construct as many empirically based computational theories as you like of sensory processes. Still, you will not capture phenomenal character. Again, that is not where phenomenal character is to be found.

To undergo a state with a certain felt or phenomenal quality is to be the subject of a state that represents a certain external quality (by being appropriately causally connected with it in optimal conditions) and that is poised for use in the formation of beliefs and/or desires (as described in the last chapter). There is a detailed psychofunctional story to be told about how the state is poised and about how it is generated from sensory stimuli. But this is not essential to the felt quality itself. And there is no reason to insist that there will be just one such scientific story for *all* possible creatures capable of phenomenal consciousness. Who knows how the *details* might vary from case to case?

Phenomenal character is not in the head, in any interesting sense, on the PANIC theory. There are no deep discoveries waiting to be made about what is going on in us neurophysiologically or computationally that will reveal to us the nature of consciousness. Neuroscientists and philosophers who suppose otherwise are looking in the wrong place.

This view is not only a consequence of the PANIC theory, but also a piece of common sense. Intuitively, there is an important aspect to our experience of the world that is not captured by internalist accounts. When we introspect our visual experiences, for example, what we are aware of are the features our experiences represent external items as having. Properties like color and shape are experienced by us as intrinsic properties of objects and surfaces. And, assuming that there is not some large-scale illusion, that is just what they are.

The account I am proposing is a broadly physical one. There is no extra, special, magical ingredient within phenomenal consciousness. The same physical stuff that makes everything else makes experiences and feelings. The PANIC proposal also provides us with a straightforward response to both the paradox of phenomenal consciousness and the problem of phenomenal causation.

On the PANIC theory, as supplemented by the causal covariation account of sensory representation, the phenomenal character of any given internal state consists in its being *a* state that is appropriately causally connected to external items and that is appropriately poised. So what it is like to undergo a given state is a broadly physical, second-order property of that state—a property of the same general sort as that of having *an* unusual shape or being *a* device that catches rats or being *a* state that causes groaning.

I argued earlier (in chapter 2) that property or state realizations must conform to the following general model: either the higher-level property or state must be a second-order property or state, that is, a property or state of the type: being a property (state) that has feature F, or it must have a conceptually sufficient condition of this sort. The lower-level property will then realize the higher-level property (in objects of the relevant kind) by itself having the feature F, as a matter of nomological necessity, so that any token of the lower-level property (within the kind) will be a token of a property having F, and hence automatically a token of the higher-level property.

The obvious suggestion, then, is that the "what it is like" aspects of phenomenal states are second-order, broadly physical properties that are realized by objective, first-order, physical properties of those states.[1] This provides us with a solution to the problem of mechanism, but it faces an immediate difficulty, of course, namely, that phenomenal states are perspectivally subjective. And where, within the proposed account, is perspectival subjectivity? Surely that has been left out by the PANIC theory.

I argue in the next section that, contrary to first appearances, perspectival subjectivity has *not* been ignored. Premise 8 of the paradox of phenomenal consciousness—the premise that asserts that if phenomenal states are perspectivally subjective, then they are neither identical with, nor realized by, objective physical types—is false. It is here that the mistake lies in the reasoning that led to the formulation of the paradox.

As far as phenomenal causation goes, there is no special difficulty in understanding how, within my approach, the felt qualities of our experiences can have effects on our behavior. Some of our inner states track external features and stand ready for cognitive use as the outputs of the sensory modules; the fact that they have these features causally influences our behavior (all being well). Since the phenomenal qualities are realized by objective physical properties, or so I am claiming, their causal efficacy is no harder to comprehend than that of higher-level physical properties generally.

Box 6.1

It is worth noting that the PANIC theory is not threatened by the following general difficulty (raised by Block [1990b]) for comprehending how *functional* properties can play causal roles. Consider the functional property F

Box 6.1 *continued*

of having some property that causes behavior *B*. It follows logically that if I instantiate *F*, I produce behavior *B*. But the connection here between *F* and *B* is logical, not nomological. How, then, can *F* cause *B*? Surely a causal connection requires a nonlogical, empirical law.

Whatever the merits of this objection to functionalism, it presents no problem for my proposal. On my view, it is not part of the nature or essence of phenomenal qualities that they cause distinctive types of behavior that are common to all creatures subject to those qualities. Admittedly, the PANIC theory does introduce a very general forward-looking element into phenomenal character that is common to all sensory states (namely, that of being appropriately poised for cognitive use), but this does not tie specific phenomenal qualities to specific pieces of behavior. Moreover, phenomenal states are distinguished from one another via the backward-looking element of the view, namely, what in the world is tracked in optimal conditions.

6.2 Perspectival Subjectivity and the Paradox

One common reaction of physicalists to the difficulty perspectival subjectivity presents for their position is to deny that phenomenal states are perspectival. I suggested in chapter 2 that this response is ultimately unsatisfactory, since it is possible to introduce and define a notion of perspectival subjectivity that makes it very hard to suppose that the notion does not apply to phenomenal states.

Consider any actual or possible state token that feels *just* the way my present hangover feels after a party last night. Call the phenomenal state type here—the one defined by reference to the phenomenal character of all such state tokens—*punishment*. There is something it is like to undergo punishment. Indeed, there is something it is essentially like to undergo punishment. So what it is like to undergo punishment is essential to it. It follows that not knowing what it is like to undergo punishment entails not knowing something *essential* to punishment, namely, what it is like to undergo it. So fully understanding the essential nature of punishment requires knowing what it is like to undergo punishment.

In general, fully understanding the essential nature of any phenomenal state *P* requires knowing what it is like to undergo *P*. Moreover, knowing what it is like to experience *P* requires adopting a certain experiential point of view. Any creature that had not experienced *P* could not know what it is like to experience *P*.[2] So fully understanding any phenomenal state *P* requires adopting a certain experiential point of view. In this way, phenomenal states are perspectivally subjective.

It seems to me that the reasoning and the conclusion reached here are extremely plausible and that any physicalist who chooses to contest them faces an uphill battle. I accept, then, the following two claims:

(1)   Fully understanding the essential nature of any phenomenal state *P* requires knowing what it is like to experience *P*.

(2)   Knowing what it is like to experience any phenomenal state *P* requires adopting a certain experiential perspective.

(1) and (2) entail

(3)   Fully understanding the essential nature of any phenomenal state *P* requires adopting the appropriate experiential perspective.

And (3) expresses the thesis of perspectival subjectivity.

What I want to argue is that the view I have developed of phenomenal character can easily accommodate and explain the truth of (3). Perspectival subjectivity is no problem at all for the position I am defending.

Let us begin with a line of reasoning that explains why, within my proposed framework, (2) is true. What it is like to undergo any phenomenal state *P* is one and the same as the phenomenal character of *P*. This is a simple definitional consequence of the expression 'phenomenal character'. But what it is like to undergo *P* is a matter of *P*'s phenomenal content (or PANIC), according to the proposal I am making. So knowing the phenomenal character of *P*, I suggest, is representing, or being capable of representing, the relevant intentional content via the appropriate concepts.

I add the qualification "via the appropriate concepts" here, since knowing the representational aspects of something intuitively requires more than simply being able to conceptualize those aspects in some way or other. For example, if you express a belief that causes one of your companions to grimace, I can conceptualize the content of your belief as the mental cause of the grimace. But in so doing, I do not know what you believe; I do not grasp the content of your belief.

I call the concepts relevant to knowing the phenomenal character of any state "phenomenal concepts." Phenomenal concepts are the concepts that are utilized when a person introspects his phenomenal state and forms a conception of what it is like for him at that time. These concepts, in my view, are of two sorts. Some of them are indexical; others are predicative.

Suppose, for example, I am having a visual experience of red$_{29}$. I have no concept *red*$_{29}$ (see chapter 5). So, how do I conceptualize my experience when I introspect it? The obvious answer is that I conceptualize it as an experience of *this* shade of red. I bring to bear the phenomenal concepts *shade of red,* and *this.* These concepts are the same ones I bring to bear when I notice the shade of red alone without attending to the fact that I am experiencing it—as, for example, when I am not introspecting but simply looking hard at the color of a red$_{29}$ object. This is why when I turn my attention inward to the experience itself, I always seem to end up scrutinizing external features. The phenomenal concepts I apply and the features to which I apply them are the same in both the perceptual and the introspective cases.

Intuitively, possessing the phenomenal concept *red* requires that one have experienced red and that one have acquired the ability to tell, in the appropriate circumstances, which things are red directly on the basis of one's experiences. On this view, a person born blind, who remains so, could not possess the phenomenal concept *red*.

These claims lay down conditions that are constitutive of possession of the above concept. In the case of predicative phenomenal concepts generally, possession consists (very roughly) in having available a state that has a causal history that links it with the relevant experiences and that enables its possessor to make the relevant discriminations, as noted above. The full story will be very complicated.

What about the phenomenal indexical concept *this?* Possessing this concept is a matter of having available a way of singling out, or mentally pointing to, particular features that are represented in sensory experiences *while* they are present in the experiences, without thereby describing those features (in foro interno). Here, then, possession of the concept does not provide one with the means to reidentify determinate sensory features as falling into certain general classes (for example, as hues of red), as in the case of predicative concepts like *red*. Conceptualizing a determinate feature one is sensing as *this* feature does not give one a way of recognizing that feature on other occasions. What one has, rather, is a way of singling out or discriminating the feature for as long as one attends to it in one's experience (and perhaps for a very short time afterward).

The way in which the phenomenal indexical operates, I might add, is very like the way in which the first-person demonstrative 'I' operates. If I think that I am thirsty, you cannot apply to me the first-person concept I apply in my thought. The reason for this is that the content of the concept precludes its possessor from applying it correctly to anyone other than himself or herself. Similarly, if I think that I am experiencing this shade of red or this bodily disturbance or this loud noise, you cannot apply the same phenomenal indexical concept to something you are not yourself experiencing.

The phenomenal indexical can only be used to single out features of sensory experience and only by the subjects of the experiences while they last (or immediately afterward). So the use of this concept does permit a range of discriminations within a single experience but not across experiences at very different times. For example, if I am presented with two patches of paint simultaneously, one having the hue red_{29} and the other the hue red_{30}, I can discriminate the hues on the basis of my indexical conceptualization of them: *this* shade of red is different from *that* one. But if the patches are presented at very different times, I have no conceptual means to draw a distinction. I have no stored concepts corresponding to the hues, only the concept *red,* which applies to both of them.

In the above examples, I have supposed that the indexical is supplemented in introspection by a predicative concept, for example, *shade of red.* This will normally be the case, but in some cases, the conceptualization will be purely indexical. I may simply think to myself that I am having an experience of *this* sort, with *this* phenomenal character. Here, I use the indexical to pick out the content of the experience, the combination of features it represents, without conceptually specifying them any further. Conceptualizations of this sort sometimes occur in the case of simple moods.

It is worth stressing here a point I made in chapter 4—that without the application of phenomenal concepts of the sort I have described, we are *oblivious* of our experiences. There is something it is like for each of us to undergo any experience, but we need not always be aware of what it is like. We need not have any Lockean conciousness of particular experiences (see chapter 1, p. 5). They can pass unnoticed without leaving any conceptual trace.

I should perhaps also note that the fact that phenomenal-concept possession is, on my view, a matter of having available a state that functions appropriately does not entail that phenomenal concepts are functional concepts. If I introspect one of my phenomenal states, I am not thereby aware of it *as* a functional state. I do not think *that* I am in a state bearing such and such causal relations to other states, inputs, and outputs. The concepts I bring to bear in my thought do not have functional *contents*. In this way, they are not functional concepts.

The point I have tried to make so far is that phenomenal concepts, as described, are crucial to knowing phenomenal character. Now, in the case of knowledge via predicative phenomenal concepts, knowing what it is like to undergo a phenomenal state type P demands the capacity to represent the phenomenal content of P under those concepts. But one cannot possess a predicative phenomenal concept unless one has actually undergone token states to which it applies. It follows that knowing the phenomenal character of P via predicative concepts requires having experienced tokens of P.[3]

In the case of knowledge via the phenomenal indexical, knowing what it is like to undergo P demands that one mentally point to the content of P while one is experiencing a token of P (or immediately afterward). Again, then, the relevant experience is required.

The conclusion we reach is that knowing what it is like to undergo any given phenomenal state requires adopting the appropriate experiential perspective. So (2) not only is consistent with my overall position but also may be derived from it, given my comments on phenomenal concepts. Since (3) is entailed by (2) and (1), the thesis of perspectival subjectivity is secure *if* (1) is true.

The problem (1) presents, of course, is as follows. It seems obvious in one way that (1) is true, because what it is like to experience any given phenomenal state P is one and the same as the phenomenal character of P. So fully understanding P requires knowing its phenomenal character. Now that, on my view of phenomenal character, requires having and/or applying the appropriate phenomenal concepts in terms of which the content of *P* can be properly conceptualized. But phenomenal states, I have argued, are states that track objective, physical properties and that stand poised for use by the cognitive centers. Apparently, then, phenomenal states can be understood without possession of the relevant phenomenal concepts. Someone who lacked the appropriate experiential perspective but who had all the right objective information could, in principle, comprehend any phenomenal state. So, on my approach, it appears that fully understanding phenomenal states does *not* require knowing what it is like to undergo the states. Something has to give: either the PANIC account, supplemented by the causal covariation approach to sensory representation (call this conjunction of views the "naturalized PANIC theory"), is retained and perspectival subjectivity goes, or perspectival subjectivity stays and the naturalized PANIC theory goes.

Not so. Thinking is always thinking under a mode of representation. Fully understanding the essence of a phenomenal state intuitively requires thinking of the state under phenomenal concepts. For the state must surely be thought of *as* a phenomenal state, *as* having a certain phenomenal character, if it is to be *totally* understood.[4] It follows that anyone who thought of the essence of the state solely in terms of its tracking certain external properties and its standing appropriately poised for cognitive response would not fully understand it. Such a person would *lack* the sort of understanding achieved from thinking of the essence under phenomenal concepts. And this is so even given that the essence is itself analyzable in the manner of the naturalized PANIC theory.

Here is another way of making the point. I can know you as the husband of my sister without knowing you as the sadistic ax murderer from Green Street, even if you are both of these things. Knowing is knowing under a (conceptual) mode of representation. What is true here for concrete people is true for abstract essences, too. I can know that the essence of knowledge is knowledge without knowing that the essence of knowledge is justified true belief, even if knowledge is justified true belief. And it is true for understanding as well as for knowing. So my understanding *that* the essence of *X* is *X*'s having such and such a naturalized PANIC is consistent with my not understanding *that* the essence of *X* is, or includes, *X*'s having such and such phenomenal character, even given that what is expressed in both of these that-clauses is true. However, if I lack the latter understanding, then it seems intuitively plausible to suppose that I do not have complete or comprehensive understanding of the essence of X. I do not *fully* understand the essence. And this is so, to repeat, notwithstanding the fact that the essence of X is identical with having such and such a naturalized PANIC. So on my view, (1) is true. Perspectival subjectivity is compatible with physicalism.

Box 6.2

Summary

According to the position I have developed—perspectival physicalism—phenomenal states have broadly physical essences of a sort that are ultimately realized by objective, microphysical types. These essences are second-order: each phenomenal state is analyzed as being *a* state that causally covaries with such and such bodily or environmental features in optimal conditions and that is poised for cognitive responses (in the way I have specified). Nonetheless, *fully* understanding the essence of any given phenomenal state requires thinking of it as a phenomenal state with a specific phenomenal character. Anyone who failed to think of the state in this way would lack a very important way of grasping or conceptualizing it and so would not fully understand it. This, in turn, requires grasping the state's phenomenal content under the appropriate concepts, since phenomenal character is phenomenal content and thinking is always thinking under some cognitive mode.

The appropriate concepts here are phenomenal concepts. Phenomenal concepts are of two sorts: indexical and predicative. These concepts are tied in somewhat different ways to experiences in the ways I have described. As a consequence, fully understanding the essence of any given phenomenal state requires adopting the appropriate experiential perspective. Phenomenal states, then, are both perspectival and physical. The problems of mechanism and perspectival subjectivity are now solved, as is the paradox of phenomenal consciousness

6.3 Mary's Room

Mary is a brilliant scientist who has spent her entire life in a black-and-white room (Jackson 1982). She views the outside world via black-and-white monitor screens, which are fed information from external cameras. She has banks of computers at her disposal. Supposedly, she knows everything there is to know about what goes on physically and functionally in human beings, and their surroundings, when they see the various colors. She knows how the light is reflected from the surfaces of objects, how it affects the retina, what the various changes in the optic nerve are, and so on. In short, she knows all the (lower-level) physical and functional facts. But there is still something she does not know, namely, what it is like to experience red, or green, or blue. She does not find this out until she leaves her room. So physicalism, understood narrowly as the doctrine that ultimately all facts are expressible in the vocabulary of microphysics, chemistry, neurophysiology, and molecular biology is incomplete. Likewise functionalism. Likewise my naturalized PANIC theory. These views, all of which I call "physicalist" hereafter, leave out what it is like.

This argument has provoked extensive discussion. Part of the difficulty in evaluating it is that it uses the very slippery term 'fact'. Let us begin, then, with a discussion of how the term 'fact' is to be understood.

Facts are sometimes taken to be as fine-grained in their individuation conditions as the contents of the propositional attitudes. Facts, in this sense, are what are expressed by the that-clauses of true beliefs. On this view, the fact that there is water ahead is not the same as the fact that there is H_2O ahead, since the beliefs are different. The one belief can be had without the other. Likewise, the fact that Tom is now asleep is not the same as the fact that Tom is asleep at 2:00 P.M. on Tuesday, even given that it is now 2:00 P.M., Tuesday. What distinguishes these facts are the different conceptual modes of representation they incorporate. The external, objective states of affairs are the same, but the ways in which they are conceptualized are different. The fact that Tom is now asleep, in the given circumstances, consists of the same real, external state of affairs as the fact that Tom is asleep at 2:00 P.M., Tuesday—in each case, there is the same real individual in the real state at the same time—but the one brings in a temporal indexical concept with reference to the individual's being in the state, whereas the other does not. Facts are identical, then, if and only if they consist of the same objective, actual states of affairs under the same concepts.

There is another, more coarse-grained view of facts that identifies them outright with states of affairs that obtain in the objective world, regardless of how those states of affairs are conceived. On this view, the fact that there is water ahead is identical with the fact that there is H_2O ahead.[5]

On the former conception of facts, the existence of facts that are neither functional nor (lower-level) physical is something that can be accepted by the functionalist or the physicalist.[6] For, there are such facts if there are concepts that are neither functional nor (lower-level) physical. And the existence of concepts of neither of these sorts can be accepted by everyone. What matters is whether there are real, nonconceptual items that cannot be accommodated within a physicalist framework.

This perhaps calls for a little further explanation. Consider the fact that I am tall. This fact is not the same as the fact that Michael Tye is tall, on the fine-grained conception of facts, since the first-person concept expressed by 'I' is not a constituent of the latter fact. Nevertheless, there is here only a single, real, external state of affairs, which consists of the individual, Michael Tye, exemplifying the property of being tall. The existence of the fact that I am tall, as distinct from the fact that Michael Tye is tall, is no objection to physicalism. One and the same thing can be conceived in different ways.

Moreover, the first-person concept is not a concept with a functional or (lower-level) physical content. In thinking of Michael Tye as me, I do not think of Michael Tye as the person who plays a certain functional role or as the bearer of certain physiological or chemical or other lower-level, physical properties. So the concept expressed by 'I' is not a physiological or chemical or functional concept. However, in my view, something in my head counts as a token of that concept if and only if it plays the right functional role. I might add that this position does not entail that the concept *I,* as I use it, really is the same as the concept *Michael Tye* after all. The concepts, like the terms that express them publicly, are syntactically different, and these syntactic differences generate fine-grained functional differences.

The question, then, is whether the case of Mary reveals any real, nonconceptual items that pose problems for physicalism. If it does, then there will be facts that cannot be accommodated by the physicalist view, even on the broader conception of facts.

Mary does not know what it is like to experience red. So, on my view, she does not know the phenomenal content of the state of experiencing red (whatever the determinate shade). She does not know this for two reasons. First, she *lacks* the phenomenal concept *red*; second, she cannot *apply* the phenomenal concept *this* to the color represented in the experience of red. After all, Mary has never had the experience of red, nor is she now having the experience of red. She is thus in no position to conceptualize the phenomenal content properly. There really is, then, something Mary does not know. Still, the state of experiencing red can have a naturalized PANIC essence, as I have argued. And Mary will know that essence (as involving such and such causal correlation, etc.) if she knows all the facts countenanced by physicalism. So there is nothing of a nonconceptual sort not known to Mary. The fact she does not know is a fine-grained one within which there are phenomenal concepts. However, the coarse-grained, nonconceptual fact it contains *is* (broadly) physical. Once the different notions of fact are sorted out, Mary creates no trouble for physicalism.[7]

6.4 Some of Mary's Philosophical Relatives

What is true for Mary is true for another old philosophical friend, the bat (Nagel 1979). One reason we cannot know what it is like to be a bat is that we lack the predicative phenomenal concepts necessary to conceptualize properly the phenomenal contents of the bat's experiences. And we lack these concepts, in part, because we are so constituted that we cannot ourselves undergo those experiences (let us concede). Another reason is that, although we do possess the phenomenal indexical concept *this*, we cannot apply it to any features except those *we* experience (while we experience them). We cannot ever say to ourselves "*This* is what the bat experiences." So there are, in one sense, certain facts about the bat that we can never know *given* the assumption that some of the features the bat's sensory states represent are not sensorily representable by us.[8] But, in a narrower sense—the one that is relevant to physicalism—we can know all the facts there are to know about the bat's experiences. In principle, we can know all the relevant nonconceptual facts.

It is sometimes suggested by physicalists that all that Mary lacks within her room are certain abilities, for example, the ability to tell when something is red by sight alone.[9] Really, Mary already knows *all* the facts. This seems to me very counterintuitive. Surely Mary makes a genuine discovery when she leaves her room. Surely, in some sense, she learns a new fact when she views a rose or gazes at a blue sky; she acquires some new information about how things look.[10] The position I am proposing can allow this so long as it is only the conceptual sense of 'fact' that is operative in these claims.

Here is another case that is supposed to create trouble for physicalism. Michael Lockwood (1989, pp. 134–37) asks us to imagine someone, Harriet, who is experiencing a throbbing headache at time *t*. We are also to imagine that we have at our disposal *all* the information there is to have about what is going on in Harriet at all physical levels. Lockwood claims that even if we have the phenomenal concepts needed to conceptualize Harriet's phenomenal state, given no further information about Harriet other than the information about what is going on in her physically, we still are not in a position to know exactly what Harriet is feeling at *t*, exactly what the phenomenal character of her state at *t* is. His conclusion is that physicalism fails.

I have already questioned one implicit assumption of this piece of reasoning, namely, that internal physical facts determine phenomenal character. As I have observed on several occasions, phenomenal character, "ain't in the head." But the assumption is not crucial to Lockwood's argument. Given as much further external physical information as you please, this still is not going to close the gap, according to Lockwood. We still are not going to be in a position to know what it is like for Harriet.

Lockwood concedes that there is a nonconceptual sense of 'fact' as well as a conceptual one (hereafter, I shall put 'fact' in capital letters when it is being used nonconceptually). But he denies that anyone who had all the physical information could know, on that basis alone, the FACT that makes it true that Harriet's state at *t* feels the way it does. Why? Because the following principle, he maintains, is true:

(P)   If one knows a FACT under one mode of presentation and one does not know it under another, then one's not knowing that it is the same

FACT that corresponds to each mode of presentation demands that one not know some further substantive FACT, under any mode of presentation.

According to Lockwood, "it scarcely seems possible to deny [P]" (p. 137). P entails that if I am unable to deduce, from my knowledge of the physical FACTS, how exactly Harriet's state at time t phenomenally felt, this cannot be simply because I am failing to conceive of the relevant physical or functional FACT in the right way. There must be some further substantive FACT that I do not know. But, ex hypothesi, I know all the physical FACTS.

There are few philosophical principles that it scarcely seems possible to deny. P is not one of them. Here is a simple counterexample. Suppose a child knows that the end of the school term is in fourteen days. Still, she need not know (or even believe) that the end of the term is in a fortnight. For she may not possess the concept *fortnight*. If she is lacking that concept, she both knows and fails to know one and the same FACT under different modes of presentation. Now what is the further substantive FACT that the child hereby fails to know? There is none.[11] So Lockwood's principle P is false.

A more plausible principle is this:

(P′) If one knows a FACT under one mode of presentation and one does not know it under another, then one's not knowing that it is the same FACT that corresponds to each mode of presentation demands that one not know some further substantive FACT, under any mode of presentation, *provided that* both modes of presentation are within one's conceptual repertoire.

P′ is not falsified by the above example, since one of the modes of presentation is not within the child's conceptual repertoire: the child lacks the concept *fortnight*. And P′ can still be applied in the case of Harriet, since we are to suppose that we possess the relevant phenomenal concepts (along with whatever concepts are necessary to understand all the physical information). What can be said in response to Lockwood's argument, understood in this way?

Suppose I am looking across the room at a group of people, and I briefly see someone who looks just like me. I take special note of the fact that he is wearing my old school tie. Unknown to me, I have actually caught a glance of myself in a mirror in the vicinity of the group of people. I know that *that* person, the one I am seeing, is wearing my old school tie. But I do not know that *I* am wearing such a tie, for I paid no attention at all to the kind of tie I put on. There is here a single FACT, the FACT that consists of Michael Tye's wearing a certain sort of tie. This FACT is known by me under one mode of presentation but not known under another. I possess all the relevant concepts. According to *P'*, my not knowing that it is the same FACT under two modes of presentation demands that I not know some further substantive FACT. But what is this FACT? The FACT that I am that person? But that is just the FACT that Michael Tye is the same as Michael Tye. And that FACT, of course, I know. Moreover, it is hardly substantive.

How, then, can I know that that person is wearing my old school tie without knowing that I am wearing such a tie? The answer obviously is that I do not know that I am that person. So there really is a relevant fact here that I do not know. But this fact is not a FACT that I do not know. So *P'*, like *P*, is false. Lockwood's argument fails again.[12]

There remains one final issue. It concerns Mary once more. Earlier, I assumed that it is possible for Mary, while she is in her room, to know all the physical FACTS.[13] But is this really possible? How this question is answered is not absolutely critical to the truth of physicalism. Still, it is of some interest. For although physicalists (and here again I include functionalists) typically accept that Mary can know all the physical FACTS, some of them appear to take the opposing view (see, for example, Harman 1990).

What sort of FACT might Mary fail to be in a position to know? Well, consider the FACT that there is a certain sensory state such that normal perceivers who view *red* objects in good lighting are caused to undergo that state. I claimed earlier that possessing the phenomenal concept *red* requires having experienced red and having acquired the ability to recognize red things directly on the basis of visual experience, given optimal viewing conditions. Mary, in her room, lacks this concept. So she cannot represent the above FACT in the way that you and I normally do—via, in part, the exercise of the phenomenal concept *red*. She cannot conceptualize redness in the way that we do when we introspect our visual experiences of red. But that does not preclude her from conceptualizing red in some nonphenomenal way, for example, as such and such a triple of spectral reflectances. So, although she cannot know the partly conceptual fact you and I know, when we represent to ourselves that there is a certain sensory state such that normal perceivers who view red objects in good lighting are caused to undergo that state, she can certainly know the corresponding FACT.

The points made here can be generalized. The conclusion I reach is that Mary can, *in principle,* know all the (salient) physical FACTS.

6.5   The Explanatory Gap

One complaint that is often raised to reductionist theories of phenomenal consciousness is that they fail to close the huge explanatory gap we intuitively feel between phenomenal experiences and brain states. I want now to explore this charge.

One way of understanding the explanatory gap between phenomenal experiences and brain states is in terms of the production of perspectivally subjective states from nonperspectival ones. How could brain states realize states with a perspectivally subjective character? I have tried to provide the outline of an answer to this question. Brain states realize states with naturalized PANIC essences in a manner that creates no special conceptual difficulty. The latter states are conceived in introspection via phenomenal concepts. Anyone who lacked such concepts would lack the sort of understanding you and I have of such states via introspective awareness. Such a person would not *fully* understand the relevant states. Therefore, states with naturalized PANIC essences are perspectivally subjective. There is, then, no deep puzzle or mystery remaining about the mechanism whereby experientially perspectival states are produced.

I am sure that it will be replied that a mystery still remains. Consider, for example, the feeling of elation. Suppose you have an autocerebroscope attached to your head at the time at which you feel elated and that you are yourself viewing, in the attached mirror, the particular firing pattern that constitutes your feeling. Is it not going to seem amazing to you that the brain state you are viewing feels the way it does, indeed that it feels any way at all? After all, many other brain states that you are capable of viewing through the autocerebroscope have no felt character.

The answer to these questions is obviously yes. But there is much that you do not know. For example, you do not know what the brain state you are viewing represents. You do not know what bodily condition it tracks (in optimal conditions). You are like the man peering hard at the word 'succubus' and trying, from that alone, to decipher its meaning.

Suppose now that you are supplied with the pertinent information about the role of the brain state and what it represents. Imagine that the information is flashed onto a screen placed before you. By reading what is on the screen, you discern the naturalized PANIC of the brain state you have been seeing via the autocerebroscope. Is it not *still* going to seem absolutely amazing to you that a state with that PANIC feels the way your present state does? Is it not *still* going to seem absolutely amazing that the brain state feels any way at all?

Why, yes. But so what? There are facts, and there are FACTS. The former are partly conceptual; the latter are not. You know, by introspection, how the state you are undergoing feels. You also know, by viewing the screen, that this state has such and such a PANIC. The concepts you apply in the two cases are very different. In the one case, the concepts are purely phenomenal; in the other, they are not. The fact you know via introspection is, therefore, very different from the fact you know as you read the screen. The one is not deducible from the other. When the pertinent information is displayed on the screen, you are entitled to be amazed. There was nothing in your initial mode of presentation that could have led you to the information you see presented before you. Nor, conversely, is there anything in the latter information, the latter fact, that could have led you to know the fact you know through introspection.

So *of course* it is amazing. In this way, *of course*, there is an explanatory gap. And *this* particular gap will never be closed. The concepts are irreducibly different. But there is still no reason to suppose that there are two different FACTS here rather than only one FACT under different modes of presentation. So there is no puzzle here for perspectival physicalism.

This point seems to me very important. The suggestion I am making is that there is no gap *in the world* between phenomenal and physical states. The gap lies in different ways of conceiving certain physical states, different concepts that we apply. Introspect your experiences for as long as you like. Say to yourself repeatedly, and with as much conviction as you are able to muster, "This cannot just be a state with such and such naturalized PANIC." You will establish nothing. The concepts you are applying to your inner states—the concepts nature has built you to apply on such occasions—do not allow you to see in what exactly, according to the naturalized PANIC theory, the phenomenal character of a particular pain or hunger pang or feeling of elation consists. That is left open by your phenomenal concepts. It is here that the gap exists, in the distance between the phenomenal and nonphenomenal modes of presentation.

My proposal, then, is ontologically *minimalist*. Yes, there is a gap, and, yes, in some ways it is a very special gap. But that does not mean that there is some spooky stuff out there in the world (the paradox of phenomenal consciousness should persuade us that *that* just can't be right, if we ever doubted it). The gap is conceptual.

There is one final way the explanatory gap is sometimes stated. Consider again the token brain event that constitutes your token feeling of elation. Suppose now that there is another brain event that, at another time, or in another person, has the same PANIC. Now why *couldn't* the latter brain event feel different (without changing or losing its PANIC)? Indeed, why *couldn't* it lack any felt quality at all? These questions surely demand informative answers. They reflect a gap in our understanding. But if the phenomenal character of your feeling of elation has, as its essence, such and such a PANIC, then it appears that these questions have no answers, that they are not genuine questions at all. For it is metaphysically impossible for anything having the appropriate *PANIC* to feel any differently from your actual experience.

The term 'could' can be used in a number of different ways. In an epistemic sense, water could turn out not to be H_2O. There is nothing in how water is represented in our ordinary water beliefs and thoughts that itself rules out or precludes water's being discovered to be something other than H_2O in the actual world. Likewise, there is nothing in the ordinary way in which people think of Hesperus as the evening star that, in and of itself, entails that it is one and the same as Phosphorus. For Phosphorus is standardly thought of under a different mode of presentation, as the morning star. In an epistemic sense, then, something *could* have just the PANIC that your feeling of elation does and yet not feel like it or not feel any way at all.

So, on an epistemic reading, the questions dissolve. Since they falsely presuppose that nothing could (epistemically) have the right PANIC and yet fail to feel the appropriate way (the way your experience of elation feels), they are really pseudoquestions. They have no answers, informative or otherwise.

There is another, nonepistemic sense that the term 'could' might have in the above questions. It might be taken metaphysically. The assumption now is that there is a serious clash between what the PANIC theory of phenomenal experience entails and what is apparently imaginable. Since we can apparently imagine something having the relevant PANIC without having the given phenomenal character, this is reason to think that it must be metaphysically possible. But the PANIC theory entails that there is no such metaphysical possibility. So, what is really being asked for is an explanation of why we shouldn't take imaginability at face value here and suppose that it really is possible for an event to be identical PANIC-wise with your experience without feeling like it.

This way of understanding what is at issue requires a more general discussion of imaginability. And in so doing, it also brings us face to face with the only two problems I have not yet addressed: the problem of duplicates and the problem of the inverted spectrum. The time has come to talk of zombies, of inversions, of what can and cannot be imagined. These are the topics of chapter 7.

Box 6.3

Summary

There is an explanatory gap between phenomenal experiences and brain states. But the gap does not concern the production of perspectivally subjective states from nonperspectival ones, because the mechanism whereby states of the former sort are generated has been specified. The gap is best viewed as a conceptual one, which presents no difficulty for physicalism. In the world itself, there is no gap, no yawning chasm, between two radically

Box 6.3 *continued*

different sorts of things. There is just good, old physical stuff that we conceptualize in different ways, depending on our mode of access to it.

The idea that a person could undergo a state with a particular PANIC but a different phenomenal quality from its actual one or no phenomenal quality at all either is merely an epistemic claim, in which case it poses no threat to the PANIC theory, or it is to be understood metaphysically. In this case, we need to look more closely at the question of whether we really can imagine the putative possibility. That we will do in the next chapter.

7

Can You Really Imagine What You Think You Can?

We have intuitions about what we can and cannot imagine, just as we have intuitions about many other things. For example, it seems to me that I can imagine myself a billionaire, a pauper, a person who can leap tall buildings in a single bound. Intuitions of this sort are standardly taken to provide reasons to believe that the things in question are possible.

It has seemed to many philosophers that they can imagine the following:

1. A microphysical duplicate of a sentient creature that experiences nothing at all.

2. A functional duplicate of a sentient creature that experiences nothing at all, for example, the China-body system we met earlier.

3. A pair of microphysical duplicates whose experiences are phenomenally inverted.

4. A person who is functionally identical with a normal human being but whose color experiences are systematically inverted in their phenomenal character.

5. A person whose mental states play the same functional roles at times t and t' (where t' is later than t) but whose color experiences at t' are phenomenally inverted relative to those at t.

6. A person whose mental states play different functional roles at times t and t' but whose color experiences are phenomenally the same at t and t'.

(1) is the hypothesis of zombie replicas, (2) the absent-qualia hypothesis, (3)–(5) variants on the inverted-spectrum hypothesis, and (6) the hypothesis of inverted earth.

In this chapter, I propose to take a close look at these hypotheses from the viewpoint of the PANIC theory. I begin by trying to clarify the *sort* of theory that I take the PANIC theory to be.

7.1   The Status of the PANIC Theory

I have justified the PANIC theory by reference to its explanatory power. It allows us to understand a variety of pieces of data that would otherwise perplex us, for example, the intensionality of "what it is like" contexts and the way in which experiences and feelings are transparent. It also allows us to solve all the various problems of consciousness we have encountered so far, and it brings a simple and persuasive solution to the paradox. No other theory or approach I am aware of can claim as many successes.

The overall proposal I am making is partly armchair-based and partly empirical. Certainly, no amount of armchair reflection on concepts will reveal the properties that enter into the PANIC of a particular exogenous feeling of depression, for example. These properties are only discoverable by us empirically. The thesis that the individual phenomenal character of that feeling is one and the same as such and such a PANIC is an a posteriori claim. This is not to say that it is not a necessary truth. Like the claim that water is H_2O, the above thesis, in my view, is true in all possible worlds if it is true at all.

Introspection provides us access to our PANIC states, of course, but in a restricted way. What happens introspectively, according to the PANIC theory, when I attend to a particular feeling, is that I think to myself that my state has *this* phenomenal character (under the simplest scenario). The phenomenal indexical here points directly to something my state has without describing it. What it points to is the particular PANIC of my state. Since the indexical 'this', as I here use it in my thought, is a rigid designator (it denotes the same thing in all possible worlds in which it denotes at all), it picks out the same PANIC in other worlds as it does in this one. So if the phenomenal character of my state is PANIC, *P*, then it is necessary that that character is *P*.

But might it not have turned out differently? Might it not have turned out that the given phenomenal character was not the given PANIC?

Certainly that is epistemically possible. We could have discovered that, in actual fact, the phenomenal quality of my state is not P at all but something else, a different PANIC, for example. This would be like discovering that water is not, in fact, H_2O, or that I am not actually Michael Tye but an impostor who murdered the real Tye many years ago. Were such discoveries not possible, there would be no substantive claims about the world here. And it seems undeniable that in each of these cases, there is such a claim.

Still, surely I can imagine my state's feeling just the way it does and yet lacking the relevant PANIC? Conversely, surely I can imagine a state having that PANIC and yet feeling different or no way at all? To address these questions, it is necessary to make some general remarks about imaginability, beginning with what seems to me to be a fruitful comparison.

7.2 Imaginability and Perception: A Parallel

As I stand in an art gallery, it visually appears to me that there is a wall before me with an oval picture of some flowers on it. This does not, of course, prove that there really is a wall or an oval picture. I might be deluded. I might be the subject of a very cleverly constructed illusion, or I might conceivably be hallucinating. Still, my visual experience gives me a reason to believe that there is a wall before me with an oval picture of some flowers. My belief is thereby warranted by my experience. But my belief may lose its warrant in the face of new evidence. Suppose, for example, I find out that the coffee I have been drinking has been doctored with a drug that produces incredibly lifelike visual hallucinations (although it has no effect on the other senses). I reach up to the wall and feel no picture in the place my visual experience represents one as being. Then my belief is no longer warranted. With the introduction of the new evidence, the old evidence is defeated. The connection between my visual experience and my belief is a defeasible one. I am entitled to believe what I do on the basis of my initial evidence, but there are possible defeaters for the evidence. And one of these defeaters later becomes actual.

Now it seems to me that I can imagine a man who runs a mile in under one minute. This certainly does not prove that there is a possible world in which our actual laws of nature obtain, and in which some man does run a mile in under one minute. We seem to be able to imagine all sorts of things that are physically impossible, for example, humans who fly, stones that do not fall, water that flows uphill, perpetual-motion machines. Nor even does my seeming to imagine a man who runs a one-minute mile prove that there is a metaphysically possible world containing such a man (a world that is nomically impossible), for I might have failed to imagine what I thought I did. For example, I might have failed to imagine a man and imagined instead a creature superficially resembling a man. Still, my seeming to imagine something P is a reason to believe that P is metaphysically possible. My belief is warranted by my apparent act of imagination, in a way that is parallel to that obtaining for perceptual beliefs and visual experiences. I am entitled to believe that P is metaphysically possible on the basis of its apparent imaginability, but the process is defeasible. With the introduction of appropriate new evidence, I may lose the warrant to my belief.

Suppose, for example, that it seems to someone that she can imagine water's not being H_2O, even given that water is, in actual fact, H_2O. Then that is a reason to believe that there is at least a *metaphysically* possible world in which water is not H_2O. But there are here, as elsewhere, possible defeaters. Does she really succeed in imagining what she thinks she does? This question, of course, is a counterpart to the question, "Did I, in the earlier example, really *see* what I thought I did?" Now although the mere existence of possible defeaters with respect to what is genuinely imagined does not entail actual defeat, still to the extent that it becomes as plausible to believe that the possible defeaters are actual as it is to believe that they are not, then the claim to be able to imagine that water is not H_2O becomes suspect. It is no longer clearly warranted.

What is it that is imagined by someone who knows that water is H_2O in the actual world but who claims to be imagining that water is not H_2O? Suppose, in response to questions, she replies that she is imagining a world in which there is a colorless, tasteless liquid that comes out of taps and fills lakes but that is not H_2O. Now we have a relevant possible defeater. In light of the new evidence, it is not unreasonable to suppose that she is really just imagining that something superficially resembling water is not H_2O rather than that water itself is not H_2O. So the belief that it is metaphysically possible that water is not H_2O is no longer clearly warranted by her apparent act of imagination.

Let us consider another example. Suppose it seems to you that you just imagined the number π's having seven consecutive sevens in its decimal expansion. Well, what exactly did you imagine? Suppose you report the following: you mentally visualized yourself sitting down with a pen and paper and doing some arithmetic, and you visualized further seven consecutive sevens showing up when you divided twenty-two by seven. Alternatively, you imagined a computer churning away at the decimal expansion of π and eventually producing seven sevens in a row. Well, then, you did not really imagine the number *itself* having seven consecutive sevens in its expansion. So there remains no clear reason *here* to believe that this is metaphysically possible.

Perhaps it will now be objected that if defeaters of the above sort are allowed, then appeals to imaginability will never provide any sort of clear warrant for claims of possibility. For there will always be alternative ways of reinterpreting what has been imagined. Suppose, for example, it seems to me that I can imagine a raccoon in the sitting room downstairs. Is that a reason to think that it is metaphysically possible that there is a raccoon in the sitting room? Intuitively, yes. But if you ask me to describe what I imagine, my description is likely to cite observable characteristics of raccoons. And it can then be replied that I did not really imagine a raccoon but only a creature superficially resembling one. So, my act of imagination does not warrant the belief that there *could* have been a raccoon in the sitting room downstairs (in the metaphysical sense of 'could').

This seems to me too hasty. Suppose you ask me some further questions about what I imagined, for example, whether I would still have counted the creature I imagined as a raccoon if its appearance had been changed dramatically so that it no longer looked like a raccoon at all. We might suppose here that I am asked whether painting a white line down its back, attaching a bushy tail, and sewing inside it a sac of smelly liquid that it can squeeze and thereby produce an extremely malodorous spray would turn the creature I am imagining into a skunk.[1] If I answer negatively, then that is reason to suppose that I did genuinely imagine that there was a raccoon in the sitting room. If I answer positively, all I imagined was there was a creature with a certain appearance (the one shared by raccoons) in the sitting room. In the former case, my act of imagination would continue to warrant the belief that a raccoon in the sitting room is metaphysically possible. In the latter case, this belief would lose its warrant; my act of imagination would warrant only that it is metaphysically possible that something with such and such observable characteristics is in the sitting room.

My suggestion, then, is that appeals to imaginability can be used to support claims of metaphysical possibility but that considerable care is needed in deciding just what has really been imagined.[2] We are now ready to return to the PANIC theory.

7.3 Troublesome Possibilities?

Consider first the claim that I can imagine my state's feeling just the way it does and yet lacking PANIC P. This is not intended as a claim about the actual world. The thought is not that, for all we know, it could still turn out that in actual fact my state lacks P. That I have already granted. Rather, the claim is that even if the felt quality of my state (call it Q) is PANIC P, I can still imagine Q's not being that PANIC. If this is true, then there is a possible world in which Q is not P. So it is not necessary that Q is P. But, I claim, the thesis that Q is P is necessarily true if it is true at all. So the conclusion to which we seem driven is that it is not true that Q is P: the PANIC theory is mistaken.

The obvious response to this argument is to challenge the claim that Q can be imagined without PANIC P. There is an equally obvious difficulty with such a reply. The problem is that the strategy that was used to defend the view that water is necessarily H_2O against the charge that we can imagine its not being H_2O (even given that water is, in fact, H_2O) is not applicable. In the latter case, it was pointed out that what we really imagine when we think we imagine water not being H_2O is something with the appearance of water not being H_2O, and that, of course, is quite different. So a possible defeater exists. Unfortunately, a defeater of this sort is not available in the case of the claim that we can imagine phenomenal character Q without PANIC P. For nothing that appeared or felt just the way the state with Q does could *fail* to have felt quality Q.

Still, the fact that a possible defeater of this sort does not exist does not show that no defeaters are possible. Consider again the claim that Q can be imagined without the specified PANIC. Why do we naturally suppose that this claim is true? The answer surely is that in thinking of a state as having phenomenal character Q, we think of it via the exercise of phenomenal concepts. The conception we form of it is the one we have when we introspect it. By contrast, in thinking of a state as having PANIC P, we bring to bear a very different set of concepts. So, we naturally infer that we are thinking of two different things: Q *and P.* But this inference is unjustified. The difference in thoughts can be accounted for solely by a difference in concepts. The one thought consists in representing the given PANIC under phenomenal concepts; the other consists in representing the same PANIC under nonphenomenal concepts.

Perhaps it will be said that if the concepts are different, then it must be possible for them to pick out, or apply to, different things. So it must be metaphysically possible for Q to be present without P after all.

Again the inference is unjustified. The concept *water* is not the same as the concept H_2O; the concept I is not the same as the concept *Michael Tye.* Nonetheless it is necessarily true that water is H_2O, and that I am Michael Tye *if* these claims are in fact true. It is worth stressing that this point holds as soon as it is granted that the terms 'water' and 'I' are rigid designators, however the details of their semantics go.

Box 7.1

Suppose, for example, that it is held that a priori reflection on the meaning of the word 'water' shows us that nothing that lacked the microstructure (whatever it might be) of the *actual* colorless, odorless, tasteless fluid filling lakes and coming out of taps could be water, that anything with a different microstructure but the same appearance would only be fool's water. On this view, the concept *water* is analytically equivalent to the concept *substance having the same microstructure (whatever it might be) of the actual colorless, odorless, tasteless fluid that comes out of taps and fills lakes* (or some concept very similar to this). Here 'actual' is taken to rigidify the definite descriptions to which it applies, so that nothing other than the actual F could be the actual F. The concept water, then, is very different from the scientific concept H_2O. But it does not follow that water might not have been H_2O. For we have discovered by empirical investigation that

Box 7.1 *continued*

the microstructure of the actual colorless, tasteless fluid coming out of taps and so on is H_2O. This factual discovery together with the structure of the concept *water* guarantees that water is necessarily H_2O.

Parallel points apply if the term 'water' is taken to be a rigid tag that refers directly to its referent without describing it at all, as Kripke (1972) and others have argued. In this case, the distinction is between a semantically simple tag and a scientific description: "stuff with molecules made up of two hydrogen atoms and one oxygen atom."

Once these points are appreciated, there seems no reason left to insist that we really can imagine Q without the given PANIC. Not only can the PANIC theorist account for the fact that we can apparently imagine Q without PANIC P in an entirely straightforward way (and one that does not presuppose the truth of the theory), but the initial presumption that Q is imaginable without the appropriate PANIC is seriously threatened by the above observations. Conceptual possibility yields apparent imaginability but not imaginability simpliciter. Some things that are conceptually possible are metaphysically impossible and hence unimaginable. The PANIC theory of phenomenal character provides an empirical view of phenomenal character that insulates it from the above appeal to imaginability.

What about the converse claim that PANIC P can be imagined without Q, or indeed without any phenomenal or "what it is like" aspect? More generally, what about the claim that we can imagine a person's having any number of states with PANIC but experiencing nothing at all? The same points apply. Certainly these things are conceivable in the sense of being apparently imaginable. But there is no good, a priori reason to think that they are *really* imaginable.

Some further observations are worth making here. In chapter 4, I made the point that without the application of concepts, our sensations are concealed from us. We are like the distracted driver who sees the road ahead, and thereby manages to avoid crashing, but who is oblivious to his visual perceptions. If we are not paying attention, if our thoughts lie elsewhere, we have no awareness of our experiences and feelings. They exist all right at such times, but for us *cognitively* they are not there.

Now when it is claimed that we can imagine a state's having some PANIC and yet no phenomenal character, what, I suggest, we really can imagine is someone who is in a state with that PANIC, but who is oblivious to its phenomenal character—someone who is like the distracted driver. Consider, for example, the case of a bad headache. I can certainly imagine someone who is in a state with the very same poised, abstract, nonconceptual content as some given headache of mine, but who does not register the way it feels. Indeed, cases like this are actual. Some headaches go on for hours on end without break, even though there are short periods when we do not notice them. At those times, the headaches continue to exist—they still have phenomenal features—but we are not conscious of them in the higher-order sense (distinguished in chapter 1). We have no higher-order consciousness of our headaches at such moments.

The suggestion I am making, then, is this. We can imagine someone in a state with the appropriate nonconceptual content. And we can also imagine or picture to ourselves that this person, *on the inside,* is in a distracted-driverlike state. That much seems to me uncontroversial. But it does not follow from this that we can imagine a PANIC state with no phenomenal character.

Perhaps it will be replied that we can further imagine the person's introspecting his state and finding no phenomenal character there (in this respect, being unlike the distracted driver). So we can imagine what I am contesting after all. But I refuse to grant this.

Consider the case of our own introspection of phenomenal states. I argued earlier that when we introspect such states and form a conception of what it is like for us, we bring to bear phenomenal concepts. Without the application of phenomenal concepts, we have no cognitive awareness of phenomenal character as such at all. Now either the person we imagine introspecting applies phenomenal concepts to his introspected state or he does not. If he does not, then he certainly will not find any phenomenal character there. But that is no reason to think that there is no phenomenal character. What follows again is simply that it is concealed from him.

On the other hand, if he does apply phenomenal concepts, then he is in precisely the state needed to generate cognitive awareness of phenomenal character, according to my view: he is bringing a PANIC state under phenomenal concepts. He is thereby aware of it as a phenomenal state.

To insist that in these circumstances he might still feel nothing seems to me incoherent. After all, given the concepts he is applying, he cannot possibly think to himself, "I feel nothing." On the contrary, he must at least think something of the following sort: "I am undergoing a state with this phenomenal character (felt quality)." And if he does think this, then how could he possibly be without any experience at all? This perhaps deserves a little further elucidation.

I believe that at this moment I am sitting on a chair and looking out of a window at a large expanse of grass and trees. There is a computer directly before me on a desk. The sun is shining; a dog is barking. But I also believe that it is metaphysically possible that last night mad scientists drugged me and took me to a laboratory, in which they removed my body, so that I am now just a brain floating in a vat. So I am prepared to grant that it is metaphysically possible that the ordinary, everyday beliefs mentioned above are false. Possibly, it merely *appears* to me that I am sitting on a chair, seeing grass, trees, the sun, a computer. Possibly, appearances are deceptive: there really is no chair, no grass, no trees, and so on, before me. But could I be radically wrong about the appearances, too? Is it metaphysically possible that I merely believe that I am seeming to see chairs, desks, trees, people, and so on, when in reality I am not even seeming to see these things? Might I now think that I am undergoing experiences but in reality feel nothing at all? What about for you? Might we *all* be radically wrong not just about the present state of the world but also about whether we have experiences and feelings?

Consider another example. One day, when I was much younger, as I was climbing aboard a train in London, the door to the carriage slammed shut on one of my thumbs. I experienced immediate, blinding pain. Or at least I strongly believed that I did. Might I have been radically mistaken? Might I, at that moment, actually have felt *nothing*?

It seems to me that we have a strong, pretheoretical conviction that error of this sort is absolutely impossible. It is simply absurd, incoherent, unimaginable to suppose that I, or we, could be wrong in these ways. In saying this, I am not denying that people can fail to discriminate phenomenal features of their experiences, if they fail to introspect carefully enough (through haste or distraction or some cognitive impairment), or if they lack (or fail to apply) the necessary concepts, or if they have been primed to expect something else. The man who is being tortured with a hot iron, which has been pressed briefly against his back twenty times in a row, and who expects to feel intense pain again as the iron is brought ever closer, may well believe (at least for a moment) that he is experiencing awful pain, even if an ice cube is substituted for the iron at the last moment. In this case, the sensation is very short-lived, and the feeling of cold is phenomenally not radically unlike the feeling of pain. Given that the man has been primed to expect pain, a mistake results.

I am not urging, then, either self-intimation or incorrigibility with respect to experience. What I am urging is the impossibility of radical error, of general hyperfallibilism, of the sort I have described.[3] First-person authority must count for *something*.

The upshot of all of this is that not only do we have no good reason to grant that we can imagine a PANIC state without phenomenal character but we also have good reason to deny it, given the virtues of the PANIC theory I have already extolled.

Let us now return to the six hypotheses with which I began the chapter. In each case, I shall take a stand on the hypothesis from the perspective of the PANIC theory. The first hypothesis I want to consider is that of the possibility of zombie replicas.

Box 7.2

Summary

The PANIC theory is justified by reference to its explanatory power. It is, at least partly, an empirical proposal. Nonetheless, the claim that a given phenomenal quality Q is one and the same as a given PANIC P is necessarily true if it is true at all.

The fact that we seem to be able to imagine Q without P can be explained by reference to a difference in concepts. It is conceptually possible for Q to be present without P, but that does not show that it is really imaginable. The fact that we seem to be able to imagine P without Q can also be explained away satisfactorily. What we really imagine in this case is the presence of P without any cognitive awareness of Q.

7.4   Zombie Replicas and Other Duplicates

On the PANIC theory, as I have elucidated it, phenomenal character ain't in the head. So the thesis that the phenomenal supervenes on the neural is false: it is metaphysically possible for microphysical duplicates to differ phenomenally. Moreover, it is metaphysically possible for there to be a microphysical duplicate of a sentient creature that lacks any experiences or feelings.

To see this, imagine a *very* simple creature that has the capacity to undergo sensations in a single sensory modality, and that phenomenal variations among these sensations are extremely limited. Imagine also that the sensory receptors with which the creature is equipped are so constructed that they *could* have been activated by a wide range of different types of physical energy, had the environment been suitably different, but that, in the environment in which the creature naturally lives, only one of these types of energy is found. Imagine finally that the creature is *not* equipped to introspect its inner states at all, but that it does respond cognitively to its sensations in very primitive ways by forming a few simple beliefs about the external environment that are only minimally discriminating among stimuli. These beliefs then interact with similarly crude desires to produce some basic movements. In other cognitive respects, the sensations have no effect.

Now imagine another creature that is a microphysical duplicate of the above creature but differs from it by living on another planet and having a dissimilar natural habitat there, in which several different sorts of physical energy impinge upon its sensory receptors. This is to be imagined to have the following consequence: whereas in the first creature, those brain states that realize its sensations covary with variations in a single external physical feature (let us suppose), for the second creature, the same brain states each standardly have several very different external causes, occurring on different occasions with equal regularity.

For the second creature, the brain states so caused do not sensorily represent anything. This is because, for each member m of the relevant set of brain states, there is no single feature such that m is tokened in the creature if and only if that feature is present and because it is present. Ex hypothesi, the second creature, like the first, is in optimal conditions:

it lives in the given environment with other members of its species and, we may suppose, no external agent is deceiving it in any way. So the relevant brain states, on the naturalized PANIC theory, are not sensory *representations*. So the second creature has *no* sensations, despite its microphysical identity with the first: it is a zombie replica.

It will not do to reply that in the second creature, each brain state B_k, in the relevant set represents a certain disjunctive property, G_k or H_k or I_k, say. Although it is true that B_k is tokened if and only if G_k or H_k or I_k is tokened, it is false that B_k is tokened *because* that disjunctive property is instantiated. Rather B_k is tokened either because G_k is tokened or because H_k is tokened or because I_k is tokened. The individual properties are causally efficacious in the production of B_k, but the disjunctive property is not. Disjunctive properties (whose disjuncts have nothing in common) play no causal role; they enter into no causal laws.

Zombie replicas are indeed possible, according to the PANIC theory. However, zombie replicas with identical causal histories and identical environments are not. In this case, there is no room for any difference in causal covariation to arise. So there is no room for any difference in sensory representation. What the one sensorily represents, the other must, too. Phenomenally the two must be identical.

There is, I suggest, no special mystery here, for the mechanism whereby phenomenal identity is guaranteed has been explained. Of course, it is epistemically possible that the PANIC theory is mistaken: there is no conceptual assurance of its truth.[4] So it is epistemically possible that there are zombie replicas with duplicate environments and histories. But if the PANIC theory is true, then it is necessarily true and replicas of the sort just mentioned are metaphysically impossible.

What about the case of functional duplicates (see Block 1980; Block and Fodor 1980; Campbell 1980; Nagel 1979)? If there can be zombie replicas of the sort I have described, then there can be *narrow* functional duplicates without any sensory experiences. For complete microphysical duplication guarantees the same responses in the sensory receptors, the same internal causal interactions, the same bodily movements—in other words, complete narrow functional duplication. But there are *wide* functional differences in the simple creatures imagined above. In the one, there is a range of brain states that causally covary with variations in a single external feature. In the other, there is no such causal covariation. This is a functional difference that brings in the environment, not an internal functional difference. And it generates the representational difference that is phenomenally relevant. Take this functional difference away, make *all* the external causal interactions, present and historical, the same, and, on the PANIC theory, there can be no phenomenal difference. So "absent qualia" in maximal functional duplicates are not possible.

Discussions of absent qualia typically focus on the case of human duplicates for no good reason, if the general question of functional duplicates without phenomenal experiences or qualia is at issue. Moreover, my admission that it is metaphysically possible for there to be a narrow functional duplicate of a sentient creature without experiences does not entail that it is metaphysically possible for there to be a narrow functional duplicate of *me* or *you* without any experiences. And, in fact, the latter claim is false.

The argument for this position goes as follows. Among my beliefs are those I form, on the basis of introspection, about my own experiences and how they resemble and differ from one another phenomenally. These beliefs manifest themselves in my actual and possible verbal and nonverbal behavior, as do all the beliefs I have. For reasons stated at the end of the last section, it seems to me conceptually impossible for these beliefs to be so badly mistaken that I really undergo *no* experiences at all. Likewise for any other being with the capacity to introspect in like fashion and to form similar beliefs.

Suppose now, contrary to fact, that neurosurgery has developed to such an extent that it is possible to replace any single neuron in the brain with a silicon chip that has exactly the same input-output functions as the neuron it replaces. It follows that no matter how many neurons are replaced, the functioning of the brain as a whole remains absolutely constant.[5]

What happens to my beliefs about my experiences, my phenomenal beliefs, as we might call them, as my neurons are replaced one by one by silicon chips, as I become less than fully carbonated, so to speak?

As more and more chips are inserted in my brain, it might be supposed that, at some stage in the procedure, I no longer exist and am replaced by someone else. This seems to me a possibility. But it need not concern us in the present context, since my interest lies with the beliefs of whomever exists in the given situation.

To begin with, it should be noted that I cannot change my responses as the chips are inserted. For example, as silicon chips are implanted in my visual cortex, I cannot report that I have suddenly gone blind or partially blind; I cannot bump into things I would not have bumped into before; my overall functioning cannot change in any way. By hypothesis, my brain functions *just* as it did before. So I must continue to behave, both verbally and nonverbally, in *exactly* the same manner.

Given that this is the case, might my phenomenal beliefs (indeed any of my beliefs) still change? Might I come to think very different thoughts, for example, that I no longer have *any* experiences, notwithstanding the absence of any change in my overt responses? Surely that is impossible. Not only are my overt responses identical to those that would have been produced had the silicon not been implanted, but I (or my successor) am also exactly the same at the microfunctional level, that is, at the level of causal interactions between neurons and their replacements. Any new or different belief I formed would have to have associated with it *some* difference in underlying causal pattern. How else could it have been produced? And how else could I have lost my old beliefs? But if the pattern of causal interactions at the neural (chip) level remains unaltered, for the same external inputs, then there is simply no way that I (or my successor) can come to any different beliefs.

Box 7.3

Suppose it is replied that it is *metaphysically* possible that the change from carbon to silicon itself produces beliefs with different contents (and simultaneously destroys the old beliefs), even though there is no change in microcausal interactions. This is a bewildering suggestion. Initially, I believe that I am experiencing three round objects in my field of view, say. As chips are implanted, I come to believe that I am losing my sight and that I now cannot tell what shapes the objects in my field of view have or even how many objects are present. What accounts for this change in what I believe? The idea that a switch from neurons to silicon could produce a difference in content of this sort *on its own*, while nothing else changes, seems to me absurd. After all, the second belief exercises concepts that are

Box 7.3 *continued*

not involved in any way in the first belief. How could I possibly undergo a state that draws on, and combines together, these new concepts if there is no alteration whatsoever in the underlying functioning, even at a very fine-grained level?

Perhaps it will now be said that, although the idea is certainly a very peculiar one, sense can still be made of it. It suffices simply to *imagine* that the new beliefs are present, notwithstanding the constancy in my internal functioning, behavior, and environmental situation. But how are we to imagine that there really are new beliefs in this case? Presumably, the idea is that we imagine that these beliefs are given to me on the inside, as it were. I know that the things I find myself saying and the ways I act are inappropriate to my beliefs inside, since I am introspectively aware of changes in what I believe.

In this imagined situation, my new beliefs have no effect on my behavior. They are cut adrift, as it were, from my public responses. Nothing that I ever say or do could give any indication whatsoever that my beliefs have altered. Indeed, they themselves make no difference at all even at the micro-functional level. For if they did, then again my brain could not continue to function *exactly* as it did before. So, any new beliefs I form must have contents that are entirely epiphenomenal with respect to anything physical.

How, then, could I even be introspectively aware of any changes in my belief contents? How could I conceptually respond to those changes? This would require that I form new second-order beliefs that are causally connected to the contents of the new beliefs I introspect. How could I do all that without *any* changes in the microcausal organization of the states in my brain? Moreover, in these circumstances, what could possibly account *metaphysically* for the contents of the new second-order beliefs? It will not do to say that these contents derive from their causal connections with the contents of the relevant introspected beliefs. This merely passes the buck. Again, what could possibly account *metaphysically* for the specific contents of the new first-order beliefs? Given that the physical inputs, the internal processing at the level of neurons, the public behavior, and the external environment are all completely unchanged, it seems to me that these questions are unanswerable. The envisaged situation, I suggest, is *not* metaphysically possible.

The conclusion that no new beliefs can be formed follows immediately, of course, if beliefs are taken to be identical with functional states, that is, states that are defined by their causal or functional role. But it holds even if this identity thesis is denied so long as it is accepted that there cannot be any change in beliefs without some microfunctional change. What the above thought experiment does, it seems to me, is make the latter claim highly plausible.

If phenomenal beliefs cannot occur without *some* experiences, and identity in phenomenal beliefs is guaranteed by microfunctional identity, it follows that any being who was an exact functional duplicate of me would *have* to have some experiences. So the absent-qualia hypothesis (hypothesis (2)) is both true and false. It is true if it is not restricted at all; it is false if it is restricted to total functional duplicates of normally functioning human beings like you and me (insofar as philosophers could ever be said to function normally). It appears that we can both have our cake and eat it.

There may be some residual uneasiness about this position as it applies to cases like that of the China-body system described by Ned Block (1980). Here a billion Chinese people communicate with one another and also with an artificial (brainless) body by two-way radio. The instructions they follow are laid out on a huge display in the sky, which is visible to all of them. Radio signals are transmitted in accordance with these instructions and thereby produce movements of various sorts in the body. The interactions of the participating Chinese people are such that together they supposedly duplicate the causal interactions between neurons in a normal human brain. Yet intuitively, according to Block and other advocates of the example, the system as a whole can be imagined to experience nothing at all.

One problem with this scenario is that the interactions between Chinese people would be much slower than those between neurons. So the system as a whole would not be microfunctionally identical with a human brain. But putting this point to one side, the example is vulnerable to the criticism that the initial intuition that the system does not feel anything may be traced to our relative size.[6] Just as a tiny, intelligent being living inside a human head might well be unable to see the forest for the trees and might leap to the false conclusion that the human did not feel anything, so humans themselves have a highly restricted perspective that easily deceives them into thinking that the China-body system could be without phenomenal experiences.

To see this, suppose some unfortunate human being's brain is removed from his skull and destroyed and that the Chinese people are replaced by tiny aliens, so that the whole group of them, together with the display of instructions, fit inside the now-empty head. Assuming that the new artificial brain has the right internal structure and is connected in the right ways (and ignoring the point about response times), the creature or system that results (call it "Homunculi Man") will be microfunctionally isomorphic to the initial human being (Original Man). The argument for the conclusion that Homunculi Man must have experiences now goes through in the same way as before, with one main difference: instead of replacing neurons with silicon chips, replace them with tiny people who duplicate the input-output functions of the neurons.

So there seems to me strong reason to believe that Homunculi Man cannot genuinely be imagined to lack experiences and feelings. This is not to deny that we can imagine Homunculi Man, from the outside, as standing before us, say, and that we can imagine further that the homunculi in the head of this person continue to do as they are instructed, so that Homunculi Man remains a functional isomorph of Original Man. Nor is it to deny that we can then imagine the person we are facing, from the inside, as feeling nothing. What it is to deny is that we can imagine all of these things *together*. The crucial point is that there are two imaginative acts here, not one (between which we may well shift back and forth). To infer that imagining the first and then imagining the second suffices to imagine the first *with* the second is effectively to commit a modal fallacy along the following lines:

Possibly *P*.
Possibly *Q*.
Therefore, possibly *P and Q*.

We have now solved the problem of duplicates. What still confronts us is the problem of the inverted spectrum and hypotheses (3)–(6), with which I began this chapter.

Box 7.4

Summary

Zombie replicas are indeed possible, on the PANIC theory, as are narrow
functional duplicates who experience nothing. However, there could not
be a narrow functional duplicate of a creature as sophisticated as a normal
human being but who experienced nothing. This is established by the
silicon-chip argument. Moreover, maximal functional duplicates—creatures that are exactly alike with respect to all their internal and external
causal interactions—must be exactly alike phenomenally.

7.5　Inverted Experiences

It has become orthodoxy in the philosophy of mind to suppose that cases
of functionally identical phenomenal color inversions are possible. The
reason is supposedly provided by imaginability. It takes no great effort
to imagine someone (Oddball) who is in a state that is typically caused
in him by viewing red things and that typically causes him to apply the
term 'red' to the seen object, but whose state is phenomenally like the
state that the rest of us are in as a result of viewing green things and that
causes us to apply the term 'green' to what we see. We also seem to be
able to imagine that other inversions obtain, so that Oddball's experiences
are overall functionally identical with ours in the above way but nonetheless phenomenally different.

Here is another case, which focuses on a different sensory modality.[7]
You and I might be alike in that we both regularly fail to discriminate
red wines on the basis of their taste. They all taste the same to me, and
they all taste the same to you, but nonetheless the way they taste to me
is different from the way they taste to you. To me they all taste like an
expensive Burgundy, say, but to you they all taste like a cheap Chianti.

Whichever of the above examples is chosen, without much further
elaboration, it is susceptible to the criticism that it commits a hasty
generalization. In each case, a range of coarse-grained functional isomor-
phisms is assumed, from which it is concluded that overall there is complete functional identity. Patently, however, there can still be some salient

fine-grained functional differences. So it has not yet been shown that the inverted spectrum hypothesis (or the above taste variant) is true.

Consider the following parallel. For any two numerical inputs M and N, a given computer always produces as outputs the product of M and N. There is a second computer that does exactly the same thing. In this way, they are functionally identical. Does it follow that they are running exactly the same program? Of course not. There are all sorts of programs that will multiply two numbers. These programs can differ dramatically. At one gross level, the machines are functionally identical, but at lower levels, the machines can be functionally different.

In the case of Oddball, then, the opponent of the inverted-spectrum hypothesis can claim that, even if he (Oddball) is functionally identical with the rest of us in the specified gross way, he will still have a very different internal, lower-level functional organization. And that is why his experiences will be phenomenally different from ours. In the wine-tasting case, the same point applies. You and I may be alike with respect to our powers of discrimination, understood in a broad or coarse-grained way—we both group all red wines together as having the same taste, and we both distinguish red wines from water, vinegar, and white wines, say—but it is not at all obvious that we are *exactly* alike in the internal functional organization of our gustatory systems.

Some wines taste fruity, others have a leathery taste, some are likened to tobacco or pepper or oak, still others have an oily flavor. These differences in taste can be brought out in various ways. For example, if you and I are presented with multifarious concoctions, some with a leathery flavor, some fruity, some peppery, and so on, and we are asked to *compare* the taste of red wine to these other tastes, we will surely *somewhere* respond differently, given a sufficiently large range of samples—if indeed red wines do not taste to you the way they taste to me. These more subtle differences in our responses reflect the fact that there are differences in the fine-grained operation of our gustatory systems. So, again, the example is unsuccessful.

Let us return to the case of inverted color experiences. How might Oddball differ functionally from the rest of us? Suppose we imagine that Oddball is as much like the rest of us as possible except that he had special inverting lenses placed in his eyes at birth. That clearly will not be enough to secure microfunctional identity, however. The state he is in when he views red objects is produced by a different narrow sensory input than the state you and I are in when we view red objects. The inverting lenses produce a different pattern of activity on his retina (a pattern that is caused by green objects in the rest of us, and also in Oddball in possible worlds in which he has his lenses removed). So there is a different causal chain operative in Oddball when he sees red things, and the state he is in accordingly plays a different narrow microfunctional role.[8]

Box 7.5

Suppose that mad scientists rewire your visual system one night while you sleep so that the neurons that used to fire in response to the retinal cells sensitive to green wavelengths of light now fire in response to the cells that used to be sensitive to the red wavelengths and vice versa. You wake up, and you are shocked to find that your lips look green, grass looks red, and so on.[9] This is reflected in your behavior, for example, in your verbal reports. Here there is clearly a functional difference accompanying the phenomenal difference. But now let us imagine that after the rewiring, you adapt to your new situation and eventually forget that it ever occurred. Alternatively, let us imagine that the rewiring was done at birth. In these cases, you will be functionally identical to the way you were earlier but phenomenally different.

This is now an intrasubjective version of the Oddball case. And it is vulnerable to the same sort of criticism. By hypothesis, it is imagined that there is some rewiring. So the internal functional organization has not been imagined to be exactly the same, even though the gross functional roles of the inner states are similar.[10]

Of course, the fact that Oddball is different from us at the microfunctional level does not entail that he is different from us at higher levels. Still, it seems highly plausible to suppose that there *will* be higher-level functional differences. To see this, consider what it is like for Oddball when he is shown a chart of colors on which a patch of saturated yellow is placed to the left of a patch of saturated blue. If Oddball's experiences are fully phenomenally inverted with respect to color, relative to the rest of us, then he will actually experience blue as being on the left and yellow as being on the right. When he is asked which color is brighter, he will say that the one on the right is, whereas the rest of us will pick the one on the left.

The point here is that yellow is a comparatively bright color at maximum saturation. Dark yellow actually has a level of brightness like that of a lighter blue. These facts are part and parcel of our experiences of the colors blue and yellow. We experience yellow *as* being a relatively bright color. So, if Oddball's experiences really are phenomenally inverted with respect to color, he must experience the right-hand patch as brighter, and this will be reflected in a difference in behavior.

A similar point is sometimes made about our experiences of red in comparison with our experiences of green. We experience red as warm and advancing, but green as cool and receding. This may well be a matter of learned associations, but if it is not, then there is again trouble for the inverted-spectrum hypothesis. For Oddball would differ functionally from the rest of us in being disposed to describe fire engines and ripe tomatoes as looking cool, but grass as looking warm.

Here is another problem. Wittgenstein once pondered the question, "Why is there no such thing as blackish yellow?"[11] The question is an interesting one, but its answer need not concern us here.[12] What matters for present purposes is its presupposition, namely, that there can be no blackish yellow. This is something we know from our experiences of lemons and other yellow things. But if red is mapped onto green and yellow onto blue, then Oddball surely will not know this from the experiences he has in viewing yellow things. He will not be disposed to respond to the question, "Can there be a blackish yellow?" in the same way as the rest of us. Since his experiences when he uses the term 'yellow' are the same as ours when we use the term 'blue', he will respond "Yes," for there can be a blackish blue.

It seems to me, then, that there is reason to deny the inverted-spectrum hypothesis, as presented in (4) and (5). And the situation is no better for the case of human taste experiences. But even if (4) and (5) are false, it does not follow that there could not be functionally identical creatures with inverted experiences or that microphysically identical creatures could not have inverted experiences (contrary to hypothesis (3)). For example, Shoemaker (1975) comments,

[E]ven if our color experience is not in fact such that a mapping of this sort [i.e., a full inversion] is possible, it seems to me conceivable that it might have been—and that is what matters for present philosophical purposes. For example, I think we know well enough what it would be like to see the world nonchromatically, i.e., in black, white, and the various shades of grey—for we frequently do see it in this way in photographs, moving pictures, and television. And there is an obvious mapping of the nonchromatic shades onto each other which satisfies the conditions for inversion. (1975)

Unfortunately, Shoemaker's example of a nonchromatic inversion does not work. If we view a white surface, as the light intensity increases, it turns glaring white and then dazzling white (the latter is higher on the brightness scale). This does not happen with a black surface. There is no glaring or dazzling black.[13] Objects that are white and hot can glow. But black objects cannot glow, and neither can gray ones. The idea that something is glowing black-hot or gray-hot is unintelligible.

These are all facts that flow from our experience of white and black. So creatures who had inverted black/white experiences like ours would again be disposed to react differently. Still, I agree with Shoemaker (and Block and others) that inverted experiences (or "qualia") *are* clearly possible in the following limited way.

Consider again a very simple creature with the capacity to undergo only a very small range of sensations in a single sensory modality. In other respects, the creature is phenomenally unconcious. Imagine that the creature lacks the capacity for introspection and that its cognitive reactions to its sensations are extremely limited: it merely responds by forming a few crude beliefs about the external environment (as in the earlier case).

Now consider another creature that is a microphysical duplicate of the first. The second creature is also a *narrow* functional duplicate. Might it undergo a different sensation? According to the PANIC theory, the answer to this question is yes. All that we need to suppose is that the evolutionary histories and natural habitats of the two creatures are different, and that the brain states that realize sensations in the first creature are causally correlated with different external features from those the same brain states are causally correlated with in the second creature. In these circumstances, their sensations will have different representational contents and different phenomenal characters.

I conclude that inverted qualia can accompany narrow functional identity. But even in the simple case just described, there is a wide functional difference on the input side: in the one creature, the sensory state has a different external cause in optimal conditions than it does in the other creature. So maximal functional identity is lacking.

Box 7.6

Summary

According to the PANIC theory, inverted qualia *are* possible in some narrow functional duplicates and also in microphysical duplicates. However, there is reason to deny that it is possible for there to be a narrow functional duplicate of a normal human being with inverted color experiences. Furthermore, inverted qualia of any sort are *not* possible in maximal (wide and narrow) functional duplicates.

7.6   Inverted Earth

I come finally to the example of Inverted Earth. In this imaginary example (Block 1990), color-inverting lenses are put in my eyes by mad scientists while I sleep, and I am transported to a planet on which things have complementary colors to those they have on earth (the sky is yellow, grass is red, fire engines are green) but are otherwise the same. The first claim is that things will look to me phenomenally just as they did on earth. The sky will look blue to me, grass will look green, and so on. Unfortunately, this is already problematic.

Consider a pair of objects O and O' on earth, such that the former is saturated yellow and the latter saturated blue. I experience the color of O as brighter than the color of O'. On inverted earth, twin O is saturated blue and twin O' is saturated yellow. So I experience the color of twin O as less bright than the color of twin O'. A parallel problem arises in connection with the earlier example of blackish blue versus blackish yellow. Clearly, some modifications are needed in the Inverted Earth hypothesis for it not to encounter immediate difficulties.

Let us be generous and allow that suitable modifications have been made and that my experiences on Inverted Earth are phenomenally *exactly* as they were on earth. Can there still be a difference in the functional roles that my visual experiences play?

Obviously, there can and will be *a* change in wide functional roles. Looking up at the sky, the visual experience I undergo on Inverted Earth will be of a sort that is typically produced by seeing yellow things and typically causes behavior with respect to yellow things, whereas on earth it was of a sort that was typically caused by viewing blue things and typically led to the manipulation of blue objects. This is possible, on the PANIC theory, without any change in phenomenal character, since I am a living creature with an evolutionary history; the environment in which I find myself on Inverted Earth is not my natural habitat and I am wearing inverting lenses. So, on Inverted Earth, optimal conditions do not obtain. The brain state in me that tracks blueness in optimal conditions (and thereby represents blueness) now tracks yellowness. But it does not now *represent* yellowness.

In my view, hypothesis (6) is therefore true; there can be a creature whose state is functionally different at two different times and yet phenomenally the same. Inverted Earth, or a slightly modified planet, is possible. This position and the earlier one adopted in connection with inverted qualia seem to me to preserve many of our intuitions and together they provide us with a solution to our final philosophical puzzle: the problem of the inverted spectrum.

That, then, is my theory of phenomenal consciousness. What I have tried to show is that, given this theory, we can solve the ten problems of consciousness. No other theory I am aware of has the resources to handle *all* the problems I have adumbrated. Admittedly, in some cases I have offered more detailed solutions than in others, and there is certainly more to be said about each of the problems, even within my own account. But there is, I believe, no reason to think that something essential to phenomenal consciousness lies beyond the reaches of my approach.

Appendix
Blindsight

How is blindsight best understood? This is an empirical question that is perhaps best left for others, but I want to make some pertinent, albeit very sketchy, concluding remarks.

My discussion is divided into two parts. I begin by examining three sorts of visual agnosia that may usefully be compared with blindsight, and I lay out a psychological model proposed by Martha Farah (1991) for understanding these visual impairments. I then briefly review some of the main experimental findings in connection with blindsight, and I present a very tentative empirical hypothesis, which makes use of Farah's model, for explaining them.

A.1 Three Sorts of Visual Agnosia

Higher-level vision begins with the combining of local elements of the visual field into contours, regions, and/or surfaces. The first thing that can go wrong, then, in higher-level vision is this process of grouping. The resulting impairment is known as apperceptive agnosia (in the narrow sense). It is typically brought about by damage to the occipital lobes and surrounding regions (by, e.g., carbon monoxide poisoning). These patients often have roughly normal visual fields, so their perception of color, brightness, and local contour is adequate. But they are strikingly impaired in the ability to recognize, match, or even copy simple shapes let alone more complicated figures.[1] In general, they have great difficulty performing any visual tasks that require combining information across local regions of the visual field.[2] For example, when shown the figure

Figure A.1
The patient read this stimulus as 7415. Reprinted with permission from M. Farah 1990. *Visual Agnosia,* Cambridge, Mass.: MIT Press, p. 14.

A.1, one patient consistently read it as 7415.[3] Evidently, he was unable to see two parts of a line with a small gap as parts of a single line.[4]

The obvious conclusion is that there is a stage in *normal* vision in which representations of the local elements of the visual field are combined or grouped into an overall representation of the surfaces visible from the given point of view. This latter representation, which specifies lines, edges, ridges, and other surface features, is a vital foundation for nearly all higher-level visual processing. It seems plausible to suppose that it has the structure of a grouped array like Marr's $2\frac{1}{2}$-D sketch (Marr, 1982), whose cells are devoted to specific lines of sight relative to the viewer (with different cells devoted to different lines). As such, it does contain information about local features of the visual field, too, for example, determinate color, texture, and orientation. That there is a representation of this sort is, of course, a hypothesis I endorsed earlier.

Now the grouped array does not itself represent the shapes of any objects visible to the viewer (e.g., whether they are squares or circles or cubes or spheres). Its concern is solely with the visible surfaces. Indeed, at this level in the processing, there is no segmentation of the visible scene into distinct objects at all. What are needed in the next levels of processing, then, are procedures that generate viewpoint-independent representations of the visible objects' shapes together with procedures that identify the objects' locations.

Ungerleider and Mishkin (1982) have hypothesized that the former procedures occur in the ventral system, which runs from area OC (primary visual cortex) through area TEO to the inferior temporal lobe (see figure A.2). This system is concerned with identifying what is present. The latter procedures are handled by a second system in the brain known as the dorsal system. It runs from circumstriate area OB to OA and then on to

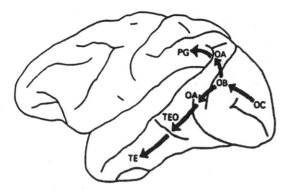

Figure A.2
The dorsal and ventral systems of the primate brain. Reprinted, by permission, from M. Mishkin, L. G. Ungerleider, and K. A. Macko, "Object Vision and Spatial Vision: Two Cortical Pathways," *Trends in Neuroscience* (1983), p. 414.

PG (in the parietal lobe). The two systems together enable us to recognize objects when they appear in different positions in the visual field.

Dorsal simultanagnosia is an impairment in the dorsal system. Patients with this impairment frequently have full visual fields, but they seem blind with respect to parts of the field. They can recognize familiar objects, but they typically can see only one at a time. For example, one patient was shown figure A.3 for two seconds. She reported that she saw mountains. When shown the same picture again for two seconds, she said that she saw a man. She apparently did not see the mountains or the camel, and she gave no indication that she realized it was the same picture. When presented with the picture for thirty seconds, she described it accurately, but she reported that she never saw it "whole." Instead, she saw "bits" of it that "faded out" (Tyler 1968). Another patient, who was watching the end of a cigarette held between his lips, is reported (Hecaen and Ajuriaguerra 1974) to have been unable to see the flame from a match offered to him one or two inches from the cigarette.

The impairment here is clearly one of attention. Dorsal simultanagnosics have a severe attentional defect, one that results in "tunnel" vision and precludes them from noticing unattended objects at all. The strongest evidence for the latter claim is that when experimenters made sudden, threatening movements toward the subjects while their attention was

Figure A.3
Tyler's (1968) patient could only pick out parts of this picture. She never noticed the camel. Reprinted with permission from M. Farah 1990, *Visual Agnosia*, Cambridge, Mass.: MIT Press, p. 19.

focused elsewhere in the field of view, they did not react at all (see Godwin-Austen 1965). However, the normal response was brought about by the same movements within the focus of attention.[5]

Since dorsal simultanagnosics can attend to only one object at a time, they cannot recognize spatial relationships among presented objects, even though they can recognize what those objects are, given appropriate shifts of attention. Nor can they adequately localize seen objects. This is shown by their failure to point correctly at the objects or to reach successfully for them.[6]

What these facts suggest is that dorsal simultanagnosia is an impairment in the dorsal system, in which attention is severely limited in its scope and not easily disengaged. The grouped array referred to earlier is itself filled in the normal manner, however. The problem, moreover, is not one that precludes object or shape recognition. When attention is properly focused, the object is recognized.

A third impairment arising in higher-level vision may be labeled "ventral simultanagnosia." Patients with this impairment have defects in their ventral systems. Like dorsal simultanagnosics, they do well at recognizing single objects, but they do badly with two or more, or with very complex objects.[7] The main difference between these patients and dorsal simultanagnosics is that they are able to *see* two or more objects. So they can accurately point to, and reach for, these objects. Moreover, given sufficient time, they can recognize multiple objects.

. The problem with ventral simultanagnosics, then, is one of object recognition.[8] Only a limited portion of the contents of the grouped array can be recognized in the period of time normally required for object recognition. Ventral simultanagnosics have no impairments in the attention system or in the processes responsible for the grouped array. Their deficit is one of slowed object recognition.

The impairment in dorsal simultanagnosia is connected with the number of objects. So it appears that the input to the attention system has already been examined at some level by the object-recognition system. Yet ventral simultanagnosics improve their performance, given appropriate spatial cuing. So, paradoxically, it appears that the input to the object-recognition system can be operated on first by attention.

Martha Farah (1991, pp. 150–153) has proposed that these facts may be explained by the general architecture shown in figure A.4, in which the grouped array is operated on directly by a spatial-attention system and an object-recognition system in parallel. The suggestion is that the spatial-attention system is set into operation either by top-down instructions (e.g., a decision to pay attention to a certain part of the visual field) or by bottom-up factors (e.g., the movement or onset of a stimulus). This system, then, selects portions of the grouped array, the result being that stimuli represented in those portions are more likely to be detected and recognized by the object/shape recognition system. It seems plausible to suppose that the process of selection here is implemented by adding activation to portions of the array. As shown in the figure, the object/shape recognition system is also hypothesized to interact with the contents

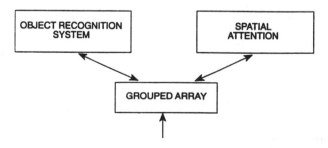

Figure A.4
A cognitive architecture for explaining dorsal and ventral simultanagnosia

of the array so that activation in certain portions of the array may increase during the course of recognition.

We can now explain how ventral simultanagnosics are able to recognize objects at spatially cued locations, among many other objects at different locations, without significant difficulty. In these cases, the spatial-attention system adds activation to the relevant parts of the array, thereby causing the object-recognition system to process those parts first. Since ventral simultanagnosics have object-recognition systems that are capable of recognizing single objects, the object at the spatially cued location will be identified.

We can also now explain one of the most puzzling facts about dorsal simultanagnosia, namely, why it is linked to the number of *objects* present. The object recognition system, in operating on the array, will cause certain portions of it to become more active—portions corresponding to objects. The activity in these portions will cause the spatial-attention system to select them. So attention will be focused on regions of the array for which there are corresponding objects. The defect in the spatial-attention system is such that attention then stays stuck to one of these regions ("sticky" attention, as Farah calls it). Only a single region corresponding to an object will be sufficiently activated for the object-recognition system to deliver a result. Once attention is disengaged from this region, it can then operate on other regions, but the same problem arises again. So only individual objects are recognized without any awareness of their spatial relationships to one another.[9]

Before we consider how this model might be applied to understanding blindsight, I should clarify one point. Object or shape recognition in vision, at least as we normally think of it, is a matter of seeing *that* such and such a type of object or shape is present. Seeing that something is the case, in turn, is a matter of forming an appropriate belief or judgment on the basis of visual experiences or sensations. Seeing that a red square is present, for example, is (in first approximation) a matter of judging correctly that a red square is present on the basis of how the scene phenomenally looks. I do not mean to suggest, of course, that there is a conscious inference from how things look to the belief. This seems obviously false in normal circumstances. What is important for my present purposes is simply that it be noted that there are two components in visual recognition, a belief component and a looking component.

Now, the looking component in seeing-that itself involves segmentation of the grouped array into the apparent shape or shapes. And this, as I noted in chapters 4 and 5, requires nondoxastic or nonconceptual categorization. So, in my view, the box labeled "object-recognition system" in figure A.4 really covers processing that is going on at several different levels: shape versus object, looking versus belief formation. For some of this processing, cognitive routines are involved (and here stored memory representations play a central role), but other aspects of it are nonconceptual.[10]

A.2 An Empirical Proposal

Blindsight subjects have a definite portion of the field with respect to which they take themselves to be blind. These portions can be marked out by slowly changing the location of a spot of light in the visual field and by asking the subjects whether they can still experience it. Why are they apparently lacking phenomenal consciousness with respect to their blind areas? If Farah's model is along the right lines, then one important requirement in the production of *normal* vision in human beings is that the spatial-attention system select the contents of a portion of the grouped array for further processing by the object/shape recognition system. It might be supposed, then, that with blindsight subjects there is an impairment that prevents their spatial-attention systems from *locking on* to a certain portion of the grouped array. So the contents of that part of the array never get selected by the attentional system.

This proposal, however, suggests that phenomenal consciousness is, at least in part, an attentional phenomenon (even if at a spatial rather than an object level). And that does not fit well with the observations in chapter 1 about the difference between attention and phenomenal consciousness. Moreover, it cannot be reconciled with what we know about the location of brain damage in blindsight subjects. Let me explain.

One major subcortical pathway from the eyes to the brain is known as the *geniculo-striate* pathway. It runs from the retina to the lateral-geniculate nucleus of the thalamus, and then from there into the occipital lobe. Patients with blindsight have damage to this pathway. By contrast, patients with defects in their spatial-attention systems have damage in the parieto-occipital regions. So, given that the grouped array itself is located in the occipital lobe,[11] the hypothesis that blindsight is due to an impairment in the linkage between the spatial-attention system and the grouped array appears to locate the problem in the wrong place, namely, beyond the geniculo-striate pathway.[12]

There is a second possible approach to blindsight that is consistent with Farah's model. We saw earlier that in the case of apperceptive agnosics, there is an impairment in the grouping processes that produce the grouped array, an impairment that leaves the array with only partial representation of nonlocal features in the visual field. Blindsight, I tentatively suggest, is a similar but more extreme impairment, one that leaves a significant portion of the grouped array completely without any representation of either local or nonlocal features. As a result, blindsight subjects are not conscious at all of the contents of their scotoma, whereas apperceptive agnosics retain consciousness of purely local features.

This proposal is consistent with the location of brain damage in blindsight subjects. What remain to be explained, of course, are the discriminatory capacities these subjects retain with respect to the contents of their scotoma. In particular, psychologists have been puzzled by the fact that accurate guesses can be made with respect to such things as presence, position, orientation, and movement of visual stimuli, and the related fact that, when a pattern is flashed into the blind field, it attracts the eye toward it just as with normally sighted subjects. There is also the intriguing phenomenon known as completion.

Under certain special conditions, if stimuli are presented to both the blind and the intact parts of the visual field, both will be registered. By contrast, if the stimulus is presented just to the blind field, nothing is reported. One psychologist who has exploited this approach to blindsight is Tony Marcel.[13] The method Marcel used was to induce afterimages of shapes with a bright photoflash. He then asked his two subjects to draw what they saw. The results are shown in figure A.5.

It may appear that the proposed model cannot accommodate either these results or the other discriminatory facts about blindsight subjects. For if the relevant portion of the grouped array is empty, then there is no information available there for processing by the object-recognition system or the spatial-attention system.

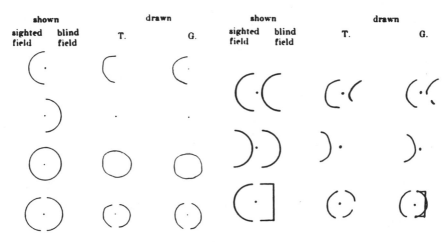

Figure A.5
Drawings by two subjects of stimuli projected to the sighted and/or blind fields. Stimuli were illuminated by brief photoflash. Adapted with permission from L. Weiskrantz 1990, "Outlooks for Blindsight: Explicit Methodologies for Implicit Processes," *Proceedings of the Royal Society London* 239, 247–278, Fig. 10–10.

This response ignores the fact that there is a second major subcortical pathway from the eyes to the brain, which is intact in blindsight subjects, and which does not feed into the grouped array. This pathway projects from the retina to the superior colliculus and continues through the pulvinar to various parts of the cortex, including both the parietal lobe and area V4 in the ventral system. It is known as the tecto-pulvinar pathway.[14]

Research with golden hamsters (Schneider 1969) suggests that one important role played by the tecto-pulvinar pathway is to orient the eyes reflexively toward a novel stimulus. It has been hypothesized that this pathway supports a wholly stimulus-based attention-shifting system whose purpose is to move the eyes appropriately (Kosslyn and Koenig 1992). In blindsight subjects, then, correct eye movements in the blind field may be traced to the proper functioning of this system.

A further hypothesis, due to Lawrence Weiskrantz (1986), is that blindsight subjects can use the tecto-pulvinar pathway to extract information about features like movement, orientation, and position with respect to stimuli in the blind field. This capacity underlies the accurate guesses blindsight subjects make (in response to instructions).[15] The information has neither the right vehicle nor the right role to count as phenomenal, however. It does not attach to activity in the grouped array (the locus, I maintain, for the output representations of the pertinent sensory module); nor is it appropriately poised. This is because the information is not accessible to those cognitive processes whose job it is to generate beliefs directly from nonconceptual representations at the interface with the conceptual domain. The cognitive processes at work when the subjects are forced to guess are not *belief*-forming processes at all.

The hypothesis that blindsight subjects can use the tecto-pulvinar pathway to acquire information about features in the blind field may also be relevant to understanding the results of Marcel's experiment cited above. It appears that such information is not sufficent on its own to trigger any shape identification. However, when combined with information about shape in the sighted field derived from processing the contents of the filled portion of the grouped array, we may suppose that it gives rise to the phenomenon I described earlier.

My proposal is consistent with the claim that in the blind field there is no phenomenal consciousness, on the view of phenomenal consciousness presented in this book. For if a portion of the grouped array is empty, then there is no sensory representation in that portion and hence no phenomenal content. Further development of the account of blindsight I have outlined must be left for future investigation.

Box A.1

Summary

I have suggested that in blindsight the portion of the grouped array corresponding to the blind field is empty. The processes responsible for filling that portion are not operative, or at least they are not operating properly. As a result, there is no processing of a region of the grouped array either by the object/shape recognition system or by the spatial-attention system. It follows that there are important underlying functional differences between blindsight subjects and normally sighted people. These differences manifest themselves in behavioral differences, in, for example, the need for instructions to guess or the failure to draw shapes presented only to the blind field.[16]

Notes

Chapter 1

1. For more on different types of experiences and feelings, see Haugeland 1985, pp. 230–35.

2. See, for example, Armstrong 1968, Rosenthal 1986, Dennett 1991.

3. See his 1991, p. 107.

4. Indeed I know of no philosopher who holds such a view. This point was made both by me and by Sydney Shoemaker in our 1993b responses to Dennett 1993. Dennett replied that "if Shoemaker and Tye want to see a card-carrying Cartesian Materialist, each may look in the mirror" (1993, p. 920)! However, neither Shoemaker nor I endorse Dennett's Cartesian Theater. Nor do I endorse the view that there is a single, privileged neural medium in which phenomenal experiences take place.

5. See Marshall and Halligan 1988.

6. For further discussion, see Nagel 1979.

7. Mary is a creation of Frank Jackson (1982).

8. The explanatory gap between phenomenal states and physical states has puzzled many philosophers. See, for example, Levine 1983, 1993; McGinn 1991, pp. 1–22; Nagel 1979; Tye 1993a; 1993b.

9. One radical response here is to deny that the phenomenal character of experiences does make any difference. For more here, see chap. 2. See also Jackson 1982.

10. Blindsight has been discussed by a number of philosophers. See, for example, Heil 1983; Dennett 1991, pp. 322–33; McGinn 1991, pp. 110–16; Tye 1993a; Block 1995.

11. This point is made by Ned Block (1993), p. 184.

12. Without this assumption, there could be what are known as *wide* functional differences between the two of us. For example, if I signal a waiter for a glass of water, and my twin lives on a planet without water but with some other liquid that looks and tastes just like it, then, in moving his arm in an identical way, he

will not be signaling for water. So, in one wide sense, there will be behavioral differences between us, even though our bodily movements, narrowly construed, will be identical.

13. For more on physicalism, see chap. 2.

14. See Ned Block 1980, p. 276.

15. One writer who is clear on these points is Chalmers (1993).

16. See, for example, Lycan 1973, Shoemaker 1982, Tye 1994b.

17. See, for example, Putnam 1981, Block 1990b.

18. Block 1990b, p. 62.

19. Nor correspondingly in intentional features of your mental states. For a discussion of intentionality, see chap. 4. I might note that Block also describes a further Inverted Earth inversion in his 1990b. Suppose on earth you have a molecule-by-molecule duplicate whom you leave behind when you depart for Inverted Earth. After sufficient time has passed, your states will remain phenomenally identical to those your twin is undergoing on earth, but they will be functionally inverted.

20. This has been remarked on by a number of authors. See, for example, Moore 1922, p. 22; McGinn 1982, p. 13; Harman 1990; Shoemaker 1990; Tye 1991, p. 119.

21. One philosopher who accepts this conclusion is Ned Block. See his 1983, p. 517. See also Jackson 1977, p. 76.

22. Thus Jerry Fodor's Tractarian remark in his 1994, "Whereof one cannot speak, thereof one must be silent."

Chapter 2

1. Here, and elsewhere, when I use the term 'perspectival', I have in mind perspectival subjectivity of the sort just described.

2. This problem is discussed by Carl Hempel (1970).

3. Compare Ned Block 1980, p. 296.

4. For more on constitution, see Richard Boyd 1980, pp. 98–103.

5. See Kim Sterelny 1990, pp. 203–6.

6. For more on realization and mechanisms, see pp. 45–8.

7. See Searle 1992, p. 105.

8. Ibid., p. 105.

9. This law is, of course, ceteris paribus (as are special science laws generally).

10. I am indebted here to Jerry Fodor's discussion of special science laws in his 1990a, pp. 144–46.

11. It might be supposed that it is possible for there to be a world just like ours microphysically, but in which some further nonphysical ectoplasms are to be found with their own biological properties, with the result that the biological laws there are not identical with ours. This complication is discussed by Terry Horgan (1983). For present purposes, it suffices to stipulate that the only possible worlds that should be considered are those like ours microphysically *and* not having such extra "alien" entities (as David Lewis [1983a] calls them).

12. If the connection is merely a posteriori and nomological, then it too requires a further mechanism.

13. The same is true if the higher-level property has a functional sufficient condition that we can discover by conceptual reflection.

14. Or, if not second-order essences, at least conceptually sufficient conditions of this type.

15. See McGinn 1991, pp. 5–17.

16. See McGinn, "The Hidden Structure of Consciousness," in his 1991, pp. 89–125.

17. Nor is it any improvement to appeal to conceptually sufficient conditions instead of hidden essences. If such conditions are to close the explanatory gap, then they must be conditions of an objective sort, whose sufficiency for perspectival subjectivity can be seen by armchair, a priori reflection alone. This seems very hard to believe. What could the relevant conditions be?

18. The points that follow against epiphenomenalism are influenced by discussion with Brian McLaughlin.

19. Assuming I can know that I myself undergo phenomenal states, on the epiphenomalist's view (something I shall shortly contest).

20. I am referring to phenomenal state *types,* of course.

21. See, for example, Jackson 1982, Chalmers 1993.

22. This is the view of, for example, Hill 1991, Flanagan 1992.

23. One defender of commonsense functionalism with respect to phenomenal states is David Lewis (although Lewis is also a defender of the type identity theory). See his 1980. Scientific functionalism is the view taken by, for example, Boyd 1980; Lycan 1987, 1990; Sober 1985; Harman 1990.

24. See Descartes 1911, Eccles 1953.

25. This is McGinn's position (1991).

26. This is the view associated most notably with Nagel (1979).

27. See, for example, Dennett 1991.

28. Fred Dretske (1981) has emphasized this point. See also Gareth Evans (1982); Diana Raffman, forthcoming; and chap. 5, p. 139.

29. See Hardin 1993, pp. 182–83; Berlin and Kay 1969.

30. This is also true of the problem of felt location and phenomenal vocabulary.

Chapter 3

1. To borrow a remark from Jerry Fodor.

2. This is the view Davidson defends in a number of articles. See, for example, his 1970, pp. 218–20. See also Parsons 1991.

3. For other virtues, see ibid.

4. For details, see Tye 1989. See also Clark 1970, Parsons 1972, Horgan 1978.

5. See Jackson 1977. Jackson calls this difficulty "the many property problem."

6. For a response to these problems, see Tye 1984, 1989.

7. See Unger 1990, pp. 177–83. Zuboff himself has not published the example.

8. See Unger 1990, pp. 183–84.

9. Cf. McLaughlin 1995.

10. For a discussion of some putative counterexamples to this last claim, see below, pp. 88–9.

11. Of course, there is an indirect cognitive sense in which you can experience my pains: you can see that I am in pain, for example, by observing my behavior. But this sense is not relevant to the claim that pains and other phenomenal objects are necessarily private to their owners. You cannot (directly) *feel* my pains. Nor, relatedly, can you have my pains.

12. For further discussion, see below, pp. 88–91.

13. Suggested to me by Dorothy Edgington.

14. If events are changes, their subjects need not *automatically* always be changes in objects. One might hold that, in some cases, spatial regions can suddenly change their properties without their being occupied by any objects.

15. Of course, this can also be denied.

16. There are replies to this problem by those who favor the Goldman/Kim approach. The usual response is to argue, contrary to what Goldman and Kim themselves originally supposed, that the property constituting an event cannot be "read out" of the description used to identify the event, even if the description is of the form "*x*'s *F*ing at *t*" (see Horgan 1980). But this reply weakens the motivation for supposing that events are complex entities that include properties at all. If the event of Sebastian's strolling does not have strolling as a constituent, why suppose that it has *any* property as a constituent?

Chapter 4

1. See Meinong 1960 (originally published in 1904).

2. Indeed, the assertion that there are objects that do not exist is a contradiction if expressed in first-order quantification theory, its formalization being "$(\exists x)\sim(\exists y)(x = y)$." One might, of course, deny that the assertion can be so

expressed. But then the onus is on one to spell out further just what is being asserted.

3. See Fodor 1975, and 1978.

4. For a detailed development of the above points concerning systematicity and productivity, see Fodor and Pylyshyn 1988.

5. One such theory is Stephen Kosslyn's pictorialism. See Kosslyn 1980.

6. The conditionals in this definition should be understood subjunctively. So the definiens is to read as follows: If optimal conditions were to obtain, S would be tokened in x if and only if P were the case; moreover, in these circumstances, S would be tokened in x because P is the case.

7. I do not mean to suggest here that the fact that the given features are represented, in and of itself, makes the states representing them sensations. More on this later.

8. These sensory modules are functionally specialized. There is no commitment here to a single, discrete neural region for each module.

9. Cf. Raffman forthcoming.

10. See pp. 114–15.

11. Other naturalistic theories include Fodor's view (1990b) of representation as asymmetric, nomic dependence and Dretske's (1988) teleological account.

12. See Smart 1959.

13. See Block 1983, esp. p. 518.

14. These virtues led me to accept the proposal until recently. See Tye 1991.

15. See Block 1983, pp. 516–17.

16. There is, I might add, a possible de re reading of this context: F-ness is such that an F image represents that something has *it*. Now, from "I have a red image" and "Red is the color of most fire engines," "I have an image the color of most fire engines" *may* be inferred.

17. I might add that, in my view, a necessary condition of any image representing that something is both F and G is that it represent that something is F. So, if I have an F, G image, I must have an F image. The argument for the premise here is straightforward: in having a blue, square image, I experience blue *as* a feature of something, a feature co-instantiated with square. *What* I experience, in part, is *that* something is blue. So my image, in part, represents that something is blue.

18. Sensory representations of this sort are determinate in a way that conceptual states are not. A blue afterimage, for example, must represent a definite shade of blue. We have concepts for the determinables (for example, blue) but not for the determinate values of these determinables (for example, blue_{37}).

19. Nor does it help to say that what the inference failure really shows is that pains themselves are ontologically suspect. Even if it were true that there are no pains, only people who are pained, this still gives us no account of why the

inference fails. After all, if 'in' means inside, and I am pained in my fingertip, then I am also pained in my mouth, assuming my fingertip is in my mouth.

20. Phantom-limb pain shows that pains do not essentially involve relations between persons and parts of their bodies. This seems to me a decisive objection to the relational view presented in Aune 1967, p. 130.

21. Cf. Armstrong 1962.

22. I do not mean to suggest that one cannot have a stabbing pain unless one has the concept of a dagger. Pains, in my view, are nonconceptual sensory representations.

23. See Pennebaker and Lightner 1980.

24. See Melzack and Wall 1965.

25. This case is due to David Armstrong. See his 1968, p. 93.

26. I deny that so-called psychological pains, for example, pains of regret or embarrassment, are really pains. I think it plausible to hold that such states are labeled 'pains' because, like (normal) pains, people are averse to them. But this usage of 'pain' is metaphorical or analogical. This is not to deny, of course, that real pains may have psychological causes. Embarrassment may certainly *cause* burning facial pain. See Stephens and Graham 1987, p. 413.

27. The constitution relation is weaker than the relation of identity. *A* can be constituted by *B* even though *A* and *B* differ in some of their modal properties. See chap. 2; Tye 1992a.

28. The same view of itches and tickles is adopted in Armstrong 1962.

29. This feeling typically elicits the desire or urge to eat, just as the feeling of pain typically causes the strong desire that it cease.

30. As noted earlier, the sensory modules are functionally specialized. There need not also be a discrete neural region for each module.

31. This is not to deny that other neural regions also play a role in some pain experiences. In particular, there are pain pathways that terminate in both the posterior parietal cortex and the superior frontal cortex.

32. For a discussion of the representational differences among sentences, pictures, and maps, see Tye 1991.

33. The characteristics of arrays are examined further in Tye 1991.

34. It need not be assumed that the proper temporal sequence referred to in the last sentence of the text *necessarily* corresponds to the real-world temporal sequence. The fact that the inspection routines treat the activity in one cell *C* as representing a later local bodily disturbance than the activity in another cell *C'* does not necessitate an implementation via an arrangement in which *C* is active after *C'*. For some illuminating comments on the representation of time that can be brought to bear on this point, see Dennett 1991, chap. 6.

35. See Kosslyn 1980, 1994.

36. I should add, within the visual buffer (and arrays generally, as I conceive them), cells representing adjacent surface regions do not *have* to be physically adjacent for the array structure to exist. It suffices that these cells be treated as if they are adjacent by the appropriate routines. See Tye 1991.

37. See Tye 1991.

38. For one possible sketch of these processes, see David Marr 1982.

39. See Damasio 1994, p. 153.

40. Cf. William James 1890.

41. This was noted by Darwin (1872) and first reported by Guillame-Benjamin Duchenne (1862). Antonio Damasio (1994) also cites Eckman's experiment. The view Damasio develops of the emotions (and moods) is similar to my own and has influenced my approach. The main difference between us is that Damasio thinks of the feeling involved in experiencing an emotion (or mood) as a matter of *cognitively monitoring* body states, whereas I think of it as a matter of *nonconceptually sensing* such states.

Chapter 5

1. The claim that substitutions fail in these examples may perhaps be resisted. But it seems to me intuitively highly plausible. Moreover, the view that there is a *further* way of reading the contexts under which the substitutions go through is no threat to the conclusion I have drawn. The embedded descriptions *can* be treated as occurring referentially or having widest scope, just as they can in other representational contexts.

2. See my discussion of painfulness in chap. 4.

3. By a primary emotion or mood, I mean one that is universally experienced from very early on in life.

4. See the earlier case of the Burning House (section 1.1).

5. Christopher Peacocke calls this layer of content "protopropositional." See his 1992, pp. 119–21.

6. For more on blindsight, see the appendix.

7. See the discussion of blindsight in the appendix.

8. The results of these experiments have been contested by some color scientists. See Young 1987.

9. Or at least that this is the case for any color we, as trichromats, can see.

10. See Amoore 1969.

11. See Amoore 1952.

12. Supervenience does not demand simply that in all possible worlds with our laws of nature, brains that are microphysically alike are also phenomenally alike. The claim rather is that in all *metaphysically* possible worlds, this is the case.

13. For more on this topic, see chap. 7.

14. The example is due to Donald Davidson (1986).

15. How the transporter beam works in the series *Star Trek* may be debated. In some of the episodes, it appears that during "transportation" from one place to another, a person's molecules are widely dispersed and then reunited. So, there is no duplication as such at all. Another possibility is that the original molecules are destroyed and duplicates created in the new place. But if this is how the beam works, there is a serious question about whether the original person still exists after transport and hence whether the person before really is one and the same as the person after.

16. I have not attempted to provide a general definition of optimal conditions; and I shall not try to do so here. It would be nice to have such a definition before us, I am happy to concede. But definitions are hard to come by for any terms, even much less abstract ones. Try to come up with a satisfactory list of necessary and sufficient conditions for being a chair, for example, or being a game or even for that old philosophical favorite, being a bachelor, for that matter. (No, being a bachelor is not being an unmarried male of maturity. Think of the pope; or a divorcé. What about males in a society that has no institution of marriage?) So I do not see it as a serious difficulty for the causal covariation approach to representation that no definition of optimal conditions has yet been supplied. It suffices that we can make reasonable decisions about what would count as optimal conditions in specific types of cases.

17. See Peacocke 1983, chap. 1.

18. See Tye 1991, 1992b. The points I make there against Peacocke are influenced by DeBellis 1991 and Harman 1990.

19. This one was suggested to me by Marcus Giaquinto.

20. For a defense of this claim, see Tye 1990.

21. Peacocke (1993) has a second problem case involving a coin presented at an oblique angle. The coin occupies an elliptical region of the visual field. This is manifest in the experience. But, according to Peacocke, the coin does not look elliptical: the visual experience does not represent it as elliptical.

This case is similar to one of Peacocke's earlier cases (1983) in which two trees of the same size are viewed, one twice as close as the other. Here, if the situation is normal, the visual experience represents the two trees as being of the same size. They look to the viewer to be the same size. But the closer tree occupies a larger region in the visual field and, in this allegedly nonrepresentational respect, looks different.

The reply in the two cases is basically the same. The closer tree is represented in the experience as being larger *from here*, that is, as subtending a larger visual angle. This is compatible with claiming that the experience represents the two trees as being of the same size, since being represented as larger from here is different from being represented as larger without qualification. Similarly, the tilted coin is represented as having boundaries that would be occluded by an elliptical shape placed in a plane perpendicular to the line of sight of the viewer. In this sense, the coin is represented as being elliptical *from here*. But it is also simultaneously represented as being at an angle and as being itself circular. This is why the tilted coin both does and does not look like the same coin held perpendicular to the line of sight.

Chapter 6

1. I am using the term 'objective' here (and throughout the chapter) to mean nonperspectivally subjective.

2. This claim is a little strong. If *P* is a complex phenomenal state, we can know what it is like to experience *P* by imagining it on the basis of what we remember of past experiences having (separately) *P*'s components.

3. For simplicity, I ignore again the complications mentioned in n. 2 above. The real requirement is somewhat weaker than the one stated.

4. Cf. Tye 1986.

5. This was the conception of facts I assumed in my 1986 discussion of Mary.

6. Here, I take lower-level physical facts to be facts expressible in the vocabulary of microphysics, chemistry, neurophysiology, or molecular biology.

7. For other responses to the case of Mary with which I am, broadly speaking, in agreement, see Horgan 1984, Churchland 1985, Lycan 1990.

8. This assumption can be contested. My point here is simply that there is no problem for physicalism, even granting the assumption.

9. See Nemirow 1980, Lewis 1983a. Not all physicalists take this view, however. For example, Loar (1990, pp. 85–6) denies it.

10. Unless Mary is a superbeing, a godlike creature who, while in her room, knows all the coarse-grained facts, past, present, *and* future, she also comes to know such new facts as, for example, that at time *t* she has her eyes directly trained on a rose (or the sky). That Mary does not know these facts *before* venturing outside can be accepted by everyone.

11. This is not to deny, of course, that there is a (fine-grained) fact the child does not know, namely, the fact that a fortnight is fourteen days.

12. In taking the above position, I am not denying that I do not know the FACT that I am seeing myself in a mirror. My ignorance of this FACT, however, is not relevant to explaining how I can know the FACT that Michael Tye is wearing a tie from a certain school under the one mode of presentation without knowing it under the other. For I equally do not know the FACT that I am seeing that person (Michael Tye) in a mirror. Nor does it help to note that I do not know that I am the person I am seeing (simpliciter). In this case, there is no FACT I do not know. For the relevant FACT here is the FACT that Michael Tye is the person Michael Tye is seeing. And that FACT is known to me under an indexical

mode of presentation, since I know that that person (the one with the familiar tie) is being seen by Michael Tye.

13. Leaving to one side the issue of whether she can know all the future FACTS. See n. 10 above.

Chapter 7

1. An example like this one has been discussed in cognitive psychology in connection with the question of how to understand concepts. See Keil 1986.

2. This point was made in Tye 1986. See also Seddon 1972, Yablo 1993.

3. Another philosopher who accepts this view is Colin McGinn (1989, pp. 85–6).

4. In my own case, if further empirical research suggests that there are phenomenally identical states that do not causally covary with a single feature in optimal conditions, the conclusion I should draw is either that there is some further, higher-level feature, as yet undiscovered, that is common to the putatively different cases and that does covary appropriately or that the PANIC theory is false. After all, empirical theories can be empirically refuted. That is their great virtue and their vulnerability.

5. The idea of silicon-chip replacement was first suggested (to my knowledge) by Zenon Pylyshyn (1980). It has also been discussed in Cuda 1985; Searle 1992, pp. 65–8; and Chalmers 1993.

6. This point has been made by a number of writers. See, for example, Lycan 1987.

7. This is suggested in Dretske 1995. Dretske and I have independently developed similar positions on consciousness (although there are some important disagreements).

8. This point is made in Levine 1988. See also Rey 1992.

9. I oversimplify here for ease of exposition. As noted in chap. 5, there is no simple connection between the wavelength of the light striking the eye and the surface color of an object.

10. For alternative criticisms, see White 1993.

11. See Wittgenstein 1978, part 3, p. 106.

12. For a good discussion, see Westphal 1987, pp. 45–6.

13. See Westphal 1987, p. 22.

Appendix

1. Movement of shapes sometimes helps these patients to identify them. See, for example, R. Efron 1968, p. 159.

2. They do better at identifying real objects (e.g., toothbrushes, safety pins) than simple shapes. However, their improved performance here is based on *inferences*

from clues provided by color, texture, and so on.

3. The patient made this identification by tracing around the figure with movements of his hand and relying on local continuity. See T. Landis et al. 1982.

4. Patients with this impairment are often classified with those who have a disorder called "simultanagnosia." In reality, the syndromes are distinct. Moreover, to confuse matters further, the term "simultanagnosia" has been used to cover two different syndromes, as we shall shortly see. The classification I shall be using is the one suggested in Farah 1991.

5. Is there something it is like for dorsal simultanagnosics with respect to unattended parts of the field? If it is indeed the case that they have full visual fields and that the deficit is a *purely* attentional one, then, on the proposed view of phenomenal consciousness, it appears that the answer to this question is yes. Dorsal simultanagnosics can shift their attentional focus, albeit with difficulty, and when they do so, they seem to become aware of phenomenal features in their experiences that had previously escaped them. There is, of course, no higher-order consciousness with respect to these phenomenal features, prior to any attentional shift.

6. The failure to localize stimuli, even when they are seen, has been labeled "visual disorientation."

7. Their reading is also severely impaired.

8. For ease of exposition, the term "object" here, and in what follows, is used broadly to include shapes. So when I refer to the object-recognition system, I have in mind the system or systems that enable us to recognize cubes, cylinders, and cones, as well as mice, men, and mountains.

9. It should be noted that, in the above framework, attention operates on the contents of the grouped array, and not relatively late in visual processing on object-based representations, as is standardly assumed. Notwithstanding this fact, Farah (1991, p. 153) maintains that it can explain the data that have been adduced in support of object-based theories of attention.

10. I might add that I see no conceptual difficulty in combining talk of symbol manipulation, inside or outside of a central executive, with my talk in this section of changing activation levels. The two sorts of talk are not directly competitive, although some have seen them so. They simply operate at different levels.

11. This is suggested not only by the location of brain damage in apperceptive agnosics but also by positron emission tomography (PET) scanning. See Stephen Kosslyn and Oliver Koenig 1992, pp. 67–70.

12. The same objection can be raised to the hypothesis that blindsight is due to a defect in the functioning of the mechanism of introspective awareness. I should perhaps add here that it is important not to confuse introspective awareness with respect to visual experiences with the operation of the spatial-attention system on the grouped array. Introspection in such cases is a process that takes visual experiences as inputs and yields beliefs about those experiences as outputs. So, introspective awareness is quite distinct from spatial attention.

13. Marcel's forthcoming work is described by L. Weiskrantz (1990). The first person to utilize this strategy was T. Torjussen (1978).

14. There are further subcortical pathways from the eyes to the brain. See Weiskrantz 1990.

15. It is a serious mistake to assume a priori, as McGinn (1991, pp. 111–12) does, that there is a common underlying causal structure at play in both sight and blindsight. If Weiskrantz's hypothesis is correct, the mechanisms responsible for the discriminations made in the two cases have little in common.

16. The fact that the responses of blindsight subjects are forced guesses cannot be accounted for by attributing to them unconscious beliefs with respect to the blind field (contra Mellor 1977, Heil 1983). This locates the problem in the wrong place: there is nothing wrong with the mechanism of introspective awareness in such subjects. See note 12 above.

References

Amoore, J. 1952. The Stereochemical Specificities of Human Olfactory Receptors. *Perfumery and Essential Oil Record and Flavours* 43:321–23.

Amoore, J. 1969. A Plan to Identify Most of the Primary Odors. In *Olfaction and Taste*. 3, ed. C. Pfaffmann, 158–71. New York: Rockefeller University Press.

Armstrong, D. 1962. *Bodily Sensations.* London: Routledge and Kegan Paul.

Armstrong, D. 1968. *A Materialist Theory of Mind,* London: Routledge and Kegan Paul.

Aune, B. 1967. *Knowledge, Mind, and Nature.* New York: Random House.

Berlin, B., and P. Kay. 1969. *Basic Color Terms: Their Universality and Evolution.* Berkeley: University of California Press.

Block, N. 1980. Troubles with Functionalism. In *Readings in the Philosophy of Psychology.* Vol. 1, ed. Ned Block, 268–305. Cambridge, Mass.: Harvard University Press.

Block, N. 1983. Mental Pictures and Cognitive Science. *Philosophical Review* 92:499–541.

Block, N. 1990a. Can the Mind Change the World? In *Meaning and Method: Essays in Honor of Hilary Putnam,* ed. George Boolos. Cambridge: Cambridge University Press.

Block, N. 1990b. Inverted Earth. *Philosophical Perspectives.* Vol. 4, ed. J. Tomberlin, 53–79.

Block, N. 1993, Review of D. Dennett, *Consciousness Explained, Journal of Philosophy* 90:181–93.

Block, N. 1995. On a Confusion about a Function of Consciousness. *Behavioral and Brain Sciences* 18:227–87.

Block, N., and J. Fodor. 1980. What Psychological States Are Not. In *Readings in the Philosophy of Psychology.* Vol. 1, ed. Ned Block, 237–50. Cambridge, Mass.: Harvard University Press.

Boyd, R. 1980. Materialism without Reductionism: What Physicalism Does Not Entail. In *Readings in the Philosophy of Psychology.* Vol. 1, ed. Ned Block, 67–106. Cambridge, Mass.: Harvard University Press.

Brentano, F. 1973. *Psychology From an Empirical Standpoint,* trans. A. Pancurello, D. Terrell, and L. McAlister. New York: Humanities. (Originally published 1874).

Brown, D. 1993. Swampman of la Mancha. *Canadian Journal of Philosophy* 23:327–47.

Campbell, K. 1969. Colours. In *Contemporary Philosophy in Australia,* ed. R. Brown and C. Rollins. New York: Humanities Press.

Campbell, K. 1980. *Body and Mind.* Notre Dame: University of Notre Dame Press.

Cannon, W., and A. Washburn. 1912. An Explanation of Hunger. *American Journal of Physiology* 29:441–54.

Chalmers, D. 1993. *Towards a Theory of Consciousness.* Doctoral dissertation. Indiana University, Bloomington, Indiana.

Chisholm, R. 1957. *Perceiving.* London: Routledge and Kegan Paul.

Churchland, P. 1985. Reduction, Qualia, and Direct Introspection of Brain States. *Journal of Philosophy* 82:8–28.

Churchland, P. 1989. *A Neurocomputational Perspective: The Nature of Mind and the Structure of Science.* Cambridge, Mass.: MIT Press, Bradford Books.

Churchland, P. 1990. *Matter and Consciousness.* Cambridge, Mass.: MIT Press.

Clark, R. 1970. Concerning the Logic of Predicate Modifiers. *Nous* 4:311–35.

Cuda, T. 1985. Against Neural Chauvinism. *Philosophical Studies* 48:111–27.

Damasio, A. 1994. *Descartes' Error.* New York: G. P. Putnam's Sons.

Darwin, C. 1872. *The Expression of the Emotions in Man and Animals.* New York: Philosophical Library.

Davies, M., and G. Humphreys. 1993. *Consciousness.* Oxford: Blackwell.

Davidson, D. 1970. The Individuation of Events. In *Essays in Honor of Carl G. Hempel.* ed. N. Rescher, 216–34. Dordrecht, Holland: Reidel.

Davidson, D. 1986. Knowing One's Own Mind. *Proceedings and Addresses of the American Philosophical Association* 60:441–58.

DeBellis, M. 1991. The Representational Content of Musical Experience. *Philosophy and Phenomenological Research* 51:303–24.

DeBellis, M. Forthcoming. *Music and Conceptualization.* Cambridge: Cambridge University Press.

Dennett, D. 1990. Quining Qualia. In *Mind and Cognition.* ed. W. Lycan, 519–48. Oxford: Blackwells.

Dennett, D. 1991. *Consciousness Explained.* Boston: Little, Brown.

Dennett, D. 1993. The Message Is: There Is No Medium. *Philosophy and Phenomenological Research* 53:919–32.

Descartes, René. 1911. *Meditations*. In *The Philosophical Works of Descartes*. trans. E. Haldane and G. Ross. Cambridge: Cambridge University Press.

Dretske, F. 1969. *Seeing and Knowing*. Chicago: University of Chicago Press.

Dretske, F. 1981. *Knowledge and the Flow of Information*. Cambridge, Mass.: MIT Press, Bradford Books.

Dretske, F. 1988. *Explaining Behavior*. Cambridge, Mass.: MIT Press, Bradford Books.

Dretske, F. 1993. Conscious Experience. *Mind* 102:263–83.

Dretske, F. 1995. *Naturalizing the Mind*. Cambridge, Mass.: MIT Press, Bradford Books.

Ducasse, C. 1942. Moore's Refutation of Idealism. In *Philosophy of G. E. Moore*. ed. P. A. Schilpp, 225–51. Chicago: Northwestern University Press.

Duchenne, G.-B. 1862. *The Mechanism of Human Facial Expression*. trans. R. A. Cuthberton. New York: Cambridge University Press.

Eccles, J. 1953. *The Neurophysiological Basis of Mind*. Oxford: Oxford University Press.

Efron, R. 1968. What Is Perception? *Boston Studies in Philosophy of Science* 4:159.

Ekman, P. 1992. Facial Expressions of Emotions: New Findings, New Questions. *Psychological Science* 3:34–38.

Evans, G. 1982. *The Varieties of Reference*. Oxford: Oxford University Press.

Farah, M. 1991. *Visual Agnosia*. Cambridge, Mass.: MIT Press.

Flanagan, O. 1992. *Consciousness Explained*. Cambridge, Mass.: MIT Press.

Fodor, J. 1975. *The Language of Thought*. New York: Thomas Crowell.

Fodor, J. 1978. Propositional Attitudes, *Monist* 61:501–23.

Fodor, J. 1983. *The Modularity of Mind*. Cambridge, Mass.: MIT Press.

Fodor, J. 1990a. Making Mind Matter More. In his *Theory of Content and Other Essays*, 137–60. Cambridge, Mass.: MIT Press.

Fodor, J. 1990b. A Theory of Content. In his *Theory of Content and Other Essays*, 89–136. Cambridge, Mass.: MIT Press.

Fodor, J. 1994. *The Elm and the Expert*. Cambridge, Mass.: MIT Press.

Fodor, J., and Z. Pylyshyn. 1988. Connectionism and Cognitive Architecture: A Critical Analysis. *Cognition* 28:3–71.

Geldard, F. 1953. *The Human Senses*. New York: John Wiley.

Godwin-Austen, R. 1965. A Case of Visual Disorientation. *Journal of Neurology, Neurosurgery and Psychiatry* 28:453–58.

Goldman, A. 1970. *A Theory of Human Action*. Englewood Cliffs, N.J.: Prentice-Hall.

Hardin, C. 1993. *Color for Philosophers*. Cambridge: Hackett.

Harman, G. 1973. *Thought*. Princeton: Princeton University Press.

Harman, G. 1990. The Intrinsic Quality of Experience. In *Philosophical Perspectives*. Vol. 4, ed. J. Tomberlin. Northridge, Calif.: Ridgeview.

Haugeland, J. 1985. *Artificial Intelligence: The Very Idea*. Cambridge, Mass.: MIT Press, Bradford Books.

Hecaen, H., and J. Ajuriaguerra. 1974. Agnosie Visuelle pour les Objets Inanimes par Lesion Unilaterale Gauche. *Revue Neurologique* 12:447–64.

Heil, J. 1983. *Perception and Cognition*. Berkeley: University of California Press.

Hempel, C. 1970. *Essays in Honor of Ernest Nagel*. eds. S. Morgenbesser, P. Suppes, and M. White. New York: St. Martin's Press.

Hilbert, D. 1987. *Color and Color Perception*. Stanford: CSLI.

Hill, C. 1991. *Sensations: A Defense of Type Materialism*. Cambridge: Cambridge University Press.

Horgan, T. 1978. The Case against Events. *Philosophical Review* 87:28–47.

Horgan, T. 1980. Humean Causation and Kim's Theory of Events. *Canadian Journal Of Philosophy* 10:663–79.

Horgan, T. 1983. Supervenience and Cosmic Hermeneutics. *The Southern Journal of Philosophy* 22. Spindel supplement on supervenience, 19–38.

Horgan, T. 1984. Jackson on Physical Information and Qualia. *Philosophical Quarterly* 34:147–83.

Huxley, T. H. 1866. *Lessons in Elementary Physiology* 8:210.

Jackendoff, R. 1989. *Consciousness and the Computational Mind*. Cambridge, Mass.: MIT Press.

Jackson, F. 1977. *Perception*, 60–81. Cambridge: Cambridge University Press.

Jackson, F. 1982. Epiphenomenal Qualia. *Philosophical Quarterly*. 32:127–36.

James, W. 1890. *The Principles of Psychology*. Vol. 2, New York: Dover (1950).

Keil, F. 1986. The Acquisition of Natural Kind and Artifact Terms. In *Language Learning and Concept Acquisition*, ed. W. Demopoulos and A. Marras, 133–53. Norwood, N.J.: Ablex.

Kim, J. 1976. Events as Property Exemplifications. In *Action Theory*, ed. M. Brand and D. Walton, 159–77. Dordrecht, Holland: Reidel.

Kim, J. 1979. Causality, Identity, and Supervenience in the Mind- Body Problem. In *Midwest Studies in Philosophy* 4:31–49.

Kosslyn, S. 1980. *Image and Mind*. Cambridge, Mass.: Harvard University Press.

Kosslyn, S. 1994. *Image and Brain: The Resolution of the Imagery Debate*. Cambridge, Mass.: MIT Press, Bradford Books.

Kosslyn, S., and O. Koening. 1992. *Wet Mind: The New Cognitive Neuroscience*. New York: Macmillan.

Kripke, S. 1972. Naming and Necessity. In *Semantics of Natural Language*, ed. D. Davidson and G. Harman, 253–355. Dordrecht, Holland: Reidel.

Land, E. 1977. The Retinex Theory of Color Vision. *Scientific American* 137:108–28.

Land, E., and J. McCann. 1971. Lightness and Retinex Theory. *Journal of the Optical Society of America* 61:1–11.

Landis, T., R. Graves, F. Benson, and N. Hebben. 1982. Visual Recognition through Kinaesthetic Mediation. *Psychological Medicine* 12:515–31.

Levine, J. 1983. Materialism and Qualia: The Explanatory Gap. *Pacific Philosophical Quarterly* 64:354–61.

Levine, J. 1988. Absent and Inverted Qualia Revisited. *Mind and Language* 3:217–87.

Levine, J. 1993. On Leaving Out What It Is Like. In Davies and Humphreys 1993.

Lewis, D. 1980. Mad Pain and Martian Pain. In *Readings in the Philosophy of Psychology*. Vol. 1, ed. Ned Block, 216–22. Cambridge, Mass.: Harvard University Press.

Lewis, D. 1983a. New Work for a Theory of Universals. *Australasian Journal of Philosophy* 61:343–77.

Lewis, D. 1983b. Postcript to 'Mad Pain and Martian Pain.' In his *Philososophical Papers*. Vol. 1, 130–32. Oxford: Oxford University Press.

Loar, B. 1990. Phenomenal States. In *Philosophical Perspectives*. Vol. 4, ed. J. Tomberlin. Northridge, Calif.: Ridgeview.

Locke, J. 1975. *An Essay Concerning Human Understanding*. New York: Oxford University Press.

Lockwood, M. 1989. *Mind, Brain, and the Quantum*. Oxford: Oxford University Press.

Lycan, W. 1973. Inverted Spectrum. *Ratio* 15:315–19.

Lycan, W. 1987. *Consciousness*. Cambridge, Mass.: MIT Press.

Lycan, W. 1990. What Is the Subjectivity of the Mental? In *Philosophical Perspectives*. Vol. 4, ed. J. Tomberlin. Northridge, Calif.: Ridgeview.

Maerz, A., and Paul, M. 1950. *A Dictionary of Color*. New York: McGraw-Hill.

Marr, D. 1982. *Vision*. San Francisco: W. H. Freeman.

Marshall, J., and P. Halligan. 1988. Blindsight and Insight in Visuospatial Neglect. *Nature* 336:766–67.

Matthen, M. 1988. Biological Function and Perceptual Content. *Journal of Philosophy* 85:5–27.

McGinn, C. 1982. *The Character of Mind*. Oxford: Oxford University Press.

McGinn, C. 1983. *The Subjective View*. Oxford: Oxford University Press.

McGinn, C. 1989. *Mental Content*. Oxford: Blackwell.

McGinn, C. 1991. *The Problem of Consciousness*. Oxford: Blackwell.

McLaughlin, B. 1995. The Public/Private Distinction. In *A Companion to Metaphysics*, ed. J. Kim and E. Sosa, 421–23. Oxford: Blackwell.

Meinong, A. 1960. The Theory of Objects. In *Realism and the Background of Phenomenology,* ed. R. Chisholm. Glencoe, Ill.: Free Press.

Mellor, H. 1977. Conscious Belief. *Proceedings of the Aristotelian Society* 68 (1977):87–101.

Melzack, R. 1961. The Perception of Pain. *Scientific American* 204.

Melzack, R. 1973. How Acupuncture Can Block Pain. *Impact of Science on Society* 23:1–8.

Melzack, R. 1990. Phantom Limbs and the Concept of a Neuromatrix. *Trends in the Neurosciences* 3:88–92.

Melzack, R., and P. Wall. 1965. Pain Mechanisms: A New Theory. *Science* 150:971–79.

Moore, G. E. 1922. The Refutation of Idealism. In his *Philosophical Studies.* London: Routledge and Kegan Paul.

Muir, F. 1976. *The Frank Muir Book: An Irreverent Companion to Social History.* London: Heinemann.

Nagel, T. 1979. *Mortal Questions.* Cambridge: Cambridge University Press.

Nemirow, L. 1980. Review of Nagel's *Mortal Questions. Philosophical Review* 89:473–77.

Parsons, T. 1972. Some Problems concerning the Logic of Grammatical Modifiers. In *Semantics of Natural Language,* ed. D. Davidson and G. Harman, 127–41. Dorderecht, Holland: Reidel.

Parsons, T. 1991. *Events in the Semantics of English.* Cambridge, Mass.: MIT Press.

Peacocke, C. 1983. *Sense and Content.* Oxford: Oxford University Press.

Peacocke, C. 1992. Scenarios, Concepts, and Perception. In *The Contents of Experience: Essays on Perception,* ed. T. Crane, 105–35. Cambridge: Cambridge University Press.

Peacocke, C. 1993. Review of M. *Tye, The Imagery Debate. Philosophy of Science* 60:675–77.

Pennebaker, J., and J. Lightner. 1980. Competition of Internal and External Information in an Exercise Setting. *Journal of Personality and Social Psychology* 39:165–174.

Poeck, K. 1964. Phantoms Following Amputation in Early Childhood and in Congenital Absence of Limbs. *Cortex* 1:269–75.

Proust, M. 1981. *Remembrance of Things Past.* New York: Random House.

Putnam, H. 1981. *Reason, Truth, and History.* Cambridge: Cambridge University Press.

Pylyshyn, Z. 1980. The Causal Power of Machines. *Behavioral and Brain Sciences* 3:442–44.

Raffman, D. Forthcoming. On the Persistence of Phenomenology. In *Conscious Experience*, ed. T. Metzinger. Paderborn, Germany: Verlag Ferdinand Schoningh.

Rey, G. 1992. Sensational Sentences Switched. *Philosophical Studies* 68:289–319.

Rosenthal, D. 1986. Two Concepts of Consciousness. *Philosophical Studies* 49:329–59.

Sacks, O. 1984. *A Leg to Stand On*. London: Duckworth.

Sacks, O. 1987. *The Man Who Mistook His Wife for a Hat*. New York: HarperCollins.

Schneider, G. 1969. Two Visual Systems. *Science* 163:895–902.

Searle, J. 1983. *Intentionality*. Cambridge: Cambridge University Press.

Searle, J. 1992. *The Rediscovery of Mind*. Cambridge, Mass.: MIT Press, Bradford Books.

Seddon, G. 1972. Logical Possibility. *Mind* 81:481–94.

Sellars, W. 1968. *Science and Metaphysics*, 9–28. London: Routledge and Kegan Paul.

Shoemaker, S. 1975. Functionalism and Qualia. *Philosophical Studies* 27:291–315.

Shoemaker, S. 1982. The Inverted Spectrum. *Journal of Philosophy* 79:357–81.

Shoemaker, S. 1990. Qualities and Qualia: What's in the Mind. *Philosophy and Phenomenological Research* 50. Supplement, 109–31.

Shoemaker, S. 1993. Lovely and Suspect Ideas. *Philosophy and Phenomenological Research* 53:905–11.

Smart, J. 1959. Sensations and Brain Processes. *Philosophical Review* 68:141–56.

Sober, E. 1985. Panglossian Functionalism. *Synthese* 64:165–93.

Stalnaker, R. 1984. *Inquiry*. Cambridge, Mass.: MIT Press.

Stampe, D. 1977. Towards a Causal Theory of Linguistic Representation. *Midwest Studies in Philosophy* 2:42–63.

Stephens, L., and G. Graham. 1987. Minding Your *P*'s and *Q*'s: Pain and Sensible Qualities. *Nous* 21:395–406.

Sterelny, Kim 1990. *The Representational Theory of Mind*. Oxford: Blackwell.

Teller, D. 1991. Color Vision. *Encyclopedia of Human Biology*. Vol. 2, 575–92. San Diego: Academic Press.

Torjussen, T. 1978. Visual Processing in Cortically Blind Hemifields. *Neuropsychologia* 16:15–21.

Tye, M. 1984. The Adverbial Approach to Visual Experience. *Philosophical Review* 93:195–225.

Tye, M. 1986. The Subjective Qualities of Experience. *Mind* 95:1–17.

Tye, M. 1989. *The Metaphysics of Mind*. Cambridge: Cambridge University Press.

Tye, M. 1990. Vague Objects. *Mind* 99:535–57.

Tye, M. 1991. *The Imagery Debate.* Cambridge, Mass.: MIT Press, Bradford Books.

Tye, M. 1992a. Naturalism and the Mental. *Mind* 101:421–41.

Tye, M. 1992b. Visual Qualia and Visual Content. In *The Contents of Experience,* ed. T. Crane, 158–76. Cambridge: Cambridge University Press.

Tye, M. 1993a. Blindsight, the Absent Qualia Hypothesis, and the Mystery of Consciousness. In *Philosophy and Cognitive Science.* Supplement to *Philosophy.* Vol. 34, ed. C. Hookway and D. Peterson, 19–40.

Tye, M. 1993b. Reflections on Dennett and Consciousness. *Philosophy and Phenomenological Research* 53:893–96.

Tye, M. 1994a. Do Pains Have Representational Content? In *Philosophy and the Cognitive Sciences, Proceedings of the Sixteenth International Wittgenstein Symposium,* ed. R. Casati et al. Vienna: Holder-Pichler-Tempsky.

Tye, M. 1994b. Qualia, Content, and the Inverted Spectrum. *Nous* 28:159–83.

Tye, M. 1995. A Representational Theory of Pains and Their Phenomenal Character. In *Philosophical Perspectives.* Vol. 9. Reprinted in *The Nature of Consciousness: Philosophical and Scientific Debates,* ed. N. Block, O. Flanagan, and G. Güzeldere. Cambridge, Mass.: MIT Press, Bradford Books. Forthcoming, 1996.

Tyler, H. 1968. Abnormalities of Perception with Defective Eye Movements (Blaint's Syndrome). *Cortex* 3:154–71.

Unger, P. 1990. *Identity, Consciousness, and Value.* Oxford: Oxford University Press.

Ungerleider, L., and M. Mishkin. Two Cortical Visual Systems. In *Analysis of Visual Behavior,* eds. D. Ingle, M. Goodale, and R. Mansfield. Cambridge, Mass.: MIT Press.

Wangensteen, O., and A. Carlson. 1931. Hunger Sensations in a Patient after Total Gastrectomy. *Proceedings of the Society of Experimental Biology* 28:545–47.

Warga, C. 1987. Pain's Gatekeeper. *Psychology Today* (August) 51–56.

Waugh, E. 1943. *Scoop.* Middlesex, England: Penguin.

Weinstein, S., and E. Sersen. 1964. Phantoms and Somatic Sensation in Cases of Congenital Aplasia. *Cortex* 1:276–90.

Weiskrantz, L. 1986. *Blindsight: A Case Study and Its Implications.* New York: Oxford University Press.

Weiskrantz, L. 1990. Outlooks for Blindsight: Explicit Methodologies for Implicit Processes. *Proceedings of the Royal Society London* 239:247–78.

Westphal, J. 1987. *Colour: Some Philosophical Problems from Wittgenstein.* Oxford: Blackwell.

White, S. 1991 *The Unity of the Self.* Cambridge, Mass.: MIT Press, Bradford Books.

White, S. 1993. Color and the Narrow Contents of Experience. Paper delivered at the Eastern Division of the American Philosophical Association.

Wittgenstein, L. 1978. *Some Remarks on Color,* ed. G. E. M. Anscombe. Oxford: Blackwell.

Yablo, S. 1993. Is Conceivability a Guide to Possibility? *Philosophy and Phenomenological Research* 53:1–42.

Young, R. 1987. Color Vision and the Retinex Theory. *Science* 238:1731–32.

Name Index

Wall, P. 223n24
Wangensteen, O. 118
Warga, C. 114
Washburn, A. 117
Waugh, E. 152
Weinstein, S. 151
Weiskrantz, L. 19, 217, 230nn.13,
    14, 15
Westphal, J. 228n12, 228n13
White, S. 228n10
Wittgenstein, L. 204, 228n11

Yablo, S. 228n22
Young, R. 225n8

Zuboff, A. 78–79, 81–82, 222n7

Subject Index